THE *portrait of a valley*
SLOCAN

Katherine Gordon

sononis WINLAW BRITISH COLUMBIA
PRESS

NATIONAL LIBRARY OF CANADA CATALOGUING IN PUBLICATION

Gordon, Katherine, 1963-

    The Slocan : portrait of a valley / Katherine Gordon.

Includes bibliographical references.

ISBN 1-55039-145-3

    1. Slocan River Valley (B.C.)—History. I. Title.

FC3845.S595G67 2004   971.1'62   C2004-902188-5

Sono Nis Press most gratefully acknowledges the support for our publishing program provided by the Government of Canada through the Book Publishing Industry Development Program (BPIDP), The Canada Council for the Arts, and the British Columbia Arts Council.

Editing by John Eerkes-Medrano
Front cover photo by Quinton Gordon
All colour photographs by Quinton Gordon unless otherwise credited
Maps by Eric Leinberger
Design by Jim Brennan

Published by
SONO NIS PRESS
Box 160
Winlaw, BC V0G 2J0

1-800-370-5228

books@sononis.com
www.sononis.com

Printed and bound in Canada by Kromar Printing.

Front cover: The Slocan River at Perry Siding.

Title page: Overlooking the village of Slocan,
where Slocan Lake drains into the Slocan River.

The Canada Council | Le Conseil des Arts
for the Arts | du Canada

Contents

for Quin

Acknowledgements

Many people have assisted me in finding the stories that are in this book.
I hesitate to single out people for special attention because everyone has
been important, but some have put a great deal of energy into supporting
me and helping me along the way. L.B. "Red" Sutherland is one of them –
a true-blue valley boy who chauffeured me around the valley, introduced
me to dozens of people, and told me stories that brought me to tears,
sometimes of sorrow but more often of laughter. Thanks, L.B. His
daughter Barbara Sutherland Coghlan, who has worked long and hard on
compiling her family's history, was also a great help, as was Ray
Kosiancic, whose energy and goodwill leave me in awe. Bob Turner, that
guru of all things to do with the history of trains, kindly reviewed what I
had written about them in Chapter 5 – a huge privilege for me. Joel Russ,
whose philosophical thinking and astute observations gave me a great
deal of food for thought as I researched the book, needs a mention here.
And speaking of food, I really want to thank Dorothy Hird for that
incredible chocolate cake.

As I mention in the "Sources" at the end of this book, I cannot praise
enough the work of the historians and archivists who have documented
and maintained the records of the valley over the years. In addition, there
are a number of dedicated volunteers who are the heart and soul of the
museums and historical societies in the small communities in which
they exist. I was overwhelmed time and again by the efforts of these folk.
The resources they painstakingly collect are a valuable asset to authors,
and my thanks go to them all.

I would also like to thank the following people:

Frog Peak dominates the valley from the Vallican area.

Mark Adams, Elsie Altman, Nancy Anderson,
Sophia Antoniuk, Larry and Mark Atherton, Larry

Avis, Donald Bain, Liz Ball, Hugh Barbour, Darcy Barisoff, Phil Best, George Bondaroff, Rhonda Bouillet, J.C. Bradford, Marcia Braundy, Edna Swanson Brown, Gary Burns, Donna and Ken Butler, Terry Clark, Agnes Clough, Eric Clough, Rosalinde Dettmar Compton, Innes Cooper, the members of the Council of Ktunaxa Elders, Greg Cran, Webb Cummings, Karen DeMeo, Jacques Dupas, Corky Evans, Larry Ewashen, Stephanie Fischer, Tom Gilgan, Carol Gordon, Ailsha Gray, Sheila Griffiths, Stan Guenther, Dorothy Haeussler, Cole Harris, Joel Harris, Nancy Harris, Kathy Hart, Sakaye Hashimoto, Nobuyoshi Hayashi, Bill and Rita Hicks, Bev Hills, ricardO Hubbs, Kay and Ted Hutton, Marilyn James of the Sinixt Nation, Mark Jordan, Mabel and Peter Kabatoff, Linda Kenny, Susan King, Evelyn Kirkaldy, Ida, Jake, and Lue Kosiancic, Sally and Barry Lamare, Shawn Lamb, Jane Leander, Bert Learmonth, Rose Legebekoff, Cris Leonard, Catherine Llewellyn, Councillor Deb Louie of Colville Confederated Tribes, Washington, Agnes Lynn, Richard Mackie, Leah Main, Fred Makortoff, Erica Mallam, Dave Martin, Laura McCoy, Colleen McCrory, Mark Mealing, Effie Mills, Mike Mills, Cam Milne, Rita Moir, Wayne Morrison, Susan Musgrave, Greg Nesteroff, Dan Nicholson, John Norris, Barry, Casey, and Toshi Obara, Lorna Obermayr, Jonathan Oldroyd, Liz O'Neill, David Orcutt, Rosemary Parent, Veronika Pellowski, Rob Riley of the *Valley Voice* newspaper, Bruce Ross, the late and missed Stan Rowe, Stuart Rush, Wayne Savinkoff, Elizabeth Scarlett, Kevin Seeley, Laurie Septav of Canadian Women in Timber, Andrei Sherstobitoff, Marion Smedbol, Bill Smith, Bonnie St. Thomas, Emby Stengar, David Suzuki, Kathryn and Margaret Teneese of Ktunaxa Nation, M.L. Thomson, Sono and Terry Tully, Carol Vanelli, John J.J. Verigin, Ryan Verigin, Walter Volovsek, Bill, Natalie, and Carey Voykin, Robert Watt of the Sinixt Nation, Edda West, Derryl White, Stan Wilson, Murray Winlaw, Gary Wright, and Elois Yaxley.

Sono Nis Press moved to the Slocan Valley in the fall of 2002, after thirty-five years of being in business on the coast of British Columbia. Like others before her, publisher Diane Morriss was looking for what the valley had to offer – a quieter existence in a very beautiful place. Diane was inspired to have this book written; and once again I offer her my thanks for her inspiration, love, and generosity. My gratitude also to John Eerkes-Medrano, my editor; and to designer Jim Brennan, who took the gorgeous image of the Slocan River made by my husband photographer Quinton Gordon and turned it into the lovely cover that graces this book. For their forbearance in listening patiently on expensive transoceanic telephone calls to all the stories, my parents Michael and Juliette Palmer deserve a salute (especially my father, who was truly shocked when I intimated that perhaps the trains weren't the most interesting subject in the book). Nobody tell Bob Turner, please.

Barrie Rodgers of B.C. Budget Rental Cars and Trucks was generous enough to assist with rental car costs on one of my research trips, which is much appreciated. Equally appreciated was the kindness of the young woman working at the Budget Rental Car desk at Castlegar Airport, who offered me – a complete stranger to her – a bed and dinner at her home in Lemon Creek because she thought I had been stranded by my ride. But then, that's the Slocan Valley for you.

INTRODUCTION:
great events, small stories

Here are just half a dozen things that happened in and
around the Slocan Valley:

The president of the Canadian Pacific Railway rode
into Sandon in 1897 in a railway carriage appointed with
velvet cushions, polished wood, and silver fittings, to visit
the most up-and-coming city in the province. He was
dressed in his usually finery, a shiny black top hat and a
greatcoat of the same sober colour. Upon his arrival, had
he so desired, he would have been able to partake of

Carpenter Creek, Sandon.

champagne and oysters for lunch, and for dessert, ice cream.

A man and his sixteen-year-old daughter went out in a three-metre boat on Christmas Day in a wild storm that was whipping up waves on Slocan Lake higher than the girl was tall, in order to repair a broken telegraph wire. It was just part of the job. Forty kilometres down the valley, a woman was out shooting rabbits for supper, having first prayed for a keen eye and good aim in the little chapel she had built in her small living room.

People caught fish in the river, which was not yet named Slocan, and ate it near their dwellings in a place that was not yet named Vallican. They buried their dead in the gravel bars of the river to rest for all eternity. A thousand years later, after the dead had been excavated by strangers in the name of science and progress, their descendants buried them again.

David Suzuki met his first girlfriend in Slocan City (or so the local folklore goes – he was, after all, a child at the time, and constrained in his activities by the fact that he was in a civilian internment camp).

Buddy Holly is rumoured to have performed at Playmor Junction in the 1950s. (It may have happened; after all, Boris Karloff played in Nelson.)

Around the same time that Buddy might or might not have played the Junction, more than one hundred children were torn from their families in night-time raids and were forced to live in an institution behind a chain-link fence for six years, before they were allowed to go home. We just want what's best for the children, the authorities said.

While researching and writing this book, I was often asked: "Why a book about the Slocan Valley?" The answer is that the thousands upon thousands of stories that occurred in the Slocan Valley and the global events that have cradled them make compelling reading. In many ways, the history of the Slocan is the history of British Columbia; indeed, it is the history of western Canada and the western United States. Various significant national events have played themselves out and continue to do so in this small amphitheatre. The actors in this drama have each created their own piece of the story, and together their stories reverberate through time and space with an intensity of emotion, tragedy, and humour that is awe-inspiring. Their stories not only echo the stories of all British Columbians over the province's checkered past, but many of them are also stories that could not have occurred in any other part of the province, let alone the country.

Although each small community in the valley enjoys a unique local history, the history of the Slocan itself is anything but local. And from time to time, the history of the province and the country – being made thousands of kilometres away in meeting rooms and legislatures full of individuals knowing little if anything of the Slocan's people – has in turn had a profound impact on the valley. The international treaties between Canada and the United States, the two world wars, the economic and political pressure to drive a transcontinental railway line across the country – all these things occurred far from the Slocan Valley but had consequences that changed its face forever.

History is dynamic, and often imprecise. The story of the Slocan Valley does not start or stop at a particular time or in a particular place. Today's event or action is tomorrow's history; and ordinary events and ordinary human beings – contradictory, temperamental, and anything but impartial – are the events and people who define the story of the Slocan as much as dramatic occurrences on the world's stage do. In time those events and people, like the flotsam in a river, converge and diverge again at different paces. Sometimes they coincide; sometimes they float in parallel but never touch each other. Occasionally, by unaccountable and accidental synergies, they are thrown together in a reservoir of someone else's design. So it has been with the Slocan Valley, where the paths of many down that river of time have led to, through, and past these places, always connected in some fashion.

Go to the Garlic Festival held in the fall each year in Hills, as long-time Winlaw resident Joel Russ points out, and these connections are amply demonstrated in the cross-section of people wandering through the stalls. There you will see farmers, loggers, environmentalists, civil servants; artists, tourists, miners, hippies, and road workers. Some members of these groups are the same people: the valley is a sturdy cradle that supports such diversity. They are aboriginal people, Doukhobors, Americans, Canadians of Japanese and Italian and Irish and American descent. All of them are drawn together by the event, and at the end of the day they will return to their homes scattered up and down the hundred-kilometre length of the valley and beyond. Some of them are newcomers, and some are descended from people who came to the valley decades, centuries, or even millennia previously; but they are all people of the Slocan Valley now.

Here is their story.

I

THE SLOCAN:
a state of mind

The question "Where is the Slocan Valley?" can be answered both in geographic terms and in human terms.

Geographically, the Slocan is a slender, blue-gold arc of water, pastures, granite, and trees lying in the western shadow of the Selkirk Mountains, in the heart of the southern interior of British Columbia. It is not a particularly large valley – barely a hundred kilometres long, if one counts only the lake and river that it shelters, and five or so kilometres wide at its broadest plateau. The Valhalla

Range of mountains forms the valley's steep and forbidding western boundary. Its eastern boundary is shaped by the lesser slopes of the Slocan Range; smaller, but no less gentle. The lake squeezes its narrow stringbean shape from north to south between their granite flanks. Every so often the mountains deign to cede to human settlement tiny deltas of flat land, fringed with maples and cottonwoods, at the mouths of creeks emptying into the lake. On the eastern shore of Slocan Lake the rock rises steadily southward from those settlements, to a crescendo at the sheer rocky bluff known as Cape Horn. There the road has been razor-cut into the vertical side of a mountain that drops hundreds of metres in freefall to the lake below.

The only illusion of security is a fragile barrier of concrete and steel that threads its way around the curve of the cliffs in tandem with the tarmac, and the driver turns her gaze west at the stunning views of the Valhalla Range at her peril. The lake pours southward into the Slocan River at the point where the valley flattens itself out once again into a narrow plateau, barely a kilometre wide but sufficient for the beginnings of human settlement after the impossibility of Cape Horn. It is a gentle river for most of its length, chuckling quietly in a series of shallow loops to its union with the Kootenay River near Shoreacres. Translucent green and sandy, overhung with willows and rimmed with bulrushes, it is the succour of the farmers and market gardeners that work along its edge, the solace of artists who gaze at it from their windows, and the joy of children who splash in its sleepy coolness or float rubber tubes through its small rapids in the heat of an August afternoon.

As the map goes, head south from the Arrow Lakes and Nakusp on provincial Highway 6 and a sign proclaiming *"Welcome to the Slocan Valley"* comes into view on the gently winding road a few kilometres south of Hills and just north of the small hamlet of Rosebery. Six kilometres further south is the picturesque and historic lakeside village of New Denver; and a few kilometres to the east of New Denver off Highway 31A is the mining ghost town of Sandon. Perched precariously on Carpenter Creek, Sandon is so many hundreds of metres higher up in the mountains than New Denver that it will still be under snow while the citizens of the latter town are admiring their new roses. Keep driving south

Previous page: Slocan Lake, looking north from Cape Horn.

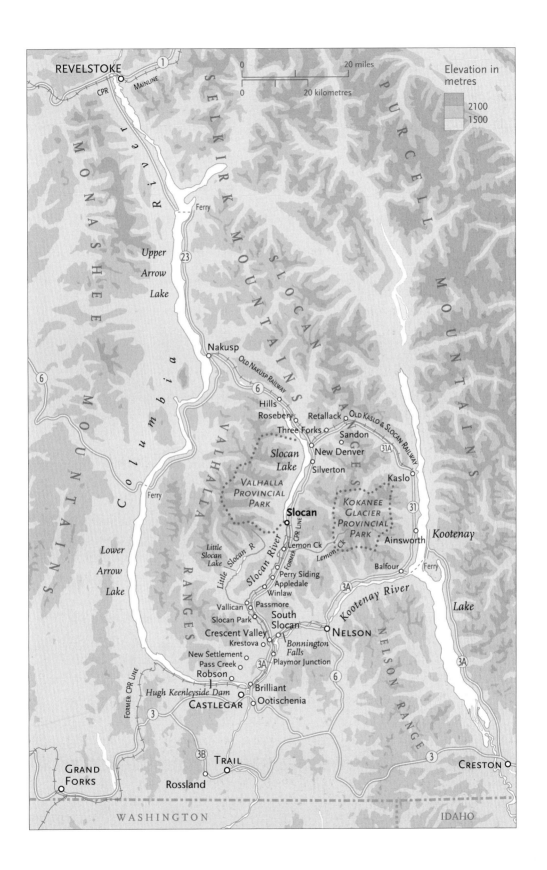

REVELSTOKE

CPR

Mainline

1

Columbia River

MONASHEE MOUNTAINS

SELKIRK MOUNTAINS

PURCELL MOUNTAINS

Ferry

Upper Arrow Lake

23

Elevation in metres
2100
1500

0   20 miles

0   20 kilometres

6

Nakusp

OLD NAKUSP RAILWAY

6

Hills

Rosebery

Three Forks

Retallack

OLD KASLO & SLOCAN RAILWAY

Sandon

New Denver

31A

Slocan Lake

Silverton

Kaslo

VALHALLA PROVINCIAL PARK

31

Ferry

VALHALLA RANGES

Slocan

FORMER CPR LINE

Lemon Ck

Little Slocan Lake

Little Slocan R

KOKANEE GLACIER PROVINCIAL PARK

Lemon Ck

Ainsworth

Kootenay

Lower Arrow Lake

Slocan River

Perry Siding

Appledale

Winlaw

Balfour

Ferry

Lake

Vallican

Passmore

Slocan Park

South Slocan

Crescent Valley

Krestova

New Settlement

Pass Creek

Robson

3A

Bonnington Falls

Playmor Junction

Kootenay River

NELSON

3A

NELSON RANGE

6

FORMER CPR LINE

Hugh Keenleyside Dam

Brilliant

Ootischenia

CASTLEGAR

3

3B

TRAIL

3

CRESTON

GRAND FORKS

Rossland

WASHINGTON

IDAHO

on Highway 6 past the exquisite village of Silverton, dreaming on the shores of Slocan Lake, and shortly afterward – before Cape Horn – the road passes a lookout west toward the stormy peaks of the Valhalla Range. The fierce faces of Gimli Peak and Gladsheim Peak glower down the Mulvey Creek watershed from their protected heights on the border of Valhalla Provincial Park. The mountain range is part of the valley's heritage, as is the valley's smaller sibling, to the southwest: the steep and dusty Little Slocan Valley, with its stone roads full of potholes and its scarcity of dwellings, its once-thick forests and its hillsides now spattered with clearcuts like shaved patches on a giant dog's back.

The highway climbs and conquers the heady cliffs of Cape Horn, now at least marginally tamed from its one lane, no-barrier days when, inches away from a free fall into the lake, trucks would have to back down the mountain in winter because they couldn't get past each other. It passes the large Slocan Forest Products sawmill at the village of Slocan, a jumbled collection of old miners' cottages and modern homes at the mouth of the Slocan River and the entrance to Valhalla Park, and continues on through overgrown cherry and apple orchards long since gone to seed, past trailers and log cabins and tidy little farms, artisan stores, and co-ops. Outside the roadside restaurant in Winlaw, six Miata sports cars of every colour of the rainbow are parked in front of a heavily loaded logging truck and an equally brightly coloured Volkswagen van, painted with flowers and spilling wild-haired children out its doors. Inside, plaid shirts and ball caps sit alongside golf shirts and tidy pastel twinsets, hemp vests and tie-dyed skirts.

At the south end of the road, the *"Welcome to the Slocan Valley"* sign is positioned immediately after the turn north onto Highway 6 at Playmor Junction, on the road between Castlegar and Nelson. The Slocan Valley does not end with Highway 6, however. Drive east past Playmor Junction and continue on a few minutes towards the city of Nelson, and a sign will invite a left turn into South Slocan. Once the busy terminus for the north–south railway route and an integral part of valley life, it is now a quiet and pleasant backwater, a bedroom community serving Nelson and Castlegar.

Cape Horn in 2003 no longer poses the terror it once did, although it is still not a road for the faint of heart. Heading in the opposite direction, twenty kilometres or so to the south another road turns west towards Brilliant and Robson before the

Nelson–Castlegar highway crosses the long bridge over the Kootenay River.

Just past Brilliant, past the small road that winds silently up towards the stately silent tombs of the dead leaders of the Doukhobors, there is an equally small and barely noticeable gravel road heading north again, at a point on the map called Raspberry. It gently meanders through a series of tiny communities and small houses hidden in the trees, their gardens scraped out of rock and clay, and eventually rejoins Highway 6 at Crescent Valley. Somewhere along its winding path, it too turns into the Slocan: perhaps at Pass Creek, or at the New Settlement, the communal land fought for so hard and so long by the Sons of Freedom; or in the arid and grassy plains of Krestova.

Ask ten different people where the Slocan Valley starts and stops, and ten different answers will be given. Strictly speaking, peripheral communities like Castlegar, Nelson, Nakusp, and Kaslo are not part of the Slocan, as geographer and Slocan aficionado Professor Cole Harris points out. But the Slocan is not defined simply by geography. Listen to a Slocan resident who commutes every day to Nelson or to an ex-Slocaner who lives in Victoria or White Rock or Washington state – but whose heart remains in the valley – and the answer departs instantly from geography and becomes: "It's a state of mind." If the Slocan Valley is defined by human beings rather than road signs, it becomes less necessary to decide where it starts and stops and what invisible lines might constrain its identity. People from the Slocan commute daily to the communities that surround the valley, shop and work in them, and depend upon them. Given the inseparable linkages the Slocan has with its eastern neighbours, and the profound impacts upon it of decision-makers in far-off Victoria and Ottawa – and even the United States – as well as the global spectrum from which its residents have come, its boundaries would certainly not stop at the ends of Highway 6, perhaps not even at the Canadian border. Indeed, to constrain its boundaries does the Slocan a disservice, and risks separating it from the fundamental role it has played in the broader history of British Columbia and of Canada.

Without a doubt, there is a region of the west Kootenays of British Columbia in Canada that is, more or less, definable as the "Slocan Valley." The boundaries of Electoral Area H in the Regional District of

Central Kootenay would suffice to define it in cartographic terms. But an electoral area consists of people; and the fact that the valley's reach is broader from time to time is clear evidence that the identity of its people has never been confined to such geographic boundaries. The Slocan is perhaps better identified by the people who have come and gone in its history, and by the strange as well as ordinary events that have occurred there, than by geography. The valley is inhabited today by people from Canada, Great Britain, the United States of America, Russia, Japan, China, Australia, New Zealand, France, and Germany – indeed, from all corners of the planet. The Slocan has been, and continues to be, a place of refuge and a place of sustenance. It has attracted all kinds of humanity over the years to its ragged mountains and its sheltered, isolated spaces. Fortune hunters, artists, recreational pleasure seekers, nature lovers, escapists, entrepreneurs, immigrants, and various refugees from war, society, or government – all have gravitated to this sheltered and bucolic region at one time or another.

As occurred throughout the Americas, aboriginal people migrated to and through the region and were using the valley's resources long before European settlers had crossed the Atlantic, let alone the continent. Their physical presence in the valley today, however, is minimal, for reasons that are at best regrettable and at worst, tragic. Marilyn James, who lives in Vallican, near the south end of the valley, is of *Sngaytskstx* descent – more readily pronounced as Sinixt ("suhn-eye-kst"). The Sinixt, commonly referred to in historical records as Lakes Indian people, once roamed through the Arrow and Slocan Lakes region in substantial numbers to hunt, fish, and winter over. James is vociferous in her defence of the contemporary presence and exclusive rights of the small number of Sinixt people in the Slocan. The Ktunaxa ("tun-a-ha") Nation, historically re-ferred to as Kutenai or Kootenay people, are on the other hand by far the largest collective group of aboriginal people in the Kootenays, with com-munities scattered throughout the eastern Rocky Mountain Trench and Columbia Basin. The Ktunaxa also maintain that theirs is a strong connec-tion to the valley, and they have included it within the maps of their traditional territory used for the purpose, among others, of treaty negotia-tions with the governments of Canada and British Columbia.

Although their visibility is small and currently appears to be peripheral to that of the majority, the distinct and resounding presence of aboriginal people within these granite walls of time is unlikely to be small and peripheral for long. There is no doubt in the minds of the descendants of the Lakes and Kootenay people who assert their connections to the valley that the thread of their history, while frayed, is far from broken. There is also no doubt that they see it extending into the future, spliced and strengthened with the threads of all the people who live there. Marilyn James and a number of others are living proof of not only the existence of native people in the valley but of their ambitions for a much greater presence and role, as they had in the past.

To think of aboriginal people, therefore, only in terms of how they lived prior to European contact – as many history books do – entirely misses the point perhaps best expressed this way by Ktunaxa Nation archivist Margaret Teneese: "This implies Ktunaxa people don't exist anymore, leaving readers to believe we have vanished. We have been in the Slocan. We are in the Slocan, and we will continue to be in the Slocan. Just because we are not visible in that area doesn't mean we are no longer there. The Slocan is and will continue to be in our traditional territory." In fact, the activities and hopes of aboriginal people flow strongly into contemporary times, and have always done so, despite adverse influences. They are no more static in their place in history than anyone else, and indeed, have strong motivation to continue to be dynamic.

In telling the stories of the passionate lives and pasts of all of the people of the valley, great sensitivities are also exposed. From a Sinixt Nation perspective, for example, it is not unreasonable to consider that it is an unarguable truth that your ancestors are the ones who used and occupied this valley from time immemorial, to the exclusion of all others – including the Ktunaxa. But from a Ktunaxa Nation perspective, it is equally the case to consider that the Slocan was and is an integral part of the way of life of at least some of its Kootenay members. The families of forestry workers who depend on their income to be able to stay in the valley where they were born and brought up can become enraged at the nerve of "newcomers" trying to stop logging. But an environmentalist who came to the Slocan twenty years ago, looking for pure water and a peaceful place to live – and indeed, one born and brought up in the valley herself – is equally outraged by a corporate giant clearcutting in his or her watershed. People who have struggled night and day for a decade to have a park established don't want to see mining taking place there, but the whispered rumour of thirty new jobs can instantly divide a community with hope and anger. There are long held painful memories that come between Doukhobor people and their own relatives, depending on whether they are Sons of Freedom or moderates; and even that last sentence presupposes that all the Sons of Freedom and all the Doukhobors were or are the same, which they are not.

Such shades of black and white do not often colour history in the valley. Some divisions remain too painful to resolve; hands are starting to reach out to each other in other cases. At one end of the valley reconciliation events are under way, while litigation is occurring at the other. Environmentalists and loggers may live as neighbours on the same street, greeting each other civilly as they pass in the morning and glaring at each other on opposite sides of a picket line in the afternoon; and youthful hippies may share a laugh with a crusty old-timer while waiting for a pay phone to come free. In the end, for the locals, this is simply the place where they grew up, fishing and swimming and playing, or where they have come or returned to find peace and a good way of life. It is their home. Perhaps who and what is the Slocan is best expressed in the words of the people of the valley themselves:

"You couldn't survive here unless you have a
good relationship with nature."
—Nancy Harris, Winlaw

"This isn't just a Sinixt issue, it's a whole world issue. I'm tired of excuses. It doesn't matter who you are, Indian or not. You have to be part of the solution. It takes commitment. A good heart and no action is no good to me."
—Marilyn James, Vallican

"We have names for those places too."
—Wilfred Jacobs, Creston

"Slocan Forest Products has benefited from [the dialogues with the anti-logging groups] but it has come at a high cost."

—Cam Milne, Village of Slocan

"People coming with fixed values have realized there is more than one point of view. For example, selective logging is OK in a place that grows trees so well."

—Nancy Harris, Winlaw

"I'll fight clearcutting until I die."

—Colleen McCrory, Silverton

"At one stage there were more Ph.D.'s here per square mile than at UBC."

—Fred Makortoff, South Slocan

"It's a wonderful community to live in. We're very proud of our town."

—Rhonda Bouillet, New Denver

"Sure I call myself Sons of Freedom. I was one then. By that I mean I am a free spirit."

—Anonymous, Slocan Valley

"There's no future in a communal lifestyle. I wouldn't do it."

—Twenty-year-old, Krestova

"A farmer never makes any money until he sells his farm for more than he paid for it."

—Ray Kosiancic, Crescent Valley

"We stand on a fine line in New Denver between the economic stability of the area and the quaintness of remaining a small historic town."
—Ken and Donna Butler, New Denver

"It's a unique place. So many influxes of immigrants have flushed out the conservative staid society with fresh blood."
—Lorna Obermayr, New Denver

"The parks around here are for visitors. The locals don't need 'em."
—Bill Hicks, Village of Slocan

"You can tell who is in the pot industry here. They pay their bills in cash and the money smells kind of – funny – if you know what I mean."
—Municipal clerk, Slocan Valley

"My kar-ma ran over your dogma."
—Bumper sticker, Winlaw

"Think fast, hippie."
—Bull bar sticker, Village of Slocan

"There's no reason to be here except for wanting to be."
—Corky Evans, Appledale

"It's just the most beautiful place in the world."
—Karen DeMeo, Victoria (formerly of Silverton)

2

LINES ACROSS THE MOUNTAINS:
the Oregon Treaty

On a pretty June day in 1846, in a small town called
Washington on the eastern seaboard of the United States
of America, a simple transaction was performed by two
men who cannot have had any idea what their actions
would mean for the future of a small and unmapped
valley lying several thousand kilòmetres away to the west
of the Rocky Mountains.

Surrounded by their officials and perhaps exchanging
some light-hearted banter in relief at having reached this

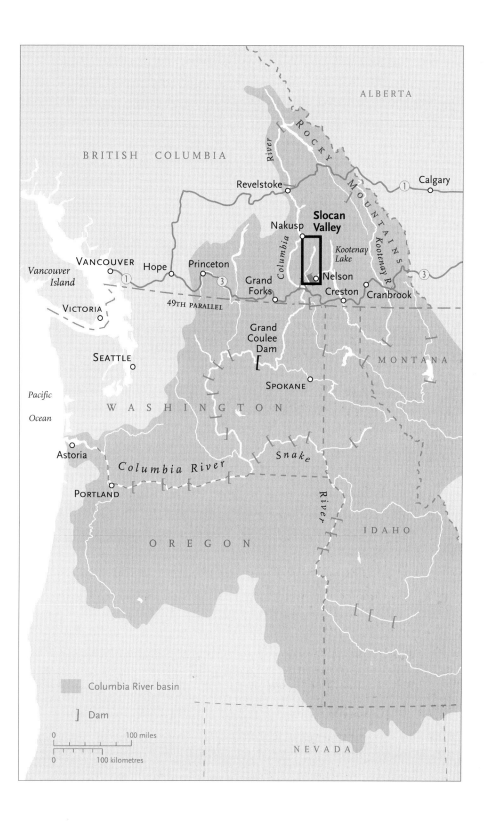

ALBERTA

BRITISH COLUMBIA

ROCKY MOUNTAINS

Columbia River

Revelstoke

Calgary

1

Slocan
Valley

Nakusp

Kootenay
Lake

Kootenay R.

Columbia

VANCOUVER

Hope

Princeton

Nelson

3

Vancouver
Island

1

3

Grand
Forks

Creston

Cranbrook

VICTORIA

49TH PARALLEL

Grand
Coulee
Dam

MONTANA

SEATTLE

Pacific

SPOKANE

Ocean

WASHINGTON

Astoria

Columbia River

Snake

PORTLAND

River

IDAHO

OREGON

Columbia River basin

] Dam

0   100 miles

0   100 kilometres

NEVADA

moment, James Buchanan, Secretary of State of the United States of America, and the Right Honourable Richard Pakenham – a member of Her Majesty's Most Honourable Privy Council, and Her Majesty's Envoy Extraordinary and Minister Plenipotentiary to the United States – each leaned forward in their chairs, picked up a pen, and signed their names to an agreement between their respective countries that would irrevocably change the way their citizens would live in the future. For the people of the area that nearly fifty years later would be known as the Slocan Valley, the impact of that agreement would continue reverberating into the 20th and 21st centuries; indeed, it could be argued that it was the most influential human event to shape the character of the valley and the lives of its people.

The Oregon Treaty of June 15, 1846 was a short document, but powerfully clear in its intent:

> "The United States of America and her Majesty the Queen of the United Kingdom of Great Britain and Ireland, deeming it to be desirable for the future welfare of both countries that the state of doubt and uncertainty which has hitherto prevailed respecting the sovereignty and government of the territory on the northwest coast of America, lying westward of the Rocky or Stony Mountains, should be finally terminated by an amicable compromise of the rights mutually asserted by the two parties over the said territory...have agreed...*the line of boundary...shall be continued westward along the...forty-ninth parallel of north latitude...*to the Pacific Ocean."

From that date forward, all the territory that now comprises the northern parts of western Montana and Idaho as well as Washington state – including everything that lay downstream of a point on the Columbia River barely thirty kilometres directly south of the Slocan Valley – would be American. This final determination of the western international border between the two countries was the culmination of several decades of tense relations between Great Britain and the United States of America over who would win control of the Pacific Northwest region. Prior to the agreement, the British government had wanted to hold all the territory west of the Rockies as far south as, and including, the

Columbia River to its mouth. The Americans, on the other hand, were determined to hold the line at no less than the 49th parallel, keeping the critical southern stretches of the powerful river under their direct control.

It was hardly surprising that in the early 19th century the two powers should have been jockeying for position over not only the Columbia River but also such a resource-rich area in general. The potential wealth to be gained from furs, minerals, trees, and fish was enormous, and both governments were under increasing pressure from corporate interests to assist them in gaining control of the Pacific Northwest. But while the scars from the War of 1812 between the two nations were still fresh, another territorial war would not have been entered into lightly by either side. No alternative resolution of the competing interests presented itself, however, and until the late 1830s it had been largely left to enterprising individuals and companies to create a presence in the West that might be sufficiently robust to justify establishing jurisdictional authority. The North West Company, and later the Hudson's Bay Company, were encouraged by the British government in their efforts to extend their corporate reach, as were their American competitors in a similar fashion by the United States administration.

Explorers, surveyors, fur traders and geologists – often one and the same people – were given mandates by their companies to find feasible east–west trading routes through the mountains as quickly as possible. But those same mountains were responsible for the relative isolation from expanding European settlement in the West of the north–south oriented valleys of the Columbia Basin and Rocky Mountain Trench. Huge tracts of the southeastern portion of British Columbia remained unmapped, let alone surveyed or settled in any fashion by British or American immigrants. On the back of the efforts, decisions, and hoped-for success of a few individuals – complete with all their human frailties, and often under immense stress in the incredibly difficult environment into which they had been sent – rode the political and strategic future of both nations. In this regard, the Americans would ultimately fare somewhat better than the British.

Over the years there had been several missed opportunities for British interests to be extended further south. Captain James Cook would arrive at the coast of what would later become British Columbia as early as 1778, but like his Spanish counterparts, Cook was a sailor, not a walker. He had islands in the South Pacific to see, and no interest in crossing mountain ranges. Without venturing further than Nootka Sound on the west coast of Vancouver Island, Cook continued his voyaging across the ocean. Captain George Vancouver would spend much of the 1790s mapping the west coast, but focused on the area north of Puget Sound up to Alaska. And on July 22, 1793, on the east side of the entrance to Elcho Harbour, in Bentinck Arm near latter-day Bella Coola, transcontinental explorer and North West Company employee Alexander Mackenzie inscribed his brief message – "from Canada, by land" – on the most famous rock in the country. But Mackenzie's arduous route had taken a more northerly bearing, avoiding what had seemed to be the impassable barrier of the Rocky Mountain Trench.

As for the Columbia River, British trading companies were aware of its potential to them as a trading route and were anxious to prevent American annexation of its navigable portions. But the British government could not possibly fully appreciate at that time the importance of that body of water to Canada's future in terms of its fisheries, hydroelectric power, and the cultural sustenance of aboriginal people. Although the realization would eventually come, it would come too late. Even the appreciation of the Columbia's value as a navigation route seemed insufficient to stimulate a strong push to establish a trading base at its mouth. As a result, in 1805 – at much the same time that the North West Company's Simon Fraser was celebrating the first British crossing of the southern Rockies from east to west by naming the region he found there "New Caledonia" – the Lewis and Clark expedition was already setting up an American flag at the mouth of the Columbia, at what would later become the border between Washington state and Oregon. David Thompson, another North West Company employee, made his first foray into the upper reaches of the Columbia River in the eastern Kootenays in 1807. He worked his way slowly through the west Kootenays, setting up trading forts for the North West Company, and not until July 15, 1811, did he complete his journey to the mouth of the Columbia. When he arrived, it was to find that an expedition financed by New York businessman John Jacob Astor had beaten him by only a few months. Fort Astoria was up and running, and American trading operations were about to commence.

However, although the Astor expedition was the first to arrive – a step that would prove crucial to the retention of jurisdiction by the United States a few years later – the American trading business would also prove, at least initially, to be far from successful. The Astorians met with a string of disasters that forced them rapidly out of business, and for about five years after 1813, the North West Company exercised a virtual monopoly throughout the Pacific Northwest. It seemed that by a matter of luck rather than through the implementation of any strategic plan, the British had been successful in establishing the level of control they wanted. But a simple bureaucratic provision would put paid to it all. Under the terms of the 1814 Treaty of Ghent ending the 1812 war between Great Britain and the United States, "All Territory, Places, and Possessions whatsoever taken by either Party from the other during the War, or which may be taken after the signing of this Treaty...shall be restored without delay." By definition, unfortunately for the British, that included Fort Astoria (by then renamed Fort George), and the Americans eventually realized that. After the United States successfully argued its case to the British, Fort George was returned to American control in 1818. There it would remain.

Jurisdiction over the all-important interior remained a matter of disagreement, however. In October 1818 the two governments had agreed on a temporary compromise, signing a formal convention to provide that for the next ten years the 49th parallel would serve as the boundary between the two countries east of the Rockies; west of the mountains, they agreed to joint occupation of the disputed border territory, respecting each other's rights and claims without dispute. The agreement was renewed in 1827, but still without a resolution of the tension between the two countries' aspirations for exclusive control of the region. During the 1830s, American settlers began flooding in great numbers into Oregon and the region to its east and immediately south of the 49th parallel, bordering the Kootenays. The United States appeared simply to be adopting a strategy of occupation – if enough American citizens settled in the territory, then it would become American by default. At the same time, American presidential candidate James Polk began campaigning on a promise to drive the U.S. border all the way north to latitude 54°40'N using "Fifty-Four Forty or Fight" as his campaign slogan.

The British appeared incapable of much resistance. In 1843, recognizing the increasing likelihood of having to withdraw from the southern Columbia region, the Hudson's Bay Company removed its trading headquarters to the newly created Fort Victoria, on the southern tip of Vancouver Island. Fearing war as a real possibility – and more importantly, the loss of any such war – the British caved and offered the compromise of settling the border at the 49th parallel, the Americans' original position. And so it was that Messrs. Buchanan and Pakenham signed and sealed the short but dramatic document before them on that summery day in Washington in 1846.

It is fair to assume that they – or at least their respective officials – would have had a reasonable sense of the topography of the landscape affected by their agreement. The British government had pushed for control of the south partly because it understood the challenges posed by the mountains in terms of connecting the country from east to west. Nevertheless, they could not have been intimate with some of the specific and immediate impacts of their document in the far western reaches of their countries. Surveys of the boundary were not begun until 1858, and took four years to complete. Separate British and American surveys had been commissioned, and when they were combined, disparities of hundreds of feet in some places were discovered. The reasons were known, even then: the gravitational pull of local land masses – like mountains – affected the accuracy of astronomical observations. The lines between boundary markers were also drawn as straight lines – not a problem for short distances, but in this case a curved line such as those used for latitude might have served better. The two countries eventually decided, several decades later, that the best approach was to agree that the international boundary would be the one physically marked on the ground even if it did not from time to time actually coincide with the 49th parallel.

Apparently unaware of that later agreement, in 2002 three optimistic American defendants charged with drug possession on the south side of a Kootenays/Washington border post attempted an enterprising defence. Their argument was that the border post lay north of the 49th parallel instead of on it – as required by the Washington state constitution – and therefore neither the state nor any other authority had jurisdiction to prosecute. Their actions, according to their lawyer, had occurred in what amounted to "no man's land." The Supreme Court of Washington, although it apparently enjoyed the opportunity to review such an interesting piece of the history of their state, wasted little time in rejecting the argument.

There would be many unforeseen consequences over the years of this drawing of an invisible but unbreakable line across the southern Columbia Mountains, separating the people who lived on either side of it permanently. As a trading route, the rights of both countries to utilize the Columbia River had been preserved in the Oregon Treaty, but the usefulness of the right would slowly be eroded over time with the advances in alternative transportation technology and the opening up of alternative travel options. The development of hydro-electric and irrigation schemes south of the border by American interests and the construction of dams along the massive river put paid to any remaining use of it as a commercial navigational route, as well as to the annual migration upriver of spawning wild Pacific salmon. The dams would also be the catalyst for the next major set of negotiations between the two jurisdictions several decades later, with both sides fighting intensely to protect their interests in the Columbia.

But of all the people and groups affected by the Oregon Treaty of 1846, the most profound and immediate impact would be felt by aboriginal people. Equally important to both the Sinixt and to the Ktunaxa people throughout the Kootenays were their north–south migratory patterns – clearly as logical a travel route for them as it was for the new occupants of their territory. For time out of mind they and their ancestors had travelled south seasonally for trading, hunting, and refuge from inclement northern weather. Their relatives and trading partners were scattered throughout communities as far south as Montana, Idaho, and eastern Washington state. Suddenly, with no advance warning and apparently no regard at all for their way of life, people who had travelled freely through the mountains, as their forebears had done for thousands of years, had their ability – and rights – to do so at will severely circumscribed, and without apparent recourse. It was to change a way of life seemingly forever, and not to their benefit.

It was a matter of little consequence for Messrs. Buchanan and Pakenham, and the governments they represented. Sadly, there was worse to come.

3

THE KEY IN THE LOCK:
building the path to
the Slocan

The Slocan Valley slumbered peacefully on for another
forty-five years, barely noticed – let alone heard of – by the
rest of the world. Until the 1890s it was not even named
as such in any European lexicon, although a number of
explorers had passed by the mouth of the Slocan River
and noted in their records, as best they could, the word
that the local native people used. Thus Palliser's expedition in 1859 thought it might be *Shlogan*, or *Schlocan*;
Dewdney captured it as *Slokèn* in 1865; and Moberly as

This image, held by the Nelson Museum, has no legend to help identify the man pictured. He is, however, fishing in what appears to be a traditional canoe utilized by both the Lakes and the Kootenay people.

Slocken in 1866. The meanings that various geographers, writers, and surveyors have ascribed to the name have ranged from "frogs" to "to pierce; strike on the head," to "a place to catch salmon." In local pioneer folklore, a dubious story circulates that it derived from an anglicized Indian phrase – *"slo-can-go,"* said to have been in use because of the difficulty of travelling in that terrain. Latter-day ethnologists Randy Bouchard and Dorothy Kennedy have recorded the name as an Okanagan-Colville Indian word, *slhu7kín*. Descendants of the Lakes Indians who travelled regularly in the area say that means "the place of the bull trout."

In any event, as far as the outside world was concerned, whatever the area was called then was immaterial. Other events of greater or lesser significance were demanding the attention of the individuals who were busy shaping the future of British Columbia, and for the present, the Slocan was left more or less alone. Its time of tranquil isolation was coming to a close, however: like the Oregon Treaty before them, each of these events would – some to a fundamental degree – influence what was to occur in the Slocan Valley several decades later. But in the years immediately following the signing of the Oregon Treaty, the nucleus of what would eventually become the province of British Columbia was still in its infancy, although already forming a strong and petulant personality. By the early 1850s, apart from the occupants of trading forts, barely 450 European settlers had colonized only two hundred hectares of land, all on Vancouver Island and all under the apparently benign dictatorship of the Hudson's Bay Company.

These settlers were vastly outnumbered in the West by the aboriginal population, but the balance would shift in a matter of a few years. By 1871, ten thousand Europeans would be clustered around the mouth of the Fraser River and Victoria and scattered throughout the interior; by the beginning of the 1880s, the census figures would record fifty thousand non-aboriginal people in British Columbia. By then, smallpox epidemics would have devastated the native population in staggering numbers, and the trend reversing the numbers would only continue, at least for the foreseeable future. One hundred years later, aboriginal people would make up about 3 percent of the population of British Columbia. In the Slocan, for all intents and purposes, there would seem to be none at all.

One of the key matters occupying government in Ottawa and Victoria during the 1850s and the years following that decade was transcontinental transportation. British Columbia had been declared a crown colony in 1858, ending the Hudson's Bay Company's virtual monopoly on exploration, settlement, and the establishment of trade routes. At the same time, gold rushes on the Fraser River brought into the B.C. interior the first real flood of permanent immigrants, increasing the demand for effective and economically viable means to travel to and from the coast as well as to Ontario and the east coast of Canada. At that time the transcontinental journey for the ordinary traveller from the east was arduous in the extreme, requiring passage by sea around the far southerly route of Cape Horn and north again to San Francisco or Victoria. For the more adventurous or the impecunious, an overland route by wagon trail was the only other option. Either one required several months' commitment of time and considerable financial resources.

Rail was the only feasible, long-term, commercially viable option. In the United States, the American Central Pacific Railway achieved a complete connection from the east coast to San Francisco by 1869. For a time, travellers to British Columbia could at least rely on this circuitous route, completing their journey by steamship to Victoria. It would be 1885 before a transcontinental link north of the border was completed by the Canadian Pacific Railway, and 1886 before the first passenger train, carrying relatively wealthy first- and second-class customers only, arrived in Port Moody on the west coast after a six-day journey from Montreal. Even at that point, there remained no cheap option for the majority of travellers, nor any direct link from the CPR line into the valleys of the Kootenays.

In Victoria, meanwhile, Governor James Douglas was busily regulating mining activity in the hope of levering some control over the wild and unruly occupants of the crown colony's gold fields. Borrowing from Australia and New Zealand, the Gold Fields Act of 1859 established mining boards and registration and licensing systems, and created the position of gold commissioner, an ad hoc extra police service in the mining regions. In an effort to improve access to the interior, Edgar Dewdney was commissioned by the government in 1861 to extend the wagon route that had already been built heading east out of Hope towards latter-day Princeton. By 1865 the Dewdney Trail had reached the Kootenays, spurred on by yet more gold strikes in the previous year, this time at Wild Horse Creek in the east Kootenays and on the Big Bend of the Columbia River.

In 1867, the Dominion of Canada was founded under the British North America Act, which gave the federal government, among other things, exclusive legislative authority over "Indians, and Lands reserved for the Indians." Four years later British Columbia succumbed to the inevitable and joined the Dominion, but subject to two significant conditions. First, Ottawa must dedicate large sums of money to railway building in the new province. In exchange, British Columbia would grant land to the railway builder for twenty miles on either side of the future tracks (for which it would receive $100,000 a year in perpetuity from Ottawa). Second, in a sign of things to come, British Columbia from the outset disclaimed any liability for its native population. Indians, it said, were the responsibility of the Canadian government in the British North America Act; and it should stay that way. Both conditions were, much later, to become sources of contention and regret for subsequent B.C. governments. In 1871, however, they seemed significant victories.

In the meantime, although the census figures for that year recorded a population of only 110 people living in the Kootenays (in addition, as the census records put it, to "139 Chinese"), the Kootenay District already had a sitting member of the B.C. legislature, Mr. R.J. Skinner. Businessman John Andrew Mara became the Kootenays' first member of Parliament; and Joseph William Trutch became British Columbia's first lieutenant-governor. Trutch had been the former colony's commissioner of crown lands since 1864, the same year that Governor James Douglas retired from service. Both Douglas and Trutch had consistent land policies that supported rapid and progressive European settlement; where they differed, at least initially, was in the matter of how aboriginal people and their lands would be treated. Douglas had started a process of treaty settlements between 1850 and 1854, reserving large tracts of land for the exclusive use of the treaty nation. The reserved lands remained in crown ownership, however, as did all the reserves laid out after 1854. Many of them were in areas into which settlers were also moving. The goal was to integrate native people into the new society by encouraging them to utilize pre-emption opportunities outside reserve lands, and eventually, to do away with reserves altogether.

It was a short-lived policy. Pre-emption – a system to allow the occupation of unsurveyed crown lots of 160 acres coupled with the ability to obtain ownership of the lot through sustained improvements rather than through purchase – was aimed at encouraging faster settlement. It had been permitted as early as the 1850s, although it was not formally established until the 1870 Land Ordinance came into effect (and was not finally abolished until as late as 1970). However, one of the first moves that Trutch made was to prohibit Indian people from pre-empting crown lands. His second and third moves were to start removing prime pieces of land from existing reserves and to limit new reserves to ten acres per family. Various legislative restrictions on the ability of native people to vote, obtain legal assistance, and access education accumulated over the years. Thus progressively disabled, and unable to readily reconcile their traditional occupation of much larger territories through seasonal migratory hunting and trading patterns with the static occupation of much smaller fixed parcels of land, native people had little chance to hold their own against the storm of incoming change.

In the west Kootenays, the problem was compounded by isolation – not even crown land reserves were set aside in those early days – and by the "Indian diaspora" that had occurred as a consequence of Hudson's Bay Company (HBC) trading activities there in the early 19th century. HBC forts had been created further south, below what would become the border between Canada and the United States. Those forts had drawn many Indian people from the Arrow and Kootenay Lakes area south to trade and to winter over, changing a habitual cold-weather pattern that had formerly seen many of them remaining further north in areas such as the Slocan Valley during the winter. The creation of the border in 1846 had the effect of separating many of these people permanently from their traditional homelands, or so it seemed at the time. Certainly the 1872 establishment by the American government of a substantial Indian reservation near Colville in Washington state, to accommodate this formerly migratory population, provided an incentive for them to remain south of the border. Although Canadian reserves were laid out further east in 1884 to accommodate Kootenay Indian bands, no equivalent was offered to native people living in the Arrow Lakes and north and west of Kootenay Lake.

The far western reaches of the Kootenays, and the Slocan Valley itself, had remained relatively empty of any other human settlement or activity during this period. Slowly but surely, however, the fingers of European exploration began to pry open its secrets. A railway charter had been granted by the provincial government to the Columbia and Kootenay Railway and Transportation Company in 1883. The company was backed by a syndicate headed by a former Mississippi River steamboat captain named J.C. Ainsworth. In exchange for building a railway line from the mouth of the Kootenay River to Kootenay Lake to bypass the non-navigable Bonnington Falls, and connecting the railway line to both Kootenay Lake and the Columbia River by steamboat, the company would receive valuable land on Kootenay Lake and Kootenay River as well as on the Columbia. By 1891 the CPR had taken over the company as well as the benefit of the charter, and the railway line was in operation. In the meantime a young Englishman named William Adolph Baillie-Grohman, with visions of an intricate system of dike building and drainage and vast agricultural development – ambitions that would be outmatched by reality – had been successful in having land set aside at the swampy south end of Kootenay Lake for the purpose of reclamation. The only thing that would be drained, however, was his bank account. In 1887, halfway up the west shore of Kootenay Lake, the tiny settlement of Ainsworth (pre-empted by J.C.'s son George in 1882) became the first town in the region to appear on a map of British Columbia.

Former Indian Land Commissioner Gilbert Malcolm Sproat travelled through the Kootenays in the mid-1880s, reporting on the climate, topography, and resources of the region. In his travels Sproat laid out the townsite of the future Nelson on the west arm of Kootenay Lake, calling it Stanley, although it was first generally known as Salisbury. Sproat's 1884 "Report on the Kootenay Country" to the minister of agriculture is eloquent and almost poetic in its descriptions of the terrain of the western region, including the Slocan Valley:

> "On the western side...particularly between the great Kootenay Lake and Slocan Lake or the Columbia River, the mountains form a broad mass rising in parts high with some snow peaks, and shedding water in all directions...The northerly and southerly trend of the Rockies, and the general though irregular parallelism of the Selkirks give necessarily a corresponding character and course to the valleys and rivers. The surface is corrugated, pressed together like the narrower part of a fan. Instead of opening westerly to the sea, the valleys are shut off by several mountain ranges...The natural facilities of intercourse are therefore greater in a north and south direction than from east to west."

Sproat continues with a poignant political comment harking back forty years, surely outside the mandate he was given:

> "It was a full knowledge of the almost insurmountable barriers to traffic presented by the north and south ranges of this north-western region of America that caused Great Britain to insist so earnestly, during the negociations [sic] ended by the Oregon Treaty of 1846, upon extending her territorial rights south so as to share at least in the benefits of the Columbia waterway...The Canadian Pacific railway [sic], cutting across the vast ribs of our land, redresses the practical failure of British diplomacy in 1846, and corrects nature."

Contrary to popular opinion, he also went on to note:

> "With the exception of Vancouver Island, Kootenay is in fact, naturally, the most accessible region in the province. But we have been fumbling about and have not put the key in the lock."

And finally, with respect to the mining prospects of the west Kootenays, Sproat had this to say:

> "Very little is known of the mineral resources of Kootenay Lake. It looks like a mining region...Galena ledges, supposed to be silver-bearing, have been discovered last year on the west side of the lake. Practical men who have been sent to examine the region generally...have been satisfied with its promising character. Almost everybody who was employed on Kootenay Lake in 1883 has what he considers to be a silver-bearing galena claim. Half a dozen men regard themselves already as Comstock millionaires. There is nothing in the facts as yet to justify any such belief..."

Sproat's caution was not justified, at least in the short term. Had he had the benefit of contemporary technology and scientific knowledge, he might have been more optimistic. In fact, the area around Kootenay Lake contained significant deposits of galena, a type of ore bearing silver, lead, and zinc in varying degrees. These deposits were also relatively accessible, for reasons of geology.

During the Jurassic Period, 210–140 million years ago, intense pressure built with infinite slowness under the Earth's crust. In the Columbia

Basin, this pressure would be to mountain-building what the 1980s was to high-rise development; just a little slower in its implementation. Over seventy millennia, the metamorphic rock and granite intrusions of the Selkirk and Purcell Mountains formed at a pace of four millimetres a year. They pushed the area that is now known as Revelstoke closer to the Rockies by three hundred kilometres and tossed up from deep within the Earth all kinds of ancient souvenirs of earlier eras. Fossil hunters would later find molluscs on the tops of mountains and squid in the shale of rivers hundreds of kilometres from the ocean. Such massive change, effected over a period of time impossible to grasp in human terms, is both astonishing and riveting. But understanding this geological change also helps to appreciate what would happen in the Slocan Valley 140 million years later, give or take a decade or two.

The language of geologists and scientists is almost invariably turgid and dense, although it can also be strangely poetic in its terminology. Here is how the provincial Ministry of Energy and Mines attempted to describe the contemporary impact of all that ancient activity:

> "The geology of the Slocan area comprises diverse lithological elements belonging to several tectonic terranes. On a regional scale, the Slocan Mining Camp is within the Kootenay Arc which lies between the Precambrian Purcell anticlinorium on the east and the Monashee and Valhalla metamorphic complexes to the west and northwest. The Kootenay Arc is a four hundred kilometre long curving belt of Cambrian to Mesozoic sedimentary, volcanic and metamorphic rocks trending northeast for 160 kilometres across Washington state into British Columbia, then north along Kootenay Lake and northwest into the Revelstoke area."

The Slocan Lake fault is described in equally disciplined terms, but in even more lyrical adjectives:

> "...A 100 kilometre long, east-dipping, linear detachment structure is exposed above the east shore of Slocan Lake. The 'upper plate' of the fault is brecciated, fractured and hydrothermally altered granite rocks of the Nelson batholith. Prolonged movement in the crushed contact zone of the batholith likely sustained a

channel way for hydrothermal solutions...silver-lead-zinc ores [galena] predominate and can be characterized as gold-silver or silver-gold with minor lead-zinc mineralization."

In simpler terms, chips and chunks of silver-rich galena could be found lying on the ground in the Slocan if one only knew where to look.

The sense of the richness of the region was certainly growing fast by the 1880s. There were legendary tales of outcroppings of galena so huge that trappers and Indians would smelt lead for bullets directly from the exposed vein. In the year immediately following Sproat's report, prospectors were already working their way down the Arrow Lakes and west from Kootenay Lake into the periphery of the Slocan watershed. In 1885, Ike Lougheed, Jack Evans, Robert Baird, and Captain John Sanderson, among others, made their way down many of the creeks in the watersheds that feed the Arrow Lakes and Kootenay River. But they were searching for the glitter of gold; the dull sheen of galena held little attraction for them at that time, and they did not stay for long. Meanwhile, the villages of Ainsworth and Nelson on Kootenay Lake were both starting to grow. The Bluebell Mine at Riondel on the east shore was operating successfully, as were the Silver King group of mines on Toad Mountain, fifteen kilometres from Nelson – notwithstanding sharp dealings, claim jumping, litigation, and even murder, perhaps indications of the value that some attributed to the potential of the Nelson region.

The effects of improved transportation technology were also slowly making themselves felt. By the end of the 1880s, small steamships and sternwheelers were operating on the Arrow Lakes and the Columbia River. The Columbia and Kootenay Steam Navigation Company, established on December 21, 1889, was striving for the successful domination of Kootenay Lake between Nelson and the mining communities further north. Travel remained a north–south enterprise rather than a lateral undertaking: no rail connection had yet been made to the main transcontinental CPR line at Revelstoke, but American interests were pushing up from the south to just below the border. The Spokane Falls & Northern, known as the Nelson and Fort Sheppard Railway in Canada, would reach Nelson by 1893.

This push from the south was not surprising. The region was prime for commercial exploitation, and, notwithstanding the border, there were no real barriers in the way of American entrepreneurs trying their luck and their money in the area. The west Kootenays were starting to capture the interest of business people in Victoria, but the area was gaining far more attention in the western United States, which was effectively much closer and its people in many ways more attuned to the economic, geographic, and social climate of the region. In 1890 the American government had passed the Sherman Silver Purchase Act, authorizing its Treasury to purchase an immense amount of silver at the prevailing market price. Accordingly, many of the prospectors and businessmen who had already come to the Kootenays were American rather than British or Canadian, and they were hungry to make a fortune.

There was an almost tangible anticipation in the air when, one day at the dawn of the 1890s, a prospector named Jim Brennan brought some ore samples into Ainsworth from an unknown source. They assayed out at 150 ounces of silver per ton – a very rich find. The excitement mounted, and increasing numbers of prospectors started to gather in the towns and villages of the west Kootenays, searching for a grubstake and perhaps a partner to share the risk and riches. It would not have been much of a surprise for the good folk of Ainsworth to open their *Hot Spring News* on the morning of October 3, 1891, and read that "the reports circulated and stories told by Jack Seaton, the Hennessy boys, Frank Flint, and John McGuygan [sic] on their return from the Kaslo-Slocan divide, on Thursday, set the town of Ainsworth wild with excitement...Bill Hennessy...says...that hundreds of tons of ore are in sight...every one of the party imagine[s] himself at once a millionaire."

The rush was on. By December 26, as the heavy bite of winter closed in on the steep, dark valleys, the Nelson *Miner* reported that "men are strung along the trail between Nelson and the lower end of Slocan Lake – some hauling boats, some pulling toboggans, some driving pack animals, some with their all on their backs – all buoyed up with the hope that the hidden wealth of the new-found Eldorado is alone for those who smilingly endure hardships and surmount obstacles." At the lower end of Slocan Lake, reported the same article, Harry Ward and Arthur Dick had a townsite surveyed and expected "to make a killing."

These hopefuls were riding on the back of one original strike, already wreathed in intrigue and the promise of vast wealth – but only for the fastest and the most ruthless. Earlier in the summer of 1891, two prospectors – one typical, the other far from it – had been prompted by finds up Kaslo Creek to venture further west towards the Slocan Valley. John L. "Jack" Seaton was an Irishman by way of Tennessee who had come to the Kootenays on the promise first of gold, then of silver. Eli Carpenter had come for the same reasons, but from a vastly different background – or so he claimed. The truth remains a mystery. Many sources claim he was French Canadian, but Carpenter's story, as recorded in newspapers and correspondence of the time, was that he hailed from northern France. There, he said, he had learned tightrope walking as an understudy to Jean-Francois "Blondin" Gravelet, the famous Frenchman who crossed Niagara Falls on a tightrope on June 30, 1859. He was also rumoured to have worked for P.T. Barnum's circus in Connecticut, with a sensational act that involved carrying his wife across the rope five storeys up. The same wife, if she existed, did not accompany Carpenter on his prospecting forays to the West. Several years later, Carpenter did show some real prowess at tightrope walking between buildings in a demonstration held in Slocan City on Victoria Day, 1897 – but his lasting fame, or infamy in the eyes of some, relates to his discovery of silver in the Slocan.

Hearing of Brennan's find, Carpenter and Seaton had formed a partnership. In July 1891, they headed west over the mountains towards Slocan Lake from Kaslo on Kootenay Lake, looking for galena. By the end of August, they had found nothing worth pursuing and were contemplating defeat. But on September 9, the two exhausted men crested a rise on a ridge that gave them sweeping views of a towering mountain named Idaho Peak and across to Slocan Lake over a deep gulch, at the bottom of which a narrow creek rushed far below them. Resting prone on the ground and on the brink of giving up, they found themselves sitting on the find of their lives. Raw chunks of galena were scattered all around them. The partners promptly staked out the four claims to which they were entitled and returned to Ainsworth to have their samples assayed and to register the claims. The results were as rich as they might have hoped, assaying out at even more than Brennan's find. But for some reason, the partnership soured. One version of the story is that Carpenter deliberately lied to Seaton, telling him the ore was worthless, and took on a German named Bielenberg as his new partner in order to secretly return to the claims and reap their riches. Kinder versions simply have the partners falling out with each other and returning separately to the claims with new partners.

If Carpenter did mislead him, Seaton appears to have worked out the truth for himself anyway. He took on not one, but four new partners – the Hennessy boys, Frank Flint, and John McGuigan – and the party scrambled to beat Carpenter back to the claims. They were successful, and on October 5 staked out a rich set of claims around the first four that would pay huge dividends over the years under the banner of the "Noble Five" Mine. Carpenter, beaten to the chase, seems to have lost heart and did not pursue his claim. He sold his interest a month later to one John Retallack for a small sum. Seaton sold out almost as quickly, also for a

modest amount. Their claims, which they had registered under the name Payne, would eventually become the richest mine in the Slocan and the seventh-highest dividend-paying operation in British Columbia. Seaton did not live long enough to learn of his poor decision. Carpenter had long since moved on by the time the wealth of the Payne had become legendary, and may also have never known of his missed fortune. Indeed, if they had known, they may not have cared.

The character of the prospector has always been quite different from that of the miner. "You must not conclude that prospecting is a soft snap and that any duffer can strike it rich," wrote New Denver's J.C. Harris three decades later. Although prospecting attracted men from all walks of life, they had one thing in common: an almost feverish obsession with the idea of the strike. To that end, they would suffer almost anything for the sake of that precious moment when they might hit paydirt. Hopeful prospectors in the thousands poured into the Slocan, the fever of excitement mounting, and the anticipation of the hunt the sole topic of barroom conversations. They came from all over Canada, from Great Britain and Europe, and overwhelmingly from south of the border, streaming north to find silver. But once the sweat and toil of the search was over and the silver found, the excitement was gone – and the history of the Slocan is full of stories of prospectors who sold their claims for just enough to grubstake them on to the next valley, and who never looked back. And, after the prospectors, came the people who really wanted to make money.

Facing page: The first claim staked in the Slocan Mining Camp was the Beaver Claim at Blue Ridge, by Lardo Jack and Andrew Jardine.

4

THE PARIS OF THE WEST:
the boom years

The *Victoria Daily Colonist* newspaper of July 14, 1897,
quoted a correspondent for the *Seattle Post-Intelligencer*
who was effervescent in his praise of the little mining
town of Sandon in British Columbia's interior: "Sandon
undoubtedly ranks as the showplace of the Kootenays, and
in its own picturesqueness and that of its surroundings,
there is no place in the world to compare with it!"

And on August 25, 1898, a correspondent for the
Spokane *Spokesman Review* could not contain his

enthusiasm: "Sandon is the centre of the greatest camp and richest silver-lead known to the world today, heralded near home as the 'Silvery Slocan'...These mines have paid more dividends and shipped more ore than any other section of the favoured Kootenays...for its size, Sandon boasts of as fine a lot of mercantile, hotel, and public buildings as any town of twice its size in the southern section of the province."

This was no mere puffery on the part of city journalists observing from a safe distance events in the Slocan Mining Camp, as the district became known. Various mining publications of the time were in excitable agreement. The *B.C. Mining Record* of October 1896 confirmed that "the country generally is showing every sign of advancement...there is an air of bustle and excitement all around," and Sandon's own *Mining Review*

Sandon at the height of its boom years, 1898.

stated emphatically that "there is no reason Sandon should not have its many thousands of people."

In the same fall of 1891 during which Carpenter and Seaton made the Payne discovery, 140 more claims were registered in the Slocan Mining Camp. That winter, despite the caution in the Nelson *Miner* that "it is not advisable for anyone, except those wishing to pass a winter breathing the purest of air and enjoying freedom from the restraints of civilization, to venture into Slocan district before the middle of March," a number of entrepreneurs had swiftly moved in to claim their ground. They were not all prospectors and miners: John R. Cook was eyeing Slocan Lake with plans to build a steamboat, Angus McIntyre was packing freight for hopeful claim stakers, Martin Fry was cooking up a storm for hungry travellers, and Gorman West set up his "Traveller's Home" lodging at a fork in the Slocan River. The Kaslo–Slocan trail that Carpenter and Seaton had more or less followed in their explorations – the latter-day route, with some variations, of Highway 31A from Kaslo to New Denver – became a regular transportation route, at least for horses and people travelling on foot. Within a year, sixteen mines were operating from the first claims; at the end of another three years, over four million kilograms of ore had been hauled out of the area.

More than three thousand claims would be registered in the Slocan Mining Camp in the next five years, during the glory days of the silver boom. In the narrow gulch of Carpenter Creek – the rushing stream that Carpenter and Seaton had seen below them when they made their discovery of the Payne site – a small settlement named Sandon started to squeeze itself into existence between the steep walls of the mountains surrounding it, on a barely discernible strip of more-or-less flat land on either side of the creek. But it was three other communities that vied at first for the envied position of becoming the Eldorado of the Silvery Slocan. Foremost – at least initially – was Three Forks, located on the Kaslo–Slocan Lake trail about twenty kilometres east of New Denver, where Seaton and Kane Creeks join Carpenter Creek as it turns west in its rush towards Slocan Lake. New Denver – at first literally named Eldorado – was situated where Carpenter Creek flows out into Slocan Lake; and Silverton, a few kilometres south of New Denver, was also considered to have the potential to outshine the others.

It would be luck, as much as anything, that would enable one community to eventually prosper over another. Almost every town in the Slocan was started by one or two individuals with grand dreams of riches and of their names being recorded in civic history forever. Their success or failure relied not only on persistence and resources but to a far greater degree on the vagaries of matters entirely beyond their control: where the railway lines would eventually be built, the destruction of random forest fires; even political actions in other countries could end dreams overnight.

Young Scotsman John Adam Watson made his way to the Slocan district in 1891 and promptly bought some acres, staking his townsite a few kilometres east of Three Forks on the Kaslo–Slocan trail, not far from the site of the Payne discovery. Watson was banking on his townsite becoming a major centre of commerce, along what he hoped would be the primary ore-shipping route from the mines: east to Kaslo. Watson wrote prolific and entertaining letters to his beleaguered fiancée Alice Clarke, waiting in England for him to make his fortune, and to his Aunt Sara, relating some of his experiences. At first, he was optimistic, writing on January 7, 1892: "I have several irons in the fire and hope to pull some of them out without scorching [my] fingers...my humble experience is this: bull-headed luck plays a very conspicuous part in the programme in this country at any rate. If putting up with discomfort, hard work, poor grub etc. entitles a man to any substantial reward in this mundane sphere then I should certainly deem there is a very front seat coming to me...I hope to see it looming up pretty soon." His enthusiasm had not faded a year later when he wrote on January 16, 1893: "Should the supply of silver emanating from the mines keep coming out in the way it has been doing, nothing can keep us back and my town of 'Watson' is right in the heart of the mining country, everything comes to he who waits..."

But by October the same year the price of silver was in disarray after the United States repealed the 1890 Silver Purchase Act, and Watson tried to sell the townsite to whoever might be convinced that the dream was still attainable. There seemed to be no sign that any railway companies had notions of using Watson as a stop-over point; and in July 1894, the last blow was struck when a wildfire roared through the area and burnt the small number of wooden buildings to the ground. "The fire left me nothing but the clothes I stood up in," he wrote to Alice, who must have been seriously reconsidering the wisdom of leaving England to marry the poor fellow at that point. "Books, papers, and everything I had was licked up by the flames...just at the moment I must question whether I could give [Watson] away." The indefatigable Scot found work eventually with the Geological Survey for fifty dollars a month, while continuing to hope that someone, somewhere, might see fit to buy his land. It was not to be. Watson Town, like its namesake, eventually simply faded out of sight.

New Denver, still going by the name of Eldorado in 1891, would fare much more profitably. Its location was attractive for both its commercial viability and its naturally amenable setting. A sheltered delta suitable for numerous building sites had formed where Carpenter Creek tumbles down the last few hundred metres of its turbulent course west towards Slocan Lake. Timber for building was readily accessible and the soil was rich, holding real potential for farming and the cultivation of fruit. The lake moderated the climate, and the settlement was hundreds of metres lower in elevation than those on the Kaslo–Slocan trail. While the late spring snows still clogged the passes through the mountains, down at the lake the wildflowers would have started to bloom. And after a hard day's work, a businessman or miner would be able to sit on the porch of his home or favourite hotel and admire the sun setting over the Valhalla Mountains across the shimmering lake.

As a jumping-off point for reaching the mining claims at the up-stream end of Carpenter Creek, New Denver also had another distinct advantage over the hopefuls setting up shop along the Kaslo–Slocan trail. Although it is only thirty kilometres in a straight line from Kaslo to the mining camps, the trail west from Kootenay Lake, challenged by large mountains and steep gullies, was almost one hundred kilometres long. Access to the claims from the New Denver side of the mountains, on the other hand, was much more straightforward, as was the ability to ship ore out and to the south. A rudimentary horse trail connected the port of Nakusp on the Arrow Lakes to Slocan Lake. As an alternative, the CPR's secondary railway line between Robson, on the Columbia River, and Nelson, following the path of the Kootenay River, was open by May 1891. It was relatively easy for entrepreneurs from Nelson to follow the trail beat by the first prospectors from the CPR siding at South Slocan on the Kootenay River. Travelling northward, along the relatively flat bench lands of the Slocan River, to Slocan Lake – a mere forty-odd kilometres – they could complete the journey over water.

When two merchants by the name of William Hunter and Bill McKinnon travelled the Slocan River trail and then rowed up Slocan Lake in the late fall of 1891, they found a number of prospectors already camped at Eldorado. Hunter and McKinnon were sold out of their supplies before they had even started building a log cabin to serve as a general store. McKinnon returned to Nelson alone to restock, and Hunter went about setting up the business while he waited for his partner to return. Within a few months hundreds more prospectors and miners had joined the Eldorado camp, preparing themselves for the strenuous trip up into the mountains in the early spring. By the following summer, a townsite had been laid out and hotels and businesses were under construction, and the prospectors' romantic name for the camp had been rejected in favour of the more solid and respectable "New Denver," after its counterpart in Colorado.

Given the ease of access from both the south and the north to the Arrow Lakes and the Columbia River, New Denver would stake its future on becoming a supply and administrative centre for the mining community. To succeed, it was necessary to do everything possible to deter the mining companies from shipping ore east to Kaslo. These companies must be persuaded instead of the merits of freighting ore through New Denver, or at least west to the Arrow Lakes or south to the CPR siding at South Slocan. An enterprising fellow called Palma Angrignon, or "French Pete," was diligently rowing passengers and freight up and down Slocan Lake in a small boat. But one man's strong back would clearly not suffice, so William Hunter and some of his colleagues formed the Slocan Trading & Navigation Company and commissioned the building of a small steamer. The *William Hunter* would provide service between the south end of Slocan Lake and Rosebery, a small town developing at the head of the lake as a nexus between the Slocan Valley and Nakusp. Even prior to the building of the steamer it had become feasible to ship ore out on this route using pack horses. But it was also already possible to send ore east to Kaslo in the same manner. Reports vary as to which mine could claim fame for being the first to ship ore out of the Carpenter Creek area, but there is no doubt that by the summer of 1892 it was on its way both to

Kaslo and to Nakusp.

As New Denver started to flourish, Silverton was becoming established a few kilometres further south. The same William Hunter who had begun the general store in New Denver had, on his first trip north, been very taken with the scenic area where Four Mile Creek emptied into Slocan Lake. With Fred Hume, a partner from Nelson, he staked out a townsite on the pretty little spot at the beginning of 1892, giving it the name Silverton. A number of galena finds had been staked on the ridges overlooking the townsite. It seemed realistic that a successful mining empire could be constructed around the infant settlement, without having to rely on persuading the miners from Carpenter Creek to come all the way down the lake from New Denver to purchase supplies or stay in a hotel. Hunter relocated his general store from New Denver to Silverton, and the community started to expand steadily.

But the real excitement lay in the mining camps. Although claims were scattered throughout the region, they were most heavily clustered around Three Forks and the growing settlement of Sandon. Since Three Forks seemed like an attractive spot to make some money,

Lake Avenue, Silverton, circa 1898.

given its strategic location along all practical transportation routes, Charles Hugonin and Eric C. Carpenter – unrelated to the eccentric Eli – pre-empted a townsite without delay. Businesses grew as more and more people flooded in. By 1893, Three Forks had its own post office, half a dozen hotels, livery stables, a butcher, a blacksmith, and a barbershop, among other thriving enterprises. With the growing rumours of trains coming to the region in the near future, Three Forks looked set to dominate the region as a centre of commerce and was becoming a real threat to the viability of New Denver.

In the meantime, a young American man named Jonathan Morgan Harris had arrived in New Denver with a pack on his back and a colourful reputation behind him. Only twenty-eight years old, "Johnny" Harris was rumoured to have already killed a man. Born in Virginia, he had spent the last few years in Wallace, Idaho, not far south of the Kootenays. Attracted by the silver strikes, he brought with him to New Denver no desire to get dirty in the dark tunnels of the mines, but rather his significant experience in property speculation, a fairly ruthless streak, and a vision, energy, and commitment that was unparalleled in the area. Harris set to work immediately. New Denver, Three Forks, and Silverton did not appeal to him; and in any event, he had been beaten to the entrepreneurial draw in all three places. In a moment that would shape its history, Harris instead fell in love immediately with Sandon.

Apart from its raw physical appeal, Sandon also held an attraction for Harris that others, less worldly, had failed to see: although numerous buildings had been constructed by the time he arrived, none of their owners had actually staked land for a townsite. They were all squatters, and Harris had no compunction in pre-empting the townsite out from underneath them. After registering his claim in the spring of 1892 and calling it Loudon after his home town in Virginia, Harris notified the incumbent occupants that they must either purchase their plots or lose them. It did not endear him to his fellow townspeople, but Harris had the law on his side and the brashness to carry it off. He beat back the lawsuits and outrage and, using the money from the sale of the existing plots, subdivided the townsite further and began buying up mines and businesses. He also started building his flagship enterprise, the Reco Hotel, on the main street of Sandon.

Calling it the "main street" makes Sandon sound like a new town in any other location, when that was anything but the case. Most new townsites in British Columbia were laid out in a grid pattern, and by 1892 a great deal of thought had been given to the most appropriate survey methods to accommodate the rapid settlement taking place in other parts of the province. Very detailed instructions were available to surveyors, who among other things were required to use instruments independent of the magnetic needle in running lines, to use marker posts of extraordinarily precise specifications, and to place pieces of charcoal under the posts as a method of later identification. But Sandon had more or less grown out of the ground in a matter of months, defying such precision in both its physical location and in the temperament of its occupants.

Sandon was, quite simply, like no other place in British Columbia. The valley it lay in is a narrow crevasse of trees, dirt, and rubble at the feet of walls of rock towering two thousand metres above the junction of Sandon and Carpenter Creeks. The road into Sandon from Three Forks climbs steadily until it reaches the townsite. "It is in a narrow gulch," wrote the correspondent for the *Seattle Post-Intelligencer*. "The sun bobs up above one mountain occasionally, says 'peep, oh,' and drops behind another mountain." And that is in the summer. In the winter, the sun's warmth is not felt down at the creek for long weeks at a time, and then only for the briefest of moments. The crackle and roar of avalanches is a constant accompaniment to winter's heavy tread, and torrents of snow regularly threaten the buildings below them. In the summer and fall, wildfires can sweep down the valley in a heartbeat, funnelled by the wind. The season for such fires is short, however: the snow does not depart until May, sometimes June – and it returns by September.

Into this hostile environment in 1892 stormed a development boom of magnificent proportions. "For a townsite," sniffed the same correspondent, "Sandon is simply ridiculous." But within four years Sandon, together with the satellite community of Cody, a few kilometres further up Sandon Creek, would have as many as two thousand permanent residents, a transient population of several thousand more, two newspapers of its own, a couple of dozen hotels, two banks, pharmacists, doctors, restaurateurs, jewellers, and fine clothiers, in addition to its industrial

The Kootenay Hotel, Sandon, circa 1896–97.

component of sawmills, lumber dealers, and hardware stores. For hundreds of metres on either side of Carpenter Creek the hillsides were scraped bare in a frenzy of building. For the first few years, the valley echoed ceaselessly to the noise of construction and revelling. For it was also possible to live a fine lifestyle – or at least, a lively one – in the town styling itself as "the Monte Carlo of Canada" and "the Paris of the West." For the aficionados of finer things, there were strawberries and oysters, ice cream, and fine wine in the hotels, and operas and plays to be enjoyed in the theatres. The more athletically inclined enjoyed sports clubs that would produce hockey players, ice skaters, curling teams, and skiers competing at an international level.

In his memoir of life in Sandon, *Window in the Rock*, old-timer Eugene Petersen recalled fondly the days of his childhood spent sledding,

Many of the Slocan Camp mines were poised on the slopes of steep mountains, like the Mammoth Mine Camp above Silverton.

snowshoeing, and generally engaging in youthful hijinks with his friends. For those inclined to a different cultural bent, there was as much liquor, gambling, and pleasure of the flesh as silver could buy. The saloons had their share of men in them with names like "Lone Jack" and "Big Al," gambling and drinking away their earnings in nights of excess and cheer. "Interspersed with [the miners and pack trains] are 'those girls' with the beautiful peroxidized tresses, mounted on blooded horses that gallop wildly, or prance and cavort in an anxiety to do so, while the fair riders ogle the [miners]," wrote the *Seattle Post-Intelligencer* correspondent enthusiastically. Sandon was the glittering jewel of the Silvery Slocan, and people just kept coming.

But Sandon's riches, like those of all the other mining towns, were

A pack train leaving Sandon to head out for the mines, late 1890s.

founded on a bitterly hard way of life. The pleasures of living near such a rollicking town, of gambling, drinking, and exchanging pleasantries with other fellows down from the mountains for a few precious hours, could not necessarily make up for the sheer hardship of working in the mines for a living.

The mining camps were mostly located far up the mountain-sides. In the very beginning, equipment and provisions had to be carried on foot up non-existent and semi-vertical trails to establish the operations, and frequently it took several exhausting trips to get everything needed on site. The sooner the miners got up there in the spring and the longer they stayed, the better. Some of them would stay all year round, but winter's tricks could easily cost a hapless soul his life. Dozens of men – and, on more than one occasion, women and children – died in ava-

A wintertime rawhiding team near Sandon. The leather-bound sacks of ore could weigh as much as a tonne each, sometimes taking horses off their feet on icy downhill slopes.

lanches, swept to oblivion in a moment's careless step. Horses, once trails had been established, fared little better than their owners. Mules and pack animals would have to carry loads of heavy equipment – cast-iron ovens and tools, sacks of provisions, and mining gear – to impossible heights. On at least one occasion a horse collapsed and died as it reached its destination, worn out by the sheer weight of the 180-kilo-gram load on its back.

But the horse was the main means to get ore from the mines out to freight depots. For the most part the horse packers took great care of their animals and obvious pride in the ability of individual animals to carry a load without any damage and in difficult conditions. In 1895 alone, according to one report, more than 8.5 million kilograms of ore was carried out of Sandon to the railheads by horses. Mines like the Payne or the Noble Five were large enough to invest in giant tramways to shift ore down the mountains – some more than two kilometres long – but smaller operators used a system called rawhiding. Stockpiling ore over the summer, miners would wait until sufficient snow had fallen to sled the heavy material down to the valley in rawhide packages weighing a tonne or more. The animal hides would be placed hair-side down to the snow and could then be laced up easily to secure the loose rock. "Leather stoneboats" was what one greenhorn observer called the rawhide packages, and it was an apt description.

Although a tonne of lead and silver ore is not as large as it may sound – perhaps the size of a large two-drawer filing cabinet – a tonne of dead weight is still a tonne of dead weight. The challenge for the horses was not to be run over by their own load as they came down the steep trails slicked to solid ice by the passage of many loads before them. Folklore relates stories of horses trained to sit back on their loads on their haunches and ride the packages down. Far more likely is the scenario that any horse on its haunches had simply been overtaken by its load. It was not that unusual, one observer noted, to see a horse "coming into town on the dead run," trying to stay ahead of its runaway cargo.

Most of the miners were young, single men. They worked long, arduous hours seven days a week, with four days off a year when employed, and were subject to layoff with no notice whenever a mine went sour. Wages were high, but so was the cost of living – twice as high as in Ontario, by comparison. These were not circumstances in which a man might feel inclined to get married and start a family, let alone bring them to live in such conditions. It was not possible to commute daily from Sandon up to most of the mines, and the company men were accommodated in bunkhouses sleeping as many as fifty. Wooden bunks were provided, but the men had to supply their own mattress and bedding. As often as not, there would be no running water and certainly no electricity, but a fee was still extracted by the company for providing the facility as well as the meals.

Days were spent underground in dark, cramped tunnels, knee-deep in cold mud, chiselling and hammering at the rock face. "There is no getting over the fact," wrote Robert Anderson from Lemon Creek to his uncle in Florida in 1902, "there is a terrible lot of rheumatism in this country." It was dangerous work on a number of counts. Apart from the risk of cave-ins and oxygen starvation when forest fires literally sucked the air out of tunnels, of falling cable-cars and death by electrocution, Anderson was quite correct that many miners suffered greatly from chronic joint pain; and in later life, they would often contract a fatal condition called silicosis, or miners' consumption. Years of breathing the rock dust in the dark tunnels would end up drowning the aging men in their own pulmonary fluids.

But these risks were known, and accepted. The appeal of the life was strong, and what money there was to spend and the time to spend it in were enjoyed by most in the bright lights, bars, and brothels of Sandon and Cody. In the middle of the 1890s, despite some setbacks, the lights seemed very bright indeed. And they appeared to be getting brighter.

Rock drilling contests were a source of entertainment in the summer months on the rare holidays miners could enjoy. This competition was held in September 1904.

*"The [Kaslo & Slocan Railway] was
doomed from the beginning."*

— Robert D. Turner, Victoria

5

SILVER AND STEEL:
the coming of the railroads

On November 7, 1885, a crowd of hirsute men dressed in heavy black coats and top hats clustered around Donald Alexander Smith, the future Lord Strathcona, as he drove into place the last spike of the transcontinental Canadian Pacific Railway. They were all standing at a remote and chilly spot called Craigellachie, in the high country between Sicamous and Revelstoke – a place that forever after would be remembered for that moment. With the striking of Smith's famous blow, the CPR's role as empire builder

in British Columbia was simultaneously hammered into history. Ironically – for Smith would also go on to become governor of the Hudson's Bay Company – it also wrote an emphatic endnote on the romance and adventure associated with the heyday of the HBC. The voyageur fur-trade era was well and truly over, and the railway companies would now become the chief instruments of land and resource development in the province.

One of the keys to the CPR's long-term commercial sustainability would be its ability to attract and keep freight custom from the interior of British Columbia. In 1892, the primary consideration for mining companies in the Slocan Camp looking for options to take their ore out for processing was cost rather than carrier or destination. The only smelters were to the south, in the United States. It did not matter who carried it there, or how, so long as they carried it for less cost than anyone else.

In an effort to reduce the amount of waste rock being shipped along with valuable ore, which was incurring needless freight costs, the mining companies would first sort the heavy ore by grade. Only the richest grades – those highest in silver and lead content – would be shipped out. Individual miners and the smaller outfits would do the sorting by hand, but the larger companies could afford to build concentrator mills to process bulk amounts of lower-grade ore into manageable quantities for shipping. The drive to find ways to keep costs down by reducing the waste content of ore required a creativity of thought and engineering: some of the processes pioneered in the Slocan, such as the flotation method of sorting minerals from waste through the use of chemically produced air bubbles, are still used in today's mining technology. This method, John Norris states in his book *Old Silverton*, is thought to have been invented by the innovative Australian wife of a miner who had observed the "muck from her husband's work-clothes" floating with the soap scum on the surface of her washing water. But regardless of such ingenuity, in the first few years the fees for freighting ore from the Slocan Camp remained almost prohibitive. The processed material could be sent out to rail connections on the Columbia River by a combination of horse-drawn transport and boats using various routes – east to Kaslo, or northwest to Nakusp, or south via Slocan

Previous page: Passengers and crew on the Kaslo & Slocan Railway braving the terrifying heights of Payne Bluff en route to Sandon, circa 1910.

Lake. But all of those routes involved circuitous, time-consuming, and difficult journeys that were limited by the available number of strong horses and the small size of the vessels.

While miners pulling silver and lead out of the ground in the Slocan could only dream of local smelters and cheap, easy transportation for their ore, two railroad companies were plotting separately to make that dream reality. Their common motivation was straightforward. The Slocan Mining Camp looked like it was going to be the richest silver-bearing region in Canada, and there was good money to be made from providing efficient rail service to the region. From the perspective of the CPR, however, its foothold as the dominant player in British Columbia was by no means assured at that time. Its biggest threat was the American-owned Great Northern Railway, a company with the two distinct advantages of having well-established southerly routes through less difficult terrain and the location of the smelters – all south of the border – on its side. It was not apparent at the time, but the Slocan Mining Camp was shortly to become the theatre in which the two corporate giants would stage their battle for control of the freight industry in southeastern British Columbia.

In 1892, the provincial legislature granted charters for two railways: first, the Nakusp & Slocan Railway, and just two weeks later, the Kaslo & Slocan Railway. The Nakusp & Slocan was backed by the CPR, which intended to drive a route southeast from the port of Nakusp on Upper Arrow Lake to a terminus at Three Forks. Ore freighted from the Slocan Camp to Nakusp via that route would then be carried north by Arrow Lakes steamers – which the CPR also planned to acquire – to connect with its main line at Revelstoke. At that stage, CPR officials did not consider it necessary to go to the considerable expense of traversing the steep and fairly treacherous section between Three Forks and Sandon: the mine owners, it was felt, could just as well bear the expense and trouble of transporting their ore as far as the terminus at the junction.

While the CPR was making its plans and preparing to begin construction, the backers of the Kaslo & Slocan Railway were also busy designing a route for their proposed line. The original investors who obtained the charter were four Canadian businessmen with considerable commercial investments. Alexander Ewen and John Hendry had become rich from timber and from fish on the Fraser – Ewen would go on to become president of the B.C. Packers' Association in later years – and Daniel James Munn was also a major player in the canneries. Robert Irving was the only one of the four with experience in the transportation industry, and that was in steamboats rather than rail. The group needed another backer with experience and serious money behind him; and they found it in James Jerome Hill of the Great Northern Railway, a man eager to take on the might of the CPR.

Hill was a Canadian who had worked for the CPR in the 1880s. During his tenure there, he had hired an American, William Cornelius Van Horne. After Hill left the CPR, Van Horne went on to become the company's president: Hill, in turn, developed the Great Northern Railway south of the border, creating an extensive system of branch lines from the American transcontinental system north into southern British Columbia. The two men shared a rivalry that was far from amiable – and now, with their respective plans for the Slocan, these adversaries were squared off directly against each other.

The Kaslo & Slocan Railway was to be built into the mining camps from the opposite direction to the CPR's line. Starting at Kaslo on Kootenay Lake, it would be forged west through the mountains, following generally the same route as the modern highway. Unlike its competitor, however, the line would go all the way to Sandon, but via a towering cliff called Payne Bluff, high above Three Forks – bypassing that town and giving its citizens every incentive to support the CPR line instead. The intention was to begin work on the Kaslo line by September 1894 and to complete the line within two years. A three-foot wide narrow-gauge track would be used. Even though the technology was already becoming a thing of the past, this track was relatively cheap to build. And, unlike the four-foot, eight-and-a-half inch standard-gauge track that the CPR intended to use on the Nakusp line, it had the added advantage of greater flexibility in navigating the sharp curves and steep grades of the route into the Slocan Camp. Despite construction delays following the economic challenges presented by the 1893 silver depression, both companies persevered with their plans, and the competing sets of tracks from Kaslo and Nakusp started to crawl over the map towards each other.

The logistics for both projects were immense and complex to manage. Apart from the difficulties involved in surveying the isolated terrain, hundreds of labourers were required to work in difficult conditions and all weathers. Supplies and materials had to be hauled in by wagon to the work sites. In the dry summers, forest fires were a constant threat and could wipe out everything that had been achieved in a matter of moments. Heavy snow and avalanches could halt work for long periods and were a serious hazard to the workers. All the same, on October 28, 1894, the first CPR train rolled over the Nakusp & Slocan Railway line into Three Forks. It was a longer line than the planned Kaslo & Slocan route by more than five kilometres, but over considerably less difficult ground; and Van Horne had beaten his rival Hill by more than a year.

Hill refused to give up, however, and by October 1895 he brought the Kaslo & Slocan line into Sandon in triumph. And clearly, despite the delay and the massive cost, it was a triumph over the CPR, whose line was now left stranded at Three Forks. A year's worth of custom had not bought it any great loyalty from the Sandon mines: the new line right into Sandon was much easier to use, and both residents and mine owners promptly started doing so. It was a hair-raising ride for passengers who braved Payne Bluff: "You can look straight down from the car window, 1,000 feet to the canyon below," reported the New Denver *Ledge* newspaper on January 16, 1896, as quoted in Robert Turner's history of the Kaslo & Slocan Railway, *The Skyline Limited*. "If you are nervous you are liable, when passing over this point, to reach for your hair and hold it down."

Its hair-raising features notwithstanding, the route was heavily utilized, and the CPR found itself in a dilemma. To extend the Nakusp & Slocan line into Sandon at this point would be hugely expensive. But not to do so would likely cost the company vastly more in strategic terms as its terminus at Three Forks became more or less redundant. The CPR acted quickly: a few weeks after the Kaslo line reached Sandon, the CPR pushed an extension of the Nakusp line through to that town as well. It spelled doom for Three Forks almost overnight. Now bypassed by both railways, the increasingly isolated little town would struggle for a few years, but Three Forks soon became a rustic backwater with a few isolated residents, and eventually it would all but disappear.

The competition between the two railway companies remained intense, and it was made acute by the proximity of the lines in Sandon.

Although there may well have been sufficient business for both, legal storm clouds started to gather immediately over the construction of the CPR's terminus in Sandon. The Kaslo outfit claimed that the terminus was situated on its right of way and demanded that it be moved. When the CPR employees refused, staff of the former company took matters into their own hands, tearing it down and destroying the adjacent sections of track. The CPR line had been operating out of Sandon for just one day. Deciding prudence was called for, the company backed off and relocated its terminus a discreet distance away.

It would be a short-lived victory for James Hill and the Kaslo & Slocan Railway. Even though Van Horne would have long since retired by then, in the end it would still be Hill's old enemy who would toast the victory of the CPR in securing control over access to and from southeastern British Columbia. Despite the increased volume of business that two cheap and accessible railway lines generated – freight costs dropped to a quarter of their former tariff, and the mines could afford to start processing much larger quantities of lower grade ore as a result – the Kaslo & Slocan Railway could not in the long run compete against the CPR, for two main reasons.

While it was extending its reach into the Slocan Camp, the CPR was also busily consolidating its corporate interests both south and north of the region. Within two years of the opening of the Nakusp & Slocan Railway, the *Nelson Tribune* newspaper reported on October 23, 1897, that Sir William van Horne had recently told the Vancouver Board of Trade: "You can readily see that with the vast amount of money that the CPR has invested in various lines in British Columbia...it cannot reasonably be expected to allow some other company to occupy the territory between the Columbia River and the Fraser Valley... Any line in such territory, other than the CPR, must, you will readily see, necessarily ally itself with the American system south of the boundary, and that will take business away from British Columbia and Vancouver. Such a line is not to be permitted."

The CPR had already done a great deal to prevent that from happening. It had by then built a branch line north from South Slocan Junction, on its line between Nelson and Robson, up to a terminus at Slocan Lake. From there the company provided a connection by boat between the two lines. It bought the Slocan Lake steamer *William Hunter* as well as two tugs, the *Arrow* and the *Denver,* to tow barges between the south end of Slocan Lake and Rosebery at the north end; and also in 1897, the CPR had a new sternwheeler built at the Rosebery shipyard for passenger service, naming it the *Slocan*. The following year it had the tug *Sandon* built, capable of carrying up to fifty passengers. It also strategically discontinued some of the services it had previously provided on Kootenay Lake to Great Northern Railway connections. And by 1898, the CPR had also taken over the small but important smelter that had been built in 1895 about fifty kilometres southwest of the junction at South Slocan, at a town called Trail on the Columbia River.

The small settlement had originally been called Trail Creek Landing. Towards the end of 1895, a mining millionaire from Montana called Fritz Augustus Heinze and his American partners had started building the smelter at Trail Creek to process copper and gold from the nearby Rossland mines. For the CPR, acquiring the smelter from Heinze had two merits: American trade tariffs were making it increasingly unprofitable for American smelters to process B.C. ore, and the freight charges required to get the ore further south were higher. The new owner of the Trail smelter immediately began improving its capacity to process lead and silver in an effort to attract what seemed like easy business from the Slocan mines. Perhaps even more importantly, in securing the ownership of the smelter the CPR had also taken over the railway rights that Heinze had acquired between Trail and Penticton, northwest of the Slocan. The CPR had just bought itself a huge competitive edge over the American-backed railway.

But it was another factor that would spell real defeat for the Kaslo & Slocan Railway, one that no amount of money could possibly overcome. The line ran through some of the most challenging terrain in the world, and in the end it was nature that destroyed the adventurous little railway line. Snow slides, avalanches, and washouts were a regular occurrence, and in just the first month of winter operations it was subjected to three complete shutdowns. Even after the railway acquired expensive snow-clearing equipment, the sheer volume of snow presented a huge problem. Photographs from the period show small black engines emerging from what look like tunnels in massive white walls of ice. Such was the regular effort required to keep the tracks clear, joked the *Kaslo Claim* newspaper on February 22, 1896, that "K&S" really meant "Keep Shovelling." In the summer, the chief enemy of the railway line was fire. Slides over the 1904 and 1908 winters almost wiped out the line; but it was a great fire in the summer of 1910 that finally brought the Kaslo & Slocan to its knees. In a conflagration that burned for days, five men died attempting to hide from the blaze inside tunnels, only to suffocate; and almost half the track, bridges, and trestles were lost to the flames.

After the financial setbacks the Kaslo & Slocan Railway had suffered over the years, combined with the increased costs of maintenance and falling metal prices, this last blow put the company beyond recovery. Hill was forced to admit defeat. The Great Northern Railway's bold attempt to include the Slocan within its empire had failed. Hill offered to sell the operation to the CPR, but the CPR, perhaps bloody-mindedly, refused the offer. In 1911, Hill sold the railway line to a syndicate of Kaslo businessmen who hoped to restart the service. But in February 1912, in a move that can only have caused Hill great resentment after the way he had been treated by the CPR, Premier Richard McBride's provincial government implemented a new railway development policy that included transferring control of the Kaslo line into the hands of his old arch-rival's company. By May the transfer was complete, and by the following year the CPR had rebuilt the line to standard-gauge width and was running trains back into Sandon again from Kaslo.

A slide caused by heavy snow on the railway tracks near the Lucky Jim Mine, circa 1906. Such natural damage eventually put paid to the Kaslo & Slocan Railway altogether.

The CPR's dominance in southeastern British Columbia appeared, once and for all, to be unassailable.

6

FOOL'S GOLD:
fragile fortunes

The 1890s were a banner decade for the Slocan Valley in terms of its modern development. This was particularly so at the valley's north end, where the silver mining camps were the raison d'être for a steady influx of entrepreneurs and settlers. But the opening up of the trail to Slocan Lake from the Kootenay River also stimulated the establishment and growth further south of businesses associated with the towns of Nelson and Castlegar, which were looking forward to a commercial boom from the Slocan mines.

Near the CPR smelter at Trail, at the little mountain town of Rossland, which had been built to service the gold mines, the West Kootenay Power & Light Company was formed in 1897 by Americans Patrick Largey and Oliver Durant and Montreal native C.R. Hosmer. The new company obtained approval from the provincial legislature on May 8 of that year to establish a hydro-electric power plant, and by July, it was supplying power to Rossland that had been generated from its dam at Bonnington Falls, on the Kootenay River. The Trail smelter would eventually become the little power company's primary customer; inevitably, the CPR would also take over West Kootenay Power & Light, in February 1905. The CPR was steadily continuing its construction of what would eventually become a seamless network of power and transportation interests to serve the Slocan Valley. The company even branched out into the recreation industry, building a fishing resort called Creel Lodge at Slocan Pool on its Robson to Nelson line, where it employed legendary pioneer fishing guide Ole Skattebo, among others, to look after its well-heeled guests.

The eccentric and passionate Johnny Morgan Harris in the Sandon Powerhouse.

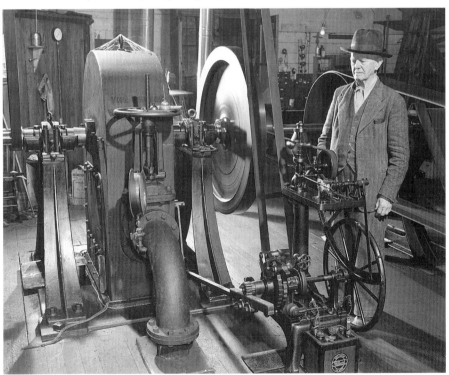

Modern technology was also available directly in the 1890s to some of the smaller communities in the Slocan Valley. In Sandon, Johnny Harris had triumphantly begun producing hydro power through his Sandon Waterworks & Light Co. by March 1897, and telephone systems were already functioning by then between many of the mines and the town. Silverton would have its own Water & Light Co. by spring 1900, and New Denver also had access to some limited telephone, electricity, and water services during the second half of the decade. By the mid-1890s, all of these communities were starting to consider the need for formal administrative structures to levy taxes, create fire protection services, and develop schools and hospitals. The leading lights of Sandon decided the town had sufficient numbers to justify taking the formal step of incorporation, and on January 1, 1898, the community officially became the city of Sandon, with postmaster E.R. Atherton as its first mayor.

Under Atherton's leadership, the new city council immediately set about making improvements to the streets. Sandon and Carpenter Creeks joined each other to flow directly through the main thoroughfare of the city, and some means was needed to constrain the turbulent streams from interfering with daily traffic. The solution was unusual, but typical of Sandon's temperament: a wooden flume, barely four metres wide and less than three deep, was constructed to straighten and contain the creeks as they ran through the city. The former channels that had meandered hap-hazardly across the face of the valley floor were filled and promptly used for building lots. And, in one stroke, the new administration solved its water-containment and waste-disposal problems simultaneously: the creeks under the wooden flume also served as the new sewage runoff system, flushing the city's waste very effectively away from the downtown area.

In the meantime, another sure sign of civilization was manifesting itself: the rise of the local newspaper. Papers in the west Kootenays started up and failed, relocated frequently, and changed names and owners as often as the seasons. But one or two persisted over the years on the strength of their publishers, who were often just individuals of strong and romantic personality and intense community loyalty. Some publications styled themselves as respectable, stolid mining journals. Others revealed their mining heritage rather more obliquely in their titles: the *New Denver Ledge*, the *Kaslo Claim*, and perhaps the most colourful of all, the *Sandon*

Paystreak, all three created by the same man, an unusual character named Robert Thornton Lowery. He was a tiny man, barely a metre and a half tall. But his words and passion exceeded his stature, and he became widely and fondly known as "Colonel" Lowery, despite never having served in the military. A native of Ontario, Lowery packed his own printing press and equipment with him as he progressed through the Kootenays, setting up and closing down a dozen newspapers in different towns and constantly moving on to the next adventure as one paper after the other failed to take off.

Possessed of a strong sense of humour and a cutting wit, Lowery was an advocate for the miners and frequently sympathized with their hard way of life in the newspaper by which he would best be remembered, his *Paystreak*. In its pages he blasted corporate greed in resounding terms: "It is upon the money that [the miner] earns that we, who live in the towns hard by, get our daily bread and other luxuries…[and] that many men of capital are enable to ride in carriages and dine with dukes in Europe…Miners may be plentiful, and some capitalists may think that their lives cut but a small figure, but we think different." Lowery treated individual hypocrisy no less harshly: "You cannot make a good, honest and pleasant citizen out of a petty, spiteful, nosey, vindictive, gluttonous individual…It is only the sneaking, cowardly, dishonourable, back-biting and blackmailing curs that writhe in mental agony when the editorial harpoon tears away their masks, exposing their detestable acts to the gaze of an outraged and indignant world."

Unfortunately, Lowery was also an alcoholic, frequently checking in to the New Denver hospital to dry out (reporting wryly in his own newspaper that he had been in "for the usual thing"). Just as unfortunately, as ardent as he was in his defence of the working man, Lowery was also un-abashedly racist. He unhesitatingly reported upon and promoted anti-Chinese sentiment in his newspapers – and he was not the only one. The *Silvertonian* reported in February 1898 that "the sooner Mongolian [sic] emigration [sic] is prohibited into Canada the better. Thank heaven we, in the Slocan, don't like the color of the breed…[We are informed] that the Chinese have located in the Slocan and Lardeau. To the best of our knowledge, this is a mistake. We are sure of it regarding the Slocan and if numerous precedents count for anything it would not be advisable for John Chinaman to come here." And an editorial in the *New Denver Ledge* of January 13, 1898, provides a commonly held view of the period: "It is to the malign influence of the CPR that we in this district, in common with the rest of the Province stand indebted for the fearful influx of Chinese which is such a curse to British Columbia today." When it was facing drastic labour shortages in the early 1880s, the CPR had brought in nearly sixteen thousand Chinese immigrants to work on completing the transcontinental railway. But with one or two courageous exceptions, these Chinese immigrants were conspicuous by their absence from the Slocan mining camps.

The treatment of Chinese immigrants in general in 19th century British Columbia had been far from stellar, and it would not improve for several decades. The first real rush of Chinese into western Canada was stimulated principally by two factors: in British Columbia, the 1858 gold strikes in the Cariboo region, and in China, the worsening of economic and social conditions to breaking point during the middle of the 19th century. Overpopulation in the Far East had led to untenable pressure on agricultural land use. At the same time, the Taiping Rebellion against the ruling Ch'ing or Manchu dynasty left millions dead in its wake between 1848 and 1865. Chinese people left their homeland in the hundreds of thousands, searching for a better way of life. Following the same pattern that occurred in California and in the later New Zealand gold rushes, the Chinese would typically follow the main strikes and work the less productive placer claims, making through sheer effort what was not achieved from "easy pickings." They were also, as the CPR knew, a low-cost service and labour supply. Those not working on the railroad or picking up placer claims were able to make a reasonable living from cooking and cleaning laundry, or occasionally from working on farms.

Anti-Chinese sentiment stemmed not only from a fear of their exotic looks and habits, but far more so from the fact that the large corporations were prepared to hire imported Chinese labour for lower wages than they were required to pay to European and Canadian workers. Fearing the loss of their members' jobs, Canadian labour unions actively – and successfully – lobbied for restrictions on Chinese immigration and employment in Canada. By 1884, Chinese immigrants were barred from buying or pre-empting land in British Columbia, and the province also attempted to

Old-timers in the Selkirk Hotel, possibly late 1920s: from left, J. Matheson, E. Batelle, B. Reese, C. Strike, T. Anderson, and Charlie Lan. Lan was one of the few Chinese Canadians who successfully became a part of the Slocan Camp in the early years of the 20th century, despite severe anti-Asian prejudice. He is the only Chinese Canadian known to be buried in the New Denver cemetery.

ban further immigration and impose an annual head tax of ten dollars on existing residents of Chinese origin. The federal government took issue with the province's attempt to usurp matters within its jurisdiction, and overturned the last two initiatives, apparently preferring to undertake them itself: it promptly passed its own laws the following year limiting further immigration and imposing a head tax five times greater than the province had contemplated. In 1887 and 1907, rioting mobs in Vancouver attempted unsuccessfully to run the Chinese population out of town. Chinese could not vote in any elections; they were barred from access to certain professions and to crown timber grants; and they could not work on municipal public works contracts. Then things got worse. The existing head tax was doubled to one hundred dollars, and then increased again by five times the amount. And in 1923, the federal Chinese Immigration Act barred further immigration altogether.

The sentiments that led to these anti-Chinese initiatives were as strongly felt in the Slocan as anywhere else in British Columbia, if not more so. One Slocan farmer admitted that he could not afford "white men" as labour but could not resort to the cheaper Chinese because none were allowed in the Slocan Camp. In her 1976 memoir of her father, Walter Clough, titled *My Dad*, Slocan City resident Phyllis Cooper surmised rather naively that "I think the reason that Chinese were not allowed in town was because the townspeople were afraid they might carry smallpox germs with them." The reality was that the Chinese were simply not welcome as cheap competition in the mining camps, except in the rare instances where they served as cooks or laundrymen in the absence of a European available to do the job. Stories are legion regarding the attempts of Chinese to disembark from steamers at the docks of communities like New Denver and Slocan City, only to be "encouraged" strongly to embark again immediately – or, in perhaps more imaginative reports, never to be seen again once they had left the boat.

In the meantime, however, for the privileged citizens of Sandon, New Denver, Silverton, and all the mining camps in the Slocan, the opportunities seemed endless, prosperity assured, and the future certain. It was a remarkably fragile framework, all the same. That assurance was based largely on hope rather than substance, on the heady excitement stimulated by the large quantities of silver that had emerged from the valley in the first three or four years of mining activity rather than on what was left behind to show for it. Many fortunes were staked on the basis of events and activities that had little sustainability and that were easily affected by matters both great and small. The famous story of the "Cockle Boulder" that appears in almost every mining-related publication in the Slocan is a good metaphor for the misguided optimism on which many hopeful entrepreneurs invested their all in places like Sandon. On July 14, 1892, a miner named James W. Cockle came across a boulder that was head-height and the arm span of two men in width, lying in a creek. The rock was almost solid galena and weighed more than 120 tonnes, and Cockle staked a claim on the creek immediately. The boulder had in fact rolled down into the water from the Slocan Star mine far above, and Cockle's claim was fairly quickly found to be worthless – but tales of hundred-tonne boulders of solid silver lying on the ground for the taking would continue to attract fortune-hunters to the Slocan for a considerable time.

Property speculation was rampant, aided by the tendency of prospectors to sell claims cheaply for a small profit rather than mine them. The trick for the speculator was to know when to sell. From one day to the next, fluctuations in the price of silver could render a claim either worthless or valuable beyond its owner's wildest dreams. Mines producing millions of dollars' worth of ore could seem worth an asking price to match – but holding out for too high a sum, or for too long, could leave a man sitting on a pretty piece of mountainside that would not fetch so much as one dollar. Several sad tales circulated to that effect. On the other hand, mine owner Al Mclure, who had bought the famous Payne mine in 1896 for less than $100,000, reputedly sold it a few years later for two and a half million dollars. As a result of this tenuous relationship with sustainability, the welfare of the towns yo-yoed dramatically in response to various events. The 1893 depression that followed the Americans' repeal of the Silver Purchase Act had only a temporary effect on Sandon, as did a sudden drop in the price of silver in the middle of 1897. But combined with a number of other factors, these fluctuations placed a strain on the high life many were living.

Avalanches were prone to destroy buildings and kill miners without warning, and in the harsh winter of 1893–94, losses were high. In 1897, news of the Klondike gold strikes emptied the Slocan's mining camps of workers briefly, but most of them came trickling back in disappointment, having arrived in the Yukon far too late to find gold. Increasingly, the realization that much of the profit generated out of the Slocan mines simply headed straight south to the United States was also sinking in. "The precious heritage of the Canadian people is being permitted to leave the country…while Uncle Sam's treasury waxes fat…" trumpeted the *B.C. Mining Record* in March 1898. It seemed that little could be done about it, however, as long as most of the big mines remained American-owned.

But by far one of the most significant issues that would face the Slocan mining camps and towns, with both negative and positive consequences, was the organization of mining labour into unions. Many of the men in the camps were Irish, Cornish, or American, fresh from the volatile atmosphere of closing mines and violent strikes in their homelands. A lot of them were lonely single men, without close family or advocates to improve the harshness of their way of life or their terms and conditions of employment. They endured a damp and unsafe working environment, high on toxic dust and low on ventilation. They were prone to serious accidents, both inside the tunnels and on the perilous mountain slopes. Tempted to work seven days a week for months on end to save money – fearing the sudden layoffs when a mining claim petered out – when they did hit town on a rare day off, more often than not they forgot any good intent of saving their hard-earned money and would simply drink and gamble it all away. It is hard to imagine the circumstances in which a man would deliberately choose such a life; and clearly, many were not there by their own preference.

Cole Harris, in his 1985 essay "Industry and the Good Life Around Idaho Peak," records the pathos of one miner's sentiments in a letter the miner wrote while on holiday in the city: "We were out last night all over the place and I tell you it makes a man feel bad to think he is living away his life in a lonely way like what we do up there." Few had anything to show for their efforts at the end of their working lives. Harris writes:

> "A young Prince Edward Islander, killed on Idaho Peak in 1902...left $11.80, a suit of clothes, two Bibles, a bundle of laundry, and a pocket book. Unless extraordinarily frugal and robust, they would likely end their working lives with paltry savings and broken health. Such men would drift to a skid road in a western city, live on a tiny union collection in a cheap room in the dry belt, where the air was thought to alleviate miners' consumption, or perhaps spend their last years in a shack somewhere at the foot of Idaho Peak."

It was a situation ripe for labour organization. The Western Federation of Miners, formed in 1892 in Butte, Montana, was an advocate not only for better wages and working conditions but also for improved circumstances generally for miners. Local 81 of the WFM was formally organized in Sandon by the spring of 1899 and was active from its inception. As much a medium to negotiate with employers as a community organization, the Sandon Miners' Union opened a hospital on the strength of its dues and a few contributions from local businessmen. The hospital was available for the use of all Sandon residents and staffed by a doctor and nurse whose names deserve to be remembered – one Miss Chisholm and Doctor William Gomm, both of whom donated their life savings and their time to the hospital to ensure it would survive through the hard times. The local was also a social club of its own kind, and the union secretary was someone a lonely miner could turn to for comfort and help. Sick miners were treated, and dead ones buried, out of union funds. Social events were organized to break the tedium of daily life. For years after they had left the mining camps, remembering the comfort of someone who cared what happened to them, former members would continue writing letters to their old secretary to keep them up to date with their movements and activities.

The union, however, was not seen in a kindly light by employers in the Slocan, many of whom were American corporations that had been embroiled in serious labour disputes in Idaho a few years previously. Characterizing the WFM as the "Western Federation of Dynamiters and Murderers," some of the mine owners retaliated by forming the Silver-Lead Mine Owners' Association in April 1899 and petitioning against pro-labour legislative initiatives. The provincial government reduced the working day from ten hours to eight; the Mine Owners' Association re-sponded by dropping wages from $3.50 a day to three dollars a day. Fred Hume, who had been William Hunter's former partner in the New Denver and Silverton general stores, was now the provincial minister of mines and was caught between the two factions. He equivocated on en-forcing the new working hours in the Slocan, raising the ire of the miners. Some started to walk off the job; the union threatened to strike, but negotiations produced no solution.

On June 21, 1899, the mine owners simply locked out the miners. "The prospects of many [have been] permanently ruined by the unfortu-nate turn affairs have taken," lamented the *B.C. Mining Record* in July. It was nine acrimonious months before a compromise was reached in Feb-ruary 1900 – the working day remained at eight hours, but for a reduced wage of $3.25. The strike's damage to the economy of a town like Sandon was permanent, however. Silverton and New Denver, although affected, were able to sustain themselves from other sources such as timber and agriculture. But in Sandon, many small mines were closed down and abandoned, their owners simply not able to survive a prolonged strike.

Miners, in desperation, looked elsewhere for work. Once gone, they would never return to the Slocan.

Slowly Sandon began pulling itself back from the brink of disaster, only to face another catastrophe within months. Early in May, just as its residents were starting to think about warmer spring days and a better summer than the year before, a fire roared through the downtown core of Sandon and destroyed every building. Two years previously, the Victoria *Daily Colonist* newspaper had reported blithely that there was little fear of fire spreading in Sandon because of the excellent water pressure and fire department. Indeed, Sandon had an impressive infrastructure in place, with fire sheds and sophisticated hydrants placed throughout the town, ready to be utilized by an experienced volunteer crew. But firefighting efforts were essentially hopeless. The dry wooden structures, built cheek by jowl to each other, caught instantly and were reduced to ashes in hours, taking the fire sheds and hydrants with them before they could be put to use.

Notwithstanding the setbacks, Sandon's leading citizens determined to rebuild "in brick and stone, with broad streets and handsome build-ings," proclaimed the *Paystreak* the day after the fire. It was an opportunity to resurvey the townsite properly and transfer the main street from its former location on Reco Avenue to the wooden flume that encased Carpenter Creek, now planked over and somewhat wider than the original. Although the city of brick and stone envisaged in the news-paper never emerged, Johnny Harris did rebuild his Reco Hotel. And a new and very impressive three-storey city hall was also built, housing a courtroom, jail, and fire hall in addition to council chambers. A larger school replaced the one demolished in the fire, and a new hospital was opened within a week. The Sandon Miners' Union built offices, a library, an auditorium and a gymnasium downtown.

The town's cultural groups and sports teams also determinedly con-tinued their activities. The men's hockey team, in particular, not only started winning local tournaments but even won the provincial champi-onship; and, according to local historian Nathaniel Thorne, one of its stars, Cecil "Tiny" Thompson, born in Sandon in 1903, would later turn pro and play goalie for a series of American teams, including the Boston Bruins and the Detroit Red Wings. The Sandon native was elected to the

The Sandon hockey team, circa 1910.

New Denver Women's hockey team, 1908–09 season.

Hockey Hall of Fame in 1959, but never returned to live in his home town. That was all far in the future, however, as Sandon grappled with rebuilding itself and its citizens threw themselves into reconstruction. The city was determined not just to recover but to prosper.

And so, by the end of the 19th century, within the space of a mere decade, the shape of pioneer settlement in the north end of the Slocan Valley had begun to emerge. The reasons for the failure of communities such as Three Forks and Watson in their attempts to establish themselves on the New Denver–Kaslo route had been recognized. Sandon, teetering on its precarious pile of silver, might either rise or fall; but either fate was as yet unpredictable. The lakeshore towns scattered along the northeast section of Slocan Lake, on the other hand, were thriving. New Denver was a solidly established little town of about five hundred people, only a few of whom were miners. The settlement that had once wanted to be the new Eldorado was instead a town comprised of shopkeepers, tradesmen, hoteliers, clerks, and agents. Born out of the mining boom, it looked set

A tea party in Silverton, date unknown.

to survive the vagaries of that industry through its diversification into administration, timber, and agriculture.

By 1898, an interesting Englishman named Joseph Colebrook Harris – no relation to Sandon's eccentric entrepreneur – had arrived in New Denver and purchased a long section of property between the town and Silverton that he called the Bosun Ranch. Shortly afterward, Harris returned briefly to England and brought home a beautiful Scottish bride. A graduate of the Agricultural College in Guelph, Ontario, Harris was a man both of action and of words. Over the next few years he would plant close to one thousand apple, cherry, and plum trees on the Bosun Ranch; become a major proponent of the Town Improvement Society – known as "T.I.S." to its members and "T.I.S.n't" to its detractors – and sell a claim on the property that would become the high-producing Bosun Mine, donating the $7,500 proceeds to build the Bosun Opera House in New Denver. A Fabian socialist, Harris also frequently made donations to assist the working members of the community. Although he ran for

The *SS Slocan* tied up at the wharf at Rosebery, 1913.

provincial election as an independent in 1909, he never actually held
political office. His views, promoting higher taxes and Crown ownership
of resources, had little support in the region.

Rosebery, a few kilometres north of New Denver, continued to prosper from the output of the Molly Hughes Mine and a local sawmill and
shipwright's yard. At the far northern tip of Slocan Lake, the settlement
of Hills was also enjoying a steady growth. The source of its name was
straightforward: the Hills brothers from New Brunswick, Alfred and Wilson, had set up a sawmill west of Bonanza Creek in 1892 and started
supplying lumber to New Denver, Silverton, and Sandon. The CPR built a

siding at Hills in 1895, consolidating the long-term viability of the little community.

At the southern end of Slocan Lake, another timber town had taken shape and would incorporate in 1901: Slocan City. Denis St. Denis, a manager who had been lured into the employ of the Ontario-Slocan Lumber Company Limited in 1903, remarked in his recollections: "Naturally, the term 'Slocan City' led me to believe that it was a place of some importance, and of considerable population. In that I was very much disappointed in both of these beliefs." St. Denis wondered to himself how the city had ever obtained a charter to incorporate. The incentive behind incorporation was to be able to obtain municipal financing to support the acquisition of land and its transfer to the Ontario-Slocan Lumber Company for the building of both a shingle mill and a sawmill; but the reason the town was successful in obtaining a charter lay in its origins. The petition was signed not so much by hopeful lumbermen, but by miners eager for alternative employment.

Like Sandon, New Denver, and Silverton, Slocan had initially sprung from the hopes and efforts of prospectors and miners. At the same time as the first rush of claims were being staked up at Carpenter Creek, a couple of prospectors named Tom Mulvey and Billy Clements were building a log shack on a pretty beach at the south end of Slocan Lake. They were quickly followed by a rush of speculators, entrepreneurs, and yet more hopeful prospectors. A townsite was staked by Frank Fletcher in 1893. By 1896, men whose family names would still appear in local directories over one hundred years later began to arrive, William and Walter Clough, Charlie Barber, and Henry Hicks among them. By the fall of that year, as many as fifteen hundred new people were living in Slocan, and like Sandon it boasted banks, a school, a number of hotels, and two or three newspapers. But in the same year, a sizeable aboriginal encampment near the mouth of Mulvey Creek departed and did not return.

A young journalist named Fred Smyth arrived in 1897 to work as a printer on the *Slocan City News*. Life in the young town was never dull, according to the young newspaperman – claims were being staked by the hundreds around nearby Springer Creek and on Lemon Creek a few kilometres south, whether or not anything had been found, and the hotels were jammed with men who were sleeping on chairs and on the pool tables. Hucksters were making a fortune out of greenhorns by pretending to be prospectors and showing them "finds" that were clearly valuable, but purporting not to know it and saying they were thinking of selling their claim. The greenhorn would avidly offer to buy the claim, which was for sale "cheap" – but still far in excess of its real value, which would be nil. In October 1897, the first CPR train rolled into town from Nelson and the sternwheeler *Slocan* rolled off the line at Rosebery, ready for service between the north and south ends of the lake. Slocan City looked set to become as robust a town as New Denver.

Directly to the east of Slocan City and almost indistinguishable from it was the little town site of Brandon, staked by W.H. "Bill" Brandon in 1896. For its first couple of years of existence, Brandon actually exceeded

The City of Sandon, circa 1905.

Slocan in size, but this was a short-lived commercial boom and Brandon rapidly became a bedroom community for Slocan. Across the river and lake, the Valhalla Mountains, named by Dr. George A. Dawson in the late 1880s, glowered at the bustle of activity taking place in their shadow. Behind the steep walls of Perry Ridge, on the west side of the river, prospectors had been exploring the Little Slocan River valley since 1894. They included among their number the legendary Bill Drinnon, for whom Drinnon Lake and Pass are named. Retiring to a reclusive existence, trapping beaver up the Little Slocan after reputedly having lost his sweetheart to his brother, Drinnon is said to have chased away unwary intruders with his gun. True or not, prospecting in the Little Slocan met with little success in any event; but even so, as many as forty families had settled in the area within a few years.

The south end of the valley remained relatively empty of settlement. A CPR siding at South Slocan provided a nexus for passengers and freight moving up and down the valley, but there was as yet no reason to stop anywhere en route between South Slocan and Slocan City. At Lemon Creek, a temporary railway camp named after prospector Bob Lemon was set up when the train tracks were being built between Nelson and Slocan in 1897. An attempt was made by a man named William Anderson to begin a settlement by setting up a store and post office to serve the active mining claims up Lemon Creek. But after the rail line was complete, there was no reason for travellers to stop only ten kilometres short of Slocan, and the little settlement vanished again quickly. Despite their relative isolation, Anderson and his two sons elected to stay on the preemption at Lemon Creek and continued to clear the farm, occasionally cutting timber for extra money.

But the days in which the south end of the valley would slumber in such peaceful and secluded activity were numbered. By the end of the next decade, things would look completely different.

7

THE GLORIOUS KOOTENAY: *fruit, farms, forests, and families*

As aboriginal people had known for thousands of years, the south end of the Slocan Valley was prime for settlement, and never more so than at the beginning of the 20th century. The boom in the north end of the valley had been the impetus for the creation of not only the rail system between Nelson and Robson on the Columbia River, with its connections south to Trail and to the United States, but also the line north through the Slocan Valley with connections to Nakusp, Revelstoke, and Kaslo. The junction with the northbound CPR line on the Kootenay River above the Slocan Pool had become generally known as South Slocan. And a few kilometres upstream on the Slocan River, in the area now called Crescent Valley, another stop on the railway line was becoming known as Bourgeois Siding.

George Bourgeois was a Québécois who had come out to homestead in the area around 1900. In 1907, Bourgeois was joined in his little log cabin by his nephew Henri and Henri's wife Hortense, together with their infant daughter Cecile. Within a few years most of Henri's family would also emigrate to the Kootenays, joining their son and brother in the farming venture. The Slocan was just starting to become known as an area with agricultural potential when Henri had packed his bags and headed west, thinking that he might find work in the mining camps or cutting timber. The young man was astute, however, and he immediately saw the prospects for dairy farming, an industry he had known in his boyhood. He bought a homestead of 360 acres, stocked it with pure bred Ayrshire cattle, and quickly established a milk trade to Nelson. Hortense created an extensive vegetable garden and started cultivating a variety of crops, including fields of turnips and potatoes.

The Bourgeois family was not the only one engaging in the dairy trade in Crescent Valley. Only a few minutes on horseback further north, at an oxbow bend in the river where the summer breezes cool the bluffs on the hottest of afternoons and a man can find some relief from the mosquitoes, was another small farm born of sweat and faith. Sometime between 1900 and 1902 Jacob and Antonia Kosiancic, immigrants to the United States from Europe, abandoned the steel mills of Pittsburgh and headed west to the Slocan. The Kosiancics purchased four hundred acres on the beautiful oxbow bend and set about building their farm with the help, as time went on, of their growing sons, Valentine, Joe, and Jack. Jacob told his grandson Ray Kosiancic many years later that there were only six families that he knew of then, including the Andersons, who lived between the Kosiancic place and Slocan City. Certainly very few people were farming; the B.C. *Henderson's Directory* for 1901 lists only nineteen people engaged in agriculture in the entire west Kootenays.

The Kosiancics, like the Bourgeois family, were beginning from scratch, living in log cabins with dirt floors. Their priorities were simple:

Jacob Kosiancic set up one of the early dairy operations in the valley. This shot was taken in 1914.

finding enough to eat and clearing the land of the thick timber that stood on either side of the railway line, in order to graze cattle and grow crops. Clearing timber was extraordinarily costly, leaving little money for purchasing food. "The land which [my father] pre-empted is by no means heavily timbered," wrote Robert Anderson in 1898 from Lemon Creek, to his uncle in Florida. "Still there is enough forest to keep us working for years to clear." Fortunately, wildlife was plentiful in the valley. "My grandmother," says Ray Kosiancic, "could handle anything. She would go out into the forest with a double-barrelled shotgun in the afternoon and shoot a rabbit for supper."

There was also at least a ready market for the timber that Jacob Kosiancic, the Andersons, and others were painstakingly hand-logging from their farms. The CPR needed railroad ties constantly to replace the worn-out ones on the line, and it could transport additional lumber out of the valley to its smelter at Trail. But if he wanted to avoid having to carry

Val Kosiancic haying, circa 1925.

the cut lumber by wagon down to another siding, Jacob Kosiancic realized, he would need a siding of his own – and he could have one only if he could ensure a proper grade for the tracks. It took him the best part of 1905 to hand-shovel hundreds of tonnes of dirt into place, but it was worth it. At the end of the year the Kosiancic Spur was put in, and Jacob was in business. Between them the Kosiancics developed an orchard, planted root crops, bred oxen, horses, and cattle, and were supplying milk to Nelson and other communities at the same time that Henri Bourgeois began his delivery business. The work was never-ending. "They always prayed for a good harvest," says their grandson Ray, "but they always kept hoeing." These enterprising jacks-of-all-trades even made four hundred kilograms of cheese a month to send to the Italian community at Trail. Then, as now, diversity was the key to economic survival in the valley. Hans Smedbol, who lives in Slocan and works in Nelson, remarks, "It's been that way forever. My grandfather [Birgir Olstad] had to roll cigars in Spokane in the winters."

With the amount of good timber that was so readily available near the railway lines – cedar, fir, hemlock, and pine, among others – and the increasing desire to clear it as more settlers started to come in to the valley, it was inevitable that logging would start to supersede mining as the next viable resource industry in the region. Some piecemeal hand- and horse-

Val and Ecla Kosiancic's wedding day, 1924.

Val Kosiancic and Pete Markin, logging in Crescent Valley in the 1930s.

logging had been under way for years, by people like Henri Bourgeois and Jacob Kosiancic. There had also been a certain amount of tension between earlier settlement and later potential forestry exploitation: both prospectors and settlers were prone to clear sites by burning off the brush, resulting in denuded landscapes no longer suitable for logging and a constant pall of smoke in the air. For many years, summer and fall in the west Kootenays were synonymous with smog in the valleys.

But now the local construction industry and the agricultural prairie markets for timber were booming. In 1905, the provincial government made timber licences transferable and renewable yearly, initiating a flood of timber staking and an increase in the number of timber licences in British Columbia from 1,500 to 15,000 in just three years. The opportunity to process cut lumber locally was presenting itself, and a number of enterprising individuals seized it. The Ontario–Slocan Lumber Co., whose prospective operations had been the stimulus for incorporation of Slocan City in 1901, bought the small Hills Brothers sawmill at the head of Slocan Lake in 1902. The company's shingle mill in Slocan City itself was short-lived, however, closing down by 1904; and it never built its promised sawmill in Slocan, eventually transferring back to the city in 1927 the land it had bought for that purpose. At Crescent Valley, Joseph Patrick and his sons Frank and Lester built the Patrick sawmill in the first decade of the 20th century. The Patrick mill dominated the local industry until 1911, when it was bought by the British Canadian Lumber Co. The Patrick brothers, like Sandon's "Tiny" Thompson, would win fame in another way: by playing ice hockey in the national leagues. Lester would go on to coach the New York Rangers from 1926 to 1937, earning himself his own place in the Hockey Hall of Fame in 1947. An annual trophy is still awarded in his name for outstanding services to hockey in the United States.

It quickly became necessary to go further and further afield for good timber as the more accessible sections along the main rail routes were cleared. Within the next few years, loggers like William "Billie" Koch started logging white pine and spruce up the headwaters of the Little Slocan, bringing the cut timber down to Koch's (pronounced "Koe's") Siding, just north of Slocan Park and close to where Peter Koch would build a sawmill at the beginning of the 1930s. By 1913, attracted by the cleared

Lumberjacks at the Wm. Koch lumber camp on the Little Slocan River, 1909–10.

Picnic at Slocan Pool on the Kootenay River, circa 1914.

land as well as the rail siding, settlers had moved into Slocan Park and the first log homes in the area were under construction. Loggers had also started working their way up the smaller watersheds and over the ridges, and the settlers were spreading further north in their wake. At another small siding on the rail line where Winlaw Creek flows into the Slocan River, there were enough people in the area for a school to be operating by 1912 in a small log building near the railway tracks by Cedar Creek. A small store and a post office had been established in 1910, as well as a large sawmill operation set up by Winlaw Creek's namesake, the irascible J.B. Winlaw, with his son Nels. The sawmill burned down twice in 1912, and the lumber yard burned again the following year. The fire risk in the dry decks of timber awaiting shipment was massive – one stray spark

One of the earliest homes and barns built in Slocan Park, circa 1913.

The mill that J.B. Winlaw built near the CPR rail siding. Although the legend accompanying the photo says "1908," according to Winlaw's daughters the mill was built around 1910.

might start a conflagration that could not be extinguished.

Transporting the cut logs to the railheads became more and more dependent on horses. And, where possible, wooden flumes were built to launch logs down to the lake, where they could be "boomed" together and towed to the rail sidings. Some were extremely long; the flume built at Mulvey Creek around 1912 was nearly two kilometres in length and crossed more than eighty ravines. Logs would roar down the flumes, sending up spray several metres into the air, occasionally jamming or soaring over the edges in their unstoppable speed. Local legend has it that one young faller rode a log down the Mulvey Creek flume for a bet, landing unscathed at the bottom – apparently on one of his luckier days.

Like mining, logging was a dangerous business and not to be taken lightly. Injuries and deaths were unfortunately common occurrences in forestry throughout British Columbia. The slip of a too-blunt blade, a stumble in handling one of the giant cross-cut saws, or a tree knocked awry by an errant gust of wind, and a man might die instantly in the freezing mud. Recognizing the need both to regulate the industry and to improve its practices, as well as to ensure that land for growing timber was permanently protected, the province passed its first Forest Act in 1912 and created a new division of the Lands Branch responsible solely for the management of trees. Things would never be the same again for the forestry industry in British Columbia.

Another kind of tree was about to change the face of the valley in a completely different manner: the fruit tree. By the time 250 apple trees were planted on the Kosiancic farm in 1913, a fruit production boom in the Slocan was already well under way. This was surprising to people familiar with the variable climate, the heavily forested landscape, and the transportation challenges of the valley in the early years of the 20th century. Weather had already proved a burden to agriculture in the west Kootenays. Harsh, "tree-killer" winters occurred on a seven- to ten-year cycle, and the wet spring weather harboured diseases and could damage fruit easily in the vigour of its downpours. Even the inaugural meeting in New Denver of the Slocan Lake Agricultural Association in 1911 was unable to proceed due to a poor turnout. "The bad weather [prevented] many from attending," the minutes recorded sadly. J.C. Harris, the socialist farmer from New Denver, had had some luck in developing his orchard on Bosun Ranch and was encouraging others to try the same, writing a regular "Fruit Growers' Column" for the *Slocan Mining Review*. But it was also a struggle – despite freight subsidies from the CPR – to compete with the more accessible and temperate fruit-producing regions of British Columbia, such as the Okanagan. "This is not much of a poor man's paradise," Robert Anderson had written to his uncle in 1902. "It is kind of a 'pay, pay, pay' affair... [A farmer] must live in the hope of great things to come, when his stumpy bonanza is under cultivation."

Nevertheless, there were those who genuinely thought the Kootenays had real potential for fruit and vegetable cultivation – and others who saw it as ripe for exploitation of a different kind. At the same time as respected agriculturalist J.T. Bealby published his *Fruit Ranching in British Columbia* in London in 1909, cautiously extolling the fitness of the Kootenays for growing fruit, property speculators in England were hawking lots in the Kootenays, sight-unseen, in pamphlets with names like *The Glorious Kootenay: Its Fruit Growing Attractions and Possibilities* and boasting "The Lake District of Southern British Columbia affords the greatest opportunity in the North American continent for a lucrative occupation and a country home." They were blatantly targeting the impoverished but genteel middle class of England, the middle sons without inheritances or vocations but with fertile imaginations, who could readily be fired with the desire to recreate their own little England in a spot like the Slocan Valley. Those gentle dreamers paid no heed to Bealby's words of warning in his lengthy and stolid publication: "The English settler, accustomed to the trim and orderly aspect of an English ploughed field, with its unbroken and level expanse of brown soil and its neat hedges or straight lines of fences, must not look to find the same things in a new country such as British Columbia."

So it was that Herbert Herridge's parents, Willie and Charlotte, came out from England in 1907 to start an apple orchard near Nakusp, only to find to their dismay that the steep plot they had purchased long-distance from England was covered in dense bush and shimmering with mosquitoes. It was barely capable of habitation, let alone cultivation. Three years later, a young Englishman called John Owen Clay arrived in Slocan City. Just a little to the south of town, he bought the Valhalla Ranch from Sophia and Harry Bathurst. It was the middle of June, and the one hundred young apple trees that Alexander Watson had planted on the property in 1906 shone a fresh, pale green in the early summer sunlight. It must have been a sight to gladden the young man's eyes; it was those apple trees that had brought him to the Slocan.

Clay was the grandson of a minister, the product of a proper English upbringing in moderate luxury – though none that he would be entitled to inherit – and a thoroughly decent gentleman. Inspired by the grand promises of the brochures and dreaming of financial independence, Clay had worked his way west with fortitude and in good spirits, despite the hardships he encountered on the way – fierce weather, a scarcity of jobs, and homesickness for a gentler way of life. Wiser than many of his compatriots, however, Clay had waited to purchase land until he arrived. Others who had not waited either struggled futilely against the impossible terrain, like the Herridges, or quailed and fled at what they found. Dave Martin's grandparents came in 1919 to a spot a little north of Winlaw on the promise of "Grow apples and grow rich in Appledale" – only to find the land they too had bought sight unseen was covered in

Left: John Owen Clay, 1908. *Right:* Owen Clay brought his sister Winnifred out to housekeep for him prior to his marriage, a custom that was common in the early 20th century. By 1911, the brother and sister could already enjoy the views of the Valhallas from the porch of the Clays' log home. *Below:* Winnifred on the log bridge over Lemon Creek, circa 1910.

huge tree stumps and was full of rocks. After considering the work in front of them and the ten years it would take to grow fruit-bearing trees, they fled to Vancouver and never looked back. But John Owen Clay rallied to his task, rolled up his properly starched white sleeves and got to work on clearing, road building, and planting as many fruit trees as possible. He brought his unmarried sister, Winnifred Ruth Clay, out to keep house in the log cabin that served as his home, and together they started to forge the way of life that he dreamed of having. Under the diligent hand of Clay and others like him up and down the valley, within a few years thick white apple blossoms were bringing vivid colour to the Slocan every spring.

Their new neighbourhood was not exactly what the new immigrants were used to in a town. Despite Slocan City's incorporation in 1901, it was no longer the bustling metropolis it had been in the late 1890s. The early optimism and confidence had gone, comments historian N.L. Barlee: "Everything, it seemed, was a little less elegant." Along with what elegance there had been would slowly disappear some of the colour and the characters: people like "Judge" Harris, the alcoholic lawyer who would all the same draw up watertight leases for illiterate miners free of charge, and "Cayuse" Brown, who would come down from the mountains and sit with his loaded pack still on his back for five hours at a stretch, drinking. Even the locals "felt he was just a little bit different," wrote Barlee. New immigrants were arriving in the place of the prospectors and miners and the speculators, gamblers, and entrepreneurs that tended to follow in the wake of glittering metal. There were fruit growers like the Clays; farmers like the Popoffs, from Manitoba, who bought a property between Slocan and Lemon Creek in 1912; the Carsons, who came to Perry Siding in 1904, and the Trozzos, to Appledale in 1912; and timber and cattle men like the Hirds, who arrived in Slocan City from Saskatchewan in 1913.

Slocan City Council faced serious problems in the early 1900s. It had been sorely disappointed by the failure of the Ontario–Slocan Lumber Co. to follow through on its promises of job creation. Denis St. Denis, appointed to act as city clerk in 1908, discovered when he looked through the records that for years unqualified aldermen had been making decisions on council. A fast trip to Victoria in 1911 to rectify the situation with the Slocan City Enabling Act solved the problem, at least temporarily. But it wasn't the first time the city had been in trouble. The price of silver had dropped again in the early 1900s, and American duties on ores being shipped south of the border were placing Canadian mines at a disadvantage. Many of the smelters also imposed a penalty on the zinc content in the ore – zinc being expensive to extract and considered of little value – depressing any profit further. Eventually, with an oversupply in the United States, most American smelters simply stopped purchasing Canadian ore at all. A lead subsidy introduced by the federal government in 1903 under the Lead Bounty Act, intended to stimulate development, did little to assist in the Slocan, where the mines were already starting to work themselves out. Increased interest in zinc and the building of a more efficient zinc smelter in Nelson in 1907 would not help, for the same reason. Even the giant Arlington Mine on Springer Creek was forced to close its operations, and it was followed by dozens more.

As the mines went, so did the miners – and the businesses that they had patronized. Many kind-hearted merchants bankrupted themselves grubstaking overly optimistic miners: "[Money] is an article very rarely handled," lamented Robert Anderson in 1902. "What takes the place of it is credit in unlimited quantities. Almost all a man has to do is ask for it and the merchants jump at the chance of getting a new customer. Consequently the business houses are often in a bad way and a mercantile life is not very desirable." The city hadn't anticipated such a progressively debilitating chain of events for its citizens. Burdened by spending that far exceeded its anticipated income, Slocan City was placed into receivership by the provincial government in 1906. Although it would recover, bolstered by the area's expanding farming development, the boom town its forefathers had envisaged was not to be.

But life was agreeable enough for both the new and the long-standing residents of Slocan City and environs in the relatively quiet years before the outbreak of World War One, and pleasures were found in simple entertainments. Robert Anderson, when not writing lengthy epistles to his uncle in Florida, was creating epic poems about pioneering life that would in later years earn him the tag "Kipling of the Kootenays," and the town was already boasting of his prowess. There was plentiful wildlife in the hills to supply supper tables, and fish were abundant in the river, making some fishermen too lazy for their own good: "The ranchers who live along the river get plenty," recounted Robert Anderson. "They use dynamite and blow the fishy denizens of the deep up. Sometimes this is dangerous for...he may accidentally forget to drop his bottle containing the dynamite stick...at the right moment. A young Swiss with whom I was acquainted did this about three years ago with the result that he is now minus one arm."

More legitimate sports also continued to be most popular, especially when competition against neighbouring towns could be found. When the Slocan Rifle Association was formed in 1901, the Football League was already up and running, as was the Slocan hockey team one year later.

Slocan City Rifle Club, 1908.

Competition between towns was fierce, and the rules of engagement strict – only residents could play. Sandon therefore rued the championship in which, having forgotten the rules, it used a non-resident "ringer" to beat Slocan City. The wily Denis St. Denis, knowing all along that Sandon would forfeit the game as a result, warned his team to keep quiet until afterwards – a ploy that left Slocan City with the trophy despite its loss of the game. The football team needed no such help – it was so good that it won the western Canadian championships in 1909 – and there was a baseball team for summer sports fans.

There may well have been boxing tournaments in the valley at this time. One native son, Vic Foley, went on to become Canadian bantamweight champion in 1925 and competed, albeit unsuccessfully, for the world lightweight championship in 1927. A churchgoing man, Foley would not train on Sundays – a major disappointment to the city folks in Toronto and Vancouver, who had expected to be able to watch him in action on their one day off from work. In Slocan City, however, horse races were frequently held on the main street regardless of the day of the week – a sure-fire way to bring whatever miners were left down from the hills to empty their pockets in betting on the winners. Another kind of racing

Slocan City horse races were a regular source of entertainment in its first few years. Here, "Pete the Packer" leads them home in 1896.

was also popular for gambling purposes: foot racing. It was so popular that even as far east as Ontario, track and field star Walter Knox heard about it and decided to come out and race for money – but under the false name of Renwick, so that he would not lose his amateur status. According to Barlee and St. Denis, Knox went on to win Olympic fame for Canada; in the Slocan, however, he won even greater infamy by allegedly colluding with a partner to earn extra money by deliberately throwing races.

The number of businesses and people slowly declined in Slocan City, but there were compensations for those who persisted. Despite its financial setbacks, the city started to modernize and had put in a water system by 1910. Supplies of every description were readily available via the railway and steamer system – although accidents occasionally happened. In the winter of 1903–04, a Consolidated Mining and Smelting Co. boxcar overshot the loading barge on Slocan Lake and ended up thirty-five metres under water, along with its brakeman, twenty-one-year-old Edward Connolly, and – allegedly – hundreds of bars of silver bullion, spawning a legend of lost silver that still has deluded fortune hunters searching for it. In 1916 a carload of silver ore was lost in the lake near

Clearing the land for farming had many challenges for the first pioneers. Bears still roam the valley, but they are no longer as plentiful as in the 1910s, when this image of a black bear was taken on the Valhalla Ranch near Slocan.

Silverton in an identical fashion; and on January 1, 1947, an entire trainload of lumber went off the barge in the middle of the lake. The freight cars, inexplicably, were said to have floated, perhaps buoyed up temporarily by the dry lumber inside them. The caboose, snowplough, and engine went straight to the bottom, two hundred metres down.

By 1900 it was possible to communicate with the outside world reasonably quickly using the telegraph system. Walter Clough had come to the Slocan in 1893 hoping to make a fortune in silver, but instead found himself a few years later looking after the telegraph line for the CPR. Using a small hand-speeder at first, he travelled the beat between Slocan City and South Slocan, repairing the lines, replacing broken insulators, and clearing the tracks of debris while he was at it. When the telegraph line was extended along the shore of the lake as far as Rosebery, his beat was likewise extended, but for no extra wage. Clough worked six days a week and on call, for sixty dollars a month. The pay was meagre but he could take his wife and children with him whenever he wanted, dropping them off to visit friends along the way or simply coming with him for a picnic on his lunch break. Occasionally, when they made it as far as South Slocan, the family might stay overnight and carry on to Nelson for a rare and much-anticipated visit. A trip to Nelson was still, in those days before the road, a rare event for most people.

Walter Clough's daughter Phyllis Clough Cooper recalled the hardships of her father's line of work in the most matter-of-fact prose in her memoir about his life. It was an incredibly demanding job, requiring him to row a small boat on the lake on the stormiest of nights to repair a broken wire or to fend off wild animals at an isolated spot on the line. And some animals not so wild: "One night dad was bringing Dr. Rose up the valley on the speeder," she wrote, "and [they] bumped into some

Ida Nettleton Collis and Douglas Percy Collis celebrated their honeymoon in traditional camping style on Slocan Lake, around 1920.

cows...it didn't hurt the cows...but it made the speeder jump the track and they both fell into the ditch...They were unhurt so they picked themselves up, hauled the speeder back on the track and continued." But if Phyllis was prosaic about her father's adventures, it was perhaps because she shared some of them herself. Her father often took her with him, especially once she became a teenager. When she reached the age of fourteen, he had already handed over the keys to his Model A Ford motorcar to her to drive; and on one memorable Christmas Day she helped him go to a line repair that was needed on the lake in the middle of a huge storm. As the storm worsened, the steering on the boat broke repeatedly, and people watching on shore had given up hope of their survival as they watched the boat disappear in the surf. "I couldn't afford to misjudge the waves," she later wrote, "or turn the wheel the slightest bit too much, or the force of the wind and waves would have swung us around into the trough and we would have capsized." But she continued to go out with him, uncomplaining. Life was difficult and lacking in amenities or luxuries; but for adults and children alike it was a constant adventure that has virtually no equal in modern society. For the same reasons that ten-year-old Phyllis Clough was able to row a boat by herself on Slocan Lake without remonstrance from her elders, J.B. Winlaw's grand-

Bill and Rita Sutherland in their cabin at Winlaw, 1922, with nine of their twelve children.

daughters Mary and Jeannette were allowed to ride on the mechanical saw cutting the giant logs in his sawmill – while it was operating. "Much to our terror, but it was so exciting," remarked Jeannette calmly in an interview with Nelson Museum curator Shawn Lamb in 1993.

As these children played in the sun and their parents struggled to tame the rocks and trees of the Slocan Valley, the days in Europe were darkening and world powers were growing increasingly troubled. British Columbia was suffering its own problems. At the turn of the century the province had been governed under the stewardship of James Dunsmuir, who had been appointed by the elected minority-party representatives to try and restore some order to a chaotic political situation. When Richard McBride was elected as premier in 1903, it had appeared that the province could look forward to prosperity and good management. But as Robert Anderson pithily observed in a letter to Florida the same year, "The only thing [the politicians] can do here is shoot off their mouths and this they do often enough. British Columbia is about the worst of all for this kind of thing and they are constantly rowing over at Victoria about something or other." When McBride finally resigned in 1915, to be succeeded by the endearingly named Attorney General William Bowser, he

Families were large and homes were small in the early days of the valley. By 1930, when the last child was born, fourteen people were living in the Sutherland family home in Winlaw.

would leave British Columbia with an accumulated debt of over ten million dollars, the legacy of his expansion schemes.

In the Slocan, while agriculture and settlement were on the rise, the heydays of the mining towns seemed, with one exception, to be coming to an end. The same wildfires that put an effective end to the ambitious Kaslo & Slocan Railway in 1910 wiped out Three Forks completely. The Sandon Miners' Union was struggling financially by 1907 as miners left to seek work elsewhere and was forced to seek financial help from the Western Federation of Miners in Colorado. Sandon's fortunes were at their lowest ebb to date, with the city going into receivership in 1913. High up in the Kokanee Mountain Range between Slocan and Kootenay Lakes, the few prospectors that had managed to scrape claims out of the lichen-covered rocks had largely abandoned them, and a whole new group of characters were invading the tarns and the creeks. This time, it was people in search of the wealth of scenery and recreation rather than silver. Using the trails that the miners had hand-carved up into the mountains, as early as 1916, members of the Kokanee Mountaineering Club were hiking up for summer camps to the miner's cabin near the old Slocan Chief claim owned by Clare Tipping, of Slocan City. On August

John Owen Clay on the tarns above Six Mile Creek in the Kokanee Glacier area: July 1921.

22, 1922, Kokanee Glacier Provincial Park was officially declared open as a Class A park by local MLA K. Campbell. It was 256 square kilometres in size, containing more than thirty lakes and half a dozen major glaciers. Mining would no longer be permitted within its boundaries, but the prohibition was almost unnecessary.

Silverton, on the other hand, was one of the few mining towns experiencing a minor revival. In 1910, a very rich vein of ore was struck at the Standard Mine, and it prompted an unexpected economic boom in the little settlement. A massive 2,400-metre tramway was built from the mine down the mountainside to Silverton, as well as a new concentrator. The opportunity for employment attracted a flood of incomers, and despite a widespread town fire in May 1911, things seemed to look very positive for Silverton and, by extension, its neighbour to the north, New Denver.

Other newcomers, heading to the valley in the years before World War One, would change its face yet again. But in the meantime, the voices of the first occupants of the area appeared to have been silenced. The last native people in the Slocan Valley had been observed in the mid-1890s near Slocan Lake. After that, none of the European memoirs or records of the time recollect their living presence anywhere in the valley. There was little to suggest that they would ever return.

While Kokanee Glacier Provincial Park was opened in 1922, Gimli Peak in the Mulvey Creek watershed was also becoming a popular climbing route at that point, at least with local enthusiasts John Owen Clay and Harry Bathurst, seen here on the summit, 1912.

Climbing in the Valhallas, 1923.

Harry Bathurst and John Clay on a camping trip in the Valhallas, 1920s. The two friends were avid campers and found time to go tenting together despite the labour-intensive challenges of ranching.

8

Rushing Towards a Ghost:
aboriginal people of the valley

In 1914, despite not being permitted to vote in provincial
or federal elections, aboriginal men who were registered
as status Indians under the Indian Act experienced the
first real freedom of choice they had been given for many
decades – in fact, since before the coming of European
settlers: they were permitted to fight for Canada in the
global conflict that broke out at the end of that year. While
they were in Europe during World War One, they were
able to travel freely when on leave, to drink in bars, and to

mix without constraint with their non-aboriginal comrades: to do all those things, in other words, that they could not do in Canada. Within their own country, however, status Indian people remained confined largely to reserves and disenfranchised.

The path by which the indigenous people of Canada had been brought to this point varied from region to region. In British Columbia, a number of key events and generic government policies affected all aboriginal groups in the province in more or less the same way; in the Slocan Valley, some of those events and policies as well as some matters specific to the area would have a devastating impact on the original occupants. When explorer David Thompson had descended the Columbia River in 1807 he was preceded, according to Cheryl Coull in *A Traveller's Guide to Aboriginal B.C.*, by a Ktunaxa prophet declaiming that the end of the world was coming. Certainly she had foreseen the end of one world: by the 1890s, there was what appeared to be a total absence of aboriginal people in the Slocan Valley, an absence that would last for nearly one hundred years.

In much the same way that an understanding of the geology of the Slocan provides the background for its relatively short resource-based history, it is useful to consider the geography of the region to appreciate the patterns of its human occupation over a much longer period. The ragged peaks that shrug their shoulders together along the roughly north–south planes of the Valhalla and Slocan Ranges are ancient beyond any recollection of humankind, either documented or oral. But within the valleys and meadows that divide the ranges, and the glaciers and rivers that have carved their character, are contained some of the key features that have shaped the face of human existence there since the last ice age ended nearly twelve thousand years ago. The Slocan Valley lies within the rocky cradle of the Selkirk Mountains, which themselves lie within the Columbia Mountains and Southern Rockies – a gigantic granite bowl of "great vertical relief," as archaeologist Gordon Mohs puts it. The steep, narrow valleys these peaks crowd around have walls of inhospitable rock and dense, dark trees that have been beaten back to the lower reaches by snowfalls of massive depth and weight. The Valhalla Range, to the west of Slocan Lake, reaches altitudes of close to three thousand metres; to the east, the Slocan Range's blunter ridges are closer to 2,500 metres in

The traditional style of sturgeon-nosed canoe was used by both the Lakes and the Kootenay people. The style is not replicated elsewhere in British Columbia.

height. Further to the west and south are the Monashees, to the east the Purcells, then the Rockies. To reach the Slocan Valley, travellers two centuries ago had to persevere across range after range of these forbidding mountains, finding a way through snow-clogged passes or down turbulent rivers that mostly preferred to take them away from the valley rather than lead them to it.

Once the valley had been reached, the geographic challenges remained, especially in the north half. Slocan Lake is a long and relatively narrow body of water flanked by rocky and precipitous shores that offer little hospitality to potential inhabitants, save for a few deltas like the one upon which New Denver is situated. Traversing the lake in the absence of modern roads and rail required a sturdy canoe and considerable nerve or a difficult detour inland to avoid the impassable bluffs at various points around the lake's circumference. The Slocan River, by comparison, provides a more welcoming environment for human occupation. For the forty-odd kilometres of its course downstream towards the Kootenay River it meanders through relatively flat bench lands. Its rich soil and gentler temperatures provide a friendly habitat for a wide range of native plants and trees, many of them edible or bearing edible fruit, and plentiful mammals, birds, and fish. At its confluence with the Kootenay River, the Slocan River offers the downstream traveller options to travel east towards Nelson and Creston and south to the Columbia River; the upstream voyager faces little challenge in the relatively moderate current and absence of difficult rapids.

It is unsurprising therefore that early explorers of the valley established their settlements in the gentler environs of the river bench lands, clustering around three main areas: Lemon Creek, Vallican, and the south end of the valley, near the confluence of the Slocan and Kootenay Rivers. All three locations benefit from southern exposure and are the broadest flat areas in the river section of the valley. In the marshlands around Lemon Creek, waterfowl, mink, and beaver could be hunted seasonally. On the ridges above Vallican, deer, elk, and caribou were plentiful; and the confluence was where people gathered to fish and to trade. There were plentiful lodgepole pines for tepee poles; western white pine to make canoes grew nearby in scattered clumps; and there were abundant berries and roots to be gathered, as well as sweet herbs for healing and for ceremonies. Travelling north to the Okanagan and south as far as Montana to visit family and friends, east to meet other groups for social events and to trade, and west to hunt and fish, groups of aboriginal people in the west Kootenays roamed back and forth seasonally through the Slocan and Arrow Lakes region.

Facing page: Traditional tepee style of temporary dwelling. Modern tepee (or tipi) making thrives as a commercial business: Wilf Jacobs's Ktunaxa Tepee Co. in Creston made the tepees seen in the film *Dances With Wolves.*

Some three thousand years ago there were people living in these places, if only from time to time, in dwellings half-buried in the earth and

thatched overhead for warmth. These pit houses were as large as many modern homes, up to ten metres across in size; and their occupants were hunters and toolmakers, utilizing local Kootenay stone to make their implements. There were not many of them then, or so it would appear from what little evidence remains. But in the same millennium that saw elsewhere the rise and fall of the Roman Empire, the birth of Christianity, and the onset of the Dark Ages in Europe, aboriginal people in the Kootenays sustained themselves with little but the passing of the seasons and the vagaries of nature to challenge their peaceful existence.

Between 450 B.C. and A.D. 750 – what archaeologists refer to, with respect to the Slocan Valley, as the "Vallican Phase" – the area seems to have increased in popularity. The pit houses became smaller, perhaps to accommodate the larger number of dwellings required. Projectile weapons made of Kootenay argillite and increasingly sophisticated cutting and perforating tools were created and used for hunting and making clothing, fishing equipment, and containers. Food was preserved against harder times and kept in well-constructed storage pits. And those who did not survive the hard times were buried in the gravel bars along the river, perhaps with some small token at their side, to be left in peace, as custom demanded, for eternity.

As time moved on, bows and arrows came into use for hunting, bone tools were made, and as the people prospered, they turned their minds to the more leisurely matter of arts and decoration. They began making bead pendants from slate, and using a thick red paint made of ochre they began to record their way of life on the rock walls of Slocan Lake. They painted men and women standing, and in canoes; floating in circles, with rays radiating out from them; stars and animals; and vivid scenes from their past. Groups of figures seem to be engaged in a migration in one image that has survived. Others could be dancing; their legs akimbo and squatting, one arm bent over their heads. And in one compelling image, across the lake from New Denver, is the story of what looks like a bear-hunting expedition gone terribly wrong. Art historian Joy Bell analyzes it this way: "The situation is out of control... the bear charged the two hunters at the upper left. One has escaped and the other hunter panics and tries to run away. The bear, enraged, is too quick for him...the two at the upper right are hopelessly out of range, weaponless, and cannot help..."

By the time that European settlers came to this western frontier, at the edge of perceived civilization, it was to share a territory in which strong civilizations had already existed for thousands of years. Who were these people, as people are defined in contemporary European terms? Explorers, historians, and ethnologists have attempted to establish the anthropology of the aboriginal people in the Slocan Valley from time to time, and indeed, contemporary aboriginal people hold strong views in this regard. They speak in terms of their past and current occupation of a "traditional territory" – an area within which they exercise rights, carry out responsibilities, and undertake traditional activities. The territory is not based on a concept of ownership as it is understood in European terms, so much as a notion of stewardship, or governance accountability. "Part of our cultural responsibility as traditional gatherers," says Sinixt spokesperson Marilyn James, "is that if we have some to spare, we will share. It's part of our reverence for the landscape and its food and its people." Or as Ktunaxa elder Leo Williams put it in an interview with researcher Nicola Harwood in 1991: "We're not allowed to 'have' land; we're here to look after the land." The Sinixt speak of the Slocan Valley as lying exclusively within the traditional territory of the Lakes people. The Ktunaxa Nation, which comprises five Kootenay Indian bands – Tobacco Plains, St. Mary's, Columbia Lakes, Shuswap, and the Lower Kootenay Indian Band, now based on a reserve near Creston – as well as two American tribes, the Confederated Salish Kooteni in Montana and the Kootenay tribe of Idaho, speak of sharing the use of the Slocan Valley with the Sinixt. They are, however, two completely distinct and separate groups of people – and their relationship to each other and the valley is, both in historical and contemporary terms, a disputed one between them.

Ethnologists tend to agree that the word "Lakes" generally refers to people in the Arrow and Slocan Lakes region that speak, or spoke, a dialect of what is known now as the Okanagan-Colville language, in turn a branch of an interior Salish tongue. Both the early explorers and the government tended to misunderstand that the Lakes people of Canada were a separate group from those people who had migrated over time to the Colville region of Washington state from various parts of the American west; and indeed also a distinct group – albeit connected through individual relationships – from the Shuswap or the Okanagan people.

Provincial government officials were entirely wrong, stated anthropologist James Teit in the early years of the 20ᵗʰ century, to class the Lakes people as "American Indians" and "interlopers in British Columbia." He also noted as "quite misleading" the Canadian Indian Department's classification of the Lakes Indian Band as being Shuswap. Much of the written analysis of the origins of the Lakes people comes from a range of such non-aboriginal sources. Fortunately, their records also include a great deal of information acquired directly from native people.

Both the Lakes people and the Ktunaxa ranged widely in their seasonal activities, travelling throughout southeastern British Columbia and the western United States, and the paths of the explorers and traders frequently crossed with theirs. Thus in 1814 a fur trader by the name of Gabriel Franchère spoke of meeting a group of native people on the Upper Arrow Lake, engaged in making heavy fringed blankets from the wool of what he referred to as mountain sheep. Hudson's Bay Company clerk John Work commented in his journal in 1830 about the presence of Lakes Indians on the Columbia River and as far north as Revelstoke. A man named William Kittson travelling in the company of a number of "Kootenay Indians" commented on the presence of Lakes Indians in the Slocan; and Teit himself, famous for his explorations of the Pacific Northwest in the early part of the 20ᵗʰ century, considered Lakes territory to include the lower Kootenay River as well as the Slocan and points both north and west of the Arrow Lakes.

Teit and others recorded the existence of six communities in the Slocan Valley – three on the lake and three on the river – and wrote down their names in awkward and oddly alphabetized versions: **SnkEmip̓**; **TakElExaitcEkst**; **Sihwîlex**; **Kāṅicāk̓**; **Nkweio'xiEn**; and **SkEtuk̓Elôx**. The Slocan itself was recorded as **slhu7k̲íṅ** or **s̓tokeṅ**. This, according to ethnologists Randy Bouchard and Dorothy Kennedy, was translated as meaning to "pierce or strike on the head" by Mary Marchand, a Lakes woman who referred to it as the way in which salmon or trout were caught. The name of the Lakes people themselves was similarly recorded, as **Sngaytskstx**, from which the anglicized Sinixt is derived.

Modern ethnologists acknowledge that the information is sketchy, and that much of the relevant history was lost and lives changed by the coming of European settlement. Nevertheless a general picture of the pre-settlement way of life for Lakes people can be painted using a combination of archaeological evidence, recorded observations, and oral history. Environmental factors were clearly a primary determinant of seasonal movement and even cultural and political organization. Because their food both moved and disappeared seasonally – fish swam upstream to spawn, animals hibernated, and plants bore fruit and then withered for the winter – Lakes people also moved with the food and migrated to other food sources at different times of year. This semi-nomadic way of life demanded strong social skills and co-operation as they travelled their regular circuits and met people from other established communities along the way. Winters were a time for larger groups to move together in temporary settlements, sharing preserved food and company; in the summers, the camps would break up into smaller, more mobile groups to travel, hunt, fish, and gather roots and fruit and berries.

Ktunaxa people were also recorded as being active, at least at the mouth of the Slocan River, where they would gather to fish and trade with the Lakes. In *A Traveller's Guide to Aboriginal B.C.*, Cheryl Coull states that Ktunaxa means "lean and fast," or alternatively "to lick the blood from the spear," which indicates their fine marksmanship. The Ktunaxa say they are descended from an original people called the **Aqɬsmakni·k** and that early Ktunaxa settlements were located throughout the Columbia Basin, among other places. They speak a unique language, not related to any other aboriginal language or other language in the world. The Lower Kootenay are called the **Ya·qan nukiy**; where the Columbia and Kootenay Rivers meet at Castlegar, they call the place **k̓iksiɬuk**, and they call Nakusp **¢aɬnuʔakuq̓nuk**. Many of the geographical features in and around Kokanee Glacier Provincial Park also have names that the Ktunaxa claim as their own: Nasokwen, or **Nasukin**, Mountain; Nalmet Lake, or **Naɬmit**, Klawala Creek, or **Kɬawɬa**. Like the Sinixt, the Ktunaxa people migrated seasonally throughout their whole territory for thousands upon thousands of years, travelling to hunt and fish and returning to settlements to preserve food for winter storage. "You moved your camp from place to place in the season," said elder Leo Williams. "The fish will be gone, finished spawning, and then you moved to another place for hunting, just before the snow comes. And then when you finished your hunting you go back to your winter quarters."

Ethno-historians have formed some contradictory views about the presence of Ktunaxa people in the Slocan from the limited amount of information available: that the Kootenay people were on good terms with the Lakes, but that the two groups appeared to have come to war around the turn of the 18th century, when the Kootenays attempted to drive the Lakes away from the prime fishing area at the mouth of the river; and that the Slocan Lake and River area are within traditional Ktunaxa territory, but that there is "no evidence" of their use of the area, other than as "guests" of the Lakes people. There is, however, also no proof presented by them that the Ktunaxa did not use or occupy the area. Maps from both the 1880s and the 1940s indicate the Slocan as being within their territory, and the Ktunaxa are adamant that their people used the area; and indeed, that they continue to do so in contemporary times to fish and to hunt. "We know what our lands are," they say. "Where we have a name for a place, those are our lands. Where we do not, it is not ours." The Sinixt are equally adamant that the Slocan Valley is exclusively within their ancestral territory.

For a distinct and dark period in the history of both groups, however, the issue of who occupied the area would become moot. With the arrival of European settlers in the area, neither the Sinixt nor the Ktunaxa people had much of a chance to retain whatever form of occupation they held at the time. "When the non-natives first came to this country," said Leo Williams, "They were rushing towards a ghost – trying to take more land before the other people came in...once they saw the land, the way it looked, they started to push the Indians into the Indian reserves. They started to claim these lands." Although the first few decades saw a reasonably amiable trading relationship, the establishment of the Hudson's Bay Company forts ultimately resulted in a change of pattern that would become permanent after the creation of the international border in 1846. Aboriginal people followed the forts south, and stayed nearby over the winter rather than returning north during the cold weather. Smallpox wreaked havoc on native populations, and the government attempted a number of regulatory manoeuvres to manage the "Indian problem." In 1857, the federal government initiated an unsuccessful assimilation effort: agreeing to give citizenship to any male aboriginal who was over the age of twenty-one, literate in English or

French, and of "good moral character and free of debt." If they wished, such men could choose to "no longer be deemed to be an Indian." Unsurprisingly, there was no great rush to take the government up on the offer. In 1876, the Canadian government passed its first comprehensive Indian Act, essentially taking control over almost every aspect of life for native people registered as "status Indians" under the legislation. Since the concept of not being aboriginal – or "Indian," as the newcomers were calling them – was simply incomprehensible to native people, most registered.

Indian band designations can fail in a number of ways to be an effective means to define a community, but they fail in the Slocan in particular for two primary reasons. First, they are a creature of a Canadian statute and do not recognize the international nature of traditional family groupings of aboriginal people like the Sinixt and the Ktunaxa. Second, should the federal government refuse for any reason to recognize a particular group of people as having the right or opportunity to form an Indian band, there is no other ready mechanism – other than a long-drawn out court process – for that group to function as an acknowledged entity in Canada and gain access to the benefits of the Indian Act, or to exercise the aboriginal rights that are affirmed under section 35 of Canada's Constitution.

In any event, the issue of what adjectives to use – Indian, aboriginal, native, or First Nations – is far more about acceptance of cultural identity than it is about terminology. This is expressed with great clarity by the Sinixt Nation's Marilyn James: "I can't switch my identity. I'm always an Indian. I have a commitment that I have no choice in, to my culture, my people, my future, past generations." And the Sinixt, of all people, are acutely aware of the problems with definition of Indian status in Canada – for the descendants of the people who once roamed the Slocan Valley for thousands of years, and who are returning there even now, do not belong to any Canadian Indian band and have no legally recognized status as an aboriginal group in Canada. There are some who even believe they have been the victims of a terrible conspiracy of targeted extermination.

Although Canadian governments have no reputation for being so well organized, a combination of neglect and bureaucratic callousness undoubtedly played a role in the position that the aboriginal people of the Slocan Valley found themselves in the early part of the 20th century. Certainly the European-introduced diseases of smallpox, influenza, and measles had played their part in reducing the native population in dramatic numbers in the 18th century. And after the HBC's Fort Colville was closed down in the early 1870s, both national governments began to consider the need to put an end to cross-border aboriginal migration in the Kootenays and elsewhere. The American government was determined to put a stop to it. Canada, in typical equivocal fashion, noted in an 1881 Privy Council report that such migratory travel for subsistence purposes was not an offence against international law, but "if restraint [was] to be sought" it would look to the United States for co-operation. Although travel had remained relatively unrestricted for some time after the international border was created in 1846, it had also become increasingly easier for Lakes people to remain in the south year-round on the Colville reservation in Washington, where they were not only welcomed but were provided with land and the protection – such as it was – of the American government. By the 1890s, when the first settlers were moving into the Slocan Valley and surrounding regions, there were virtually no Lakes people left there. Ironically, many of the new settlers thought that the few Indians they saw coming north to hunt and fish were trespassing on Canadian soil; they urged their politicians to send these "Americans" back home where they belonged.

A gold commissioner by the name of W.G. Cox had in 1861 posted an unofficial reserve at the site where the modern community of Brilliant is located, at the confluence of the Kootenay and Columbia Rivers. The reserve was never formalized, however, and within a few years the land was in private hands. Instead, in November 1902 the federal government finally set aside some land as a reserve for the Lakes Indian Band, at Oatscott on the east shore of Lower Arrow Lake. But the area was remote, and the total registered population in Canada of the Lakes Indian Band at the time was a mere twenty-six people. Rather than go to a designated reserve that had so few people, one Lakes man named Baptiste Christian and his family continued to lobby to retain the land that had notionally been designated for a reserve at Brilliant, which was where he and his family were living.

Archaeological investigations would later establish the site as having been occupied for at least 4,500 years, which in contemporary times would present a compelling argument to pay serious attention to the issue. In the meantime, even without such evidence, Christian had considerable support from a number of concerned individuals, including James Teit and the Reverend John MacDougall. A flurry of correspondence ensued between the Department of Indian Affairs and local officials to investigate the matter and consider the options, and it seemed that at least a small reserve would be created. It was not to be, however. The Christians would be defeated in their aspirations, and finally, they too would depart for the Colville Reservation in Washington. For in 1912, despite the Canadian government having agreed to make part of the land at Brilliant an Indian reserve, Baptiste Christian and his family awoke one morning to find themselves being told by strangers that they had three weeks to leave their home. The property had been sold, to a Russian immigrant named Peter Vasiliyevitch Verigin.

As he left, Christian reminded the Indian agent that he was a "King George man" – a British subject. Some day, said Christian, I will come back here.

"The fabric of our community is only as strong as all its pieces, including its leaders. In the past, we had some very strong individual leaders. But such leaders can often be accused of other things."

— John "J.J." Verigin Jr., Grand Forks

9

BREAD, SALT, AND WATER: *the Doukhobors*

In 1908, a group comprising several thousand Russian immigrants moved west to British Columbia in a mass exodus from Saskatchewan. Many of these immigrants settled in the Slocan Valley. Like every other settler in the province, they were in search of a better place to live and a better future. They were also quite unlike any immigrants who had preceded them, or indeed, would come after them. They were Doukhobors, and what that means is perhaps only truly understood by the Doukhobors themselves.

In that respect they have much in common with their aboriginal neighbours, despite the differences the two groups have had over the years.

They are remembered by many Canadians in the 21st century only for the most sensationalized aspects of their culture, if they are remembered at all: for the burnings and the bombings that took place at the hands of the Sons of Freedom Doukhobors. The actions of the Sons of Freedom were described in 1947 as "terrorist" by one provincial judge. But the principles behind terrorism, if those can even be defined comprehensively, are extremely blurry. The Sons of Freedom protests were certainly founded on a self-directed and passionate sense of the rightness of their beliefs. But the complexity of the experiences that led to those protests is profound; and simplistic labels obscure a proper understanding of their history. Because the story of the Doukhobors – including the Sons of Freedom – is about a people and their way of life, it is both too complex and too interesting to be captured in mere generalizations. To abridge their story to a series of violent or sensational actions is unjust at worst and superficial at best. Just as importantly, equating the story of the Doukhobors as a whole with the tale of the Sons of Freedom is akin to assuming the tip is the whole iceberg. Rather, it is a story about a vibrant culture that overcame significant hardship to persevere in holding to its values and that has enriched the history of British Columbia and Canada significantly. The story is also a sad one, encompassing painful rifts between Doukhobors and their neighbours as well as between Doukhobor and Doukhobor, and including actions that are sometimes hard to understand; but the colours of right and wrong are, all the same, difficult to select from the palette of their history.

By the time the Doukhobors arrived in the west Kootenays and settled in the Slocan Valley and Castlegar area, they had been in Canada for less than a decade. They were, however, already carrying with them the considerable baggage of a past going back more than two hundred years. Originally members of the Russian Orthodox Church, Doukhobors were a Christian group whose predecessors had started to emerge in Russia as early as the mid-17th century. They held strong views about the nature of God and the way in which people should behave. In particular, they believed that the spirit of God resides within each man and woman and is manifested by people behaving towards each other with goodwill and understanding. This belief in the inherent goodness of mankind carried with it a consequent belief in pacifism: there was no need to be trained in the arts of war if men agreed not to fight each other but to respect the Holy Spirit within each other instead. Since such a simple formula for behaviour would in itself constitute sufficient regulation of society, there was also therefore no need to worship icons or to obey artificial rituals and ceremonies invented by priests. Nor was there a need for any formal structure of government. Formal schooling, a tool of the authorities, was also regarded with suspicion.

It was a simple and attractive attitude that, needless to say, did not sit well with the intensely hierarchical leaders of the Orthodox Church and the Russian Tsarist government. The authorities regarded these dissident beliefs as heretical and as a danger to good order – and perhaps, therefore, a danger to themselves. In short, they considered – in the time-honoured tradition of powerful and dominant governments throughout history – that something had better be done about these uppity peasants who thought that living communally, forgoing the need for any ceremonies such as weddings, and renouncing war were all good things. The authorities adopted the strategies first of ridicule, then of force and persecution. When neither of these strategies worked, the Doukhobors themselves would eventually solve the problem.

In an attempt to humiliate the renegades, around 1785 a church official labelled the group with the derogatory name *Dukhobortsi*, or people fighting against the Holy Spirit of God – the "Spirit Wrestlers." But the bestowal of the supposedly disparaging name turned out to be a tactical error on the part of the church. Far from being embarrassed, the Doukhobors simply claimed the title as their own and celebrated its meaning in a different way: as people who wrestled for a better way of life with the spirit of God in them. Rather than serving to send them packing with their tail between their legs, the new name united and strengthened the dissident group. The Doukhobors also adopted three simple symbols of their philosophy – bread, salt, and water, the three staples of existence – and continued to practise their unregulated way of life. It was perhaps less a religion than a spiritual and social movement; and neither governments nor churches in any period or on any part of this planet have ever dealt with such movements gracefully. Before the end of the 18th century the Russian government began deporting Doukhobor dissidents to remote regions of Siberia. In 1825, the newly installed Tsar Nicolas I ordered the enforcement against the Doukhobors of compulsory military conscription. His officials began to instigate increasingly repressive measures against them.

The harder the government tried to quell the Doukhobors, however, the more determined they seemed to become. Fairly early on in their emergence as a definable group, a number of dynamic leaders had surfaced and succeeded each other in what would eventually become a hereditary role. Under what seemed like the divine guidance of those leaders, the Doukhobor community clung together in the latter half of the 19th century, growing in numbers despite its treatment at the hands of the government. By 1882 the principal spokesperson for the group was a forceful woman named Lukeria Vasiliyevna Kalmakova, the childless widow of the previous leader. Perhaps prescient of her own impending death within less than five years, and determined not to let the Doukhobor community fall into disarray for lack of an heir, this resolute and powerful woman selected her successor and brought him into her home to groom him for the leadership. His name was Peter Vasiliyevitch Verigin. He was twenty-four years old, a young man so committed to his future role that in order to fulfil his duties he was prepared to leave behind him indefinitely his wife, Evdokeya Grigorevna, and their young son, Peter Petrovitch.

In 1886, Kalmakova died and Verigin succeeded to the leadership. Almost immediately, he was exiled and imprisoned by the government; he would spend the next fifteen years of his life in prisons in Georgia and Siberia, consolidating his beliefs and issuing long-distance directives to followers hundreds of kilometres away. One of those directives would unwittingly be the catalyst that would eventually turn the Doukhobors towards Canada, as unlikely a destination as might have been conceived – a secular country committed to regulation and the rule of law, enforced by the hand of government. On June 29, 1895, thoughts of Canada had not thus far been entertained by the Doukhobors, for as yet there was no need or desire to leave their homeland. But on that eventful day, following Verigin's orders, every weapon in their possession was burned in a massive rejection of the use of force for military purposes. It was the last straw for the authorities, and the consequences were severe. Hundreds were killed and exiled, and their property was confiscated. Those in exile suffered greatly from malnutrition and disease, and further hundreds died – in all, a thousand people would be lost as a result of the government's revenge for the actions of the community. In the midst of this persecution, an unexpected saviour appeared: the already-famous novelist Leo Tolstoy, who had converted to Christianity in the late 1870s and espoused a similar philosophy to the Doukhobors in terms of pacifism. He donated the proceeds of his novel *Resurrection* to the cause, and with a number of supporters began an active campaign abroad to publicize the persecution of the Doukhobors.

In the end, it was clear to all that the only feasible solution to save the Doukhobors was voluntary exile, and Canada was the destination of choice. The relieved Russian government gladly gave the Doukhobors permission to go, although at a high cost: they were forbidden ever to return to Russia, on pain of swift and severe punishment if they should do so. An advance guard was sent to the prairies of western Canada to review the possibilities. It was known that plentiful land was there to homestead and that Mennonite communities had already settled there in collective organizations with little apparent difficulty. In its turn, the Canadian government was most encouraging, as was the omnipresent Canadian Pacific Railway. It was in the best interests of both institutions, after all, to bring good farmers west to tame the prairies and create revenue-producing settlements. A straightforward deal was negotiated. Clifford Sifton, the minister for the interior of Canada, agreed that the Doukhobors would be exempt from military service, free to practise their religious beliefs, and permitted to farm communally in the same manner as the Mennonites. It seemed ideal, and in 1899 about 7,500 Doukhobor men, women, and children arrived in their newly adopted country, establishing villages on large homestead properties in the territory that would in a few years become the province of Saskatchewan.

But while each of the parties to the agreement thought they knew what it meant, they also each thought something different. Sifton had intended that like the Mennonites, the Doukhobors would register their homesteads individually, to comply with the Dominion Lands Act, and simply farm them communally. The Doukhobors had no such intention, however – the bureaucracy of individual property ownership was contrary to their beliefs. There were also two other seriously ambiguous components to the agreement. Although education was a provincial responsibility, it was not yet a statutory requirement in the relatively remote territory in which the Doukhobors had settled – an important influence upon the choice of location, as philosophically the notion of organized schooling aroused both confusion and distrust in equal proportions. The semi-military style of public schools repelled the Doukhobors in their mimicry of the government authority and practices. And, although he never specifically prohibited school attendance, in correspondence that Peter Verigin wrote while imprisoned he disparaged formal education systems and advocated that Doukhobors teach themselves what they needed to know. In any event, when they arrived on the prairies the Doukhobors did not seem to have envisaged that their children would need to enrol in the public school system. The Canadian government saw no need to confront the issue at that point, and the matter was not pressed.

The second ambiguity in the agreement was more fundamental. A homesteader in Canada wanting to prove title on his or her property was required, if not already a British citizen, to swear allegiance to the Queen of England before the expiry of three years from the date of the pre-emption. It is uncertain whether the Doukhobors had any notion of this requirement, or if they believed it had been waived for them. Clearly, their decision to travel to Canada was based on a belief, however mistaken, that they were coming to a place where government controls would differ in every respect from those of the regime they were escaping and, moreover, an understanding that they would be free from government controls. It seems likely that the government decided not to press that issue either, in the equally mistaken belief that by the time the requirement to swear allegiance became due, the Doukhobors would have been fully assimilated into Canada and would be ready to comply.

The communities faced more immediate and compelling problems. For a start, their leader had remained in Russia, still in prison. They were extremely poor and had little means to improve their situation in the short term. They had also arrived, without knowing it, into a local atmosphere of tension and distrust. They were already reputed to be anti-government and anarchistic, and there was a great deal of resentment on the part of previous settlers at the ease with which the Doukhobors were allowed to acquire free land as well as the exemptions they had been given by the government. But in fact the government immediately began placing pressure on the Doukhobors to register their homesteads individually. This requirement threw them into great confusion. At the same time, inflammatory documents promoting resistance to government and the concept of private property were circulating in the communities.

In this climate of uncertainty and turmoil, divisions began to emerge within the group almost immediately. A faction of zealous individuals formed on one fringe, their passion for the purity of their principles intensified by the isolation they were experiencing in their new country. This group lobbied for the utmost simplicity in the approach that the Doukhobors should take to establishing their communal villages. Luxuries or mechanical assistance should be completely forsworn, they believed; and they condemned as unchristian a number of practices such as the use of cattle and horses – even the paid employment of other human beings – to assist in breaking ground or carrying loads. At the other end of the spectrum were some Doukhobors who could see how well off their Canadian neighbours seemed to be, and the option of striking out on their own grew increasingly attractive. The situation was ripe for rapid disintegration of the community.

In 1902, Peter Vasiliyevitch Verigin was finally released from his Russian prison. He did not stay with his wife and son in Russia, but instead set out immediately for Canada and his flock, arriving in time to apply his strong and charismatic personality to smooth the troubled waters. For Verigin was, without question, a compelling man. The newspaper accounts of his arrival in Canada are effusive in praise of this impressive and articulate man, lingering in glowing terms over his good looks and impeccable clothing. Government officials were apparently similarly swayed by his impressive demeanour. In a difficult and delicate negotiation, Verigin simultaneously persuaded the Canadian government to accept him as the proper representative of the Doukhobors and to have patience while the Doukhobors adjusted to the new regime they lived under, while

Facing page: **Peter Vasiliyevitch "Lordly" Verigin, 1922.**

Copyright 1922.

Campbell Art Gallery.
Nelson. BC.

persuading the Doukhobors to accept the individual registration of homestead title. The government readily agreed, hoping that Verigin would persuade his people eventually to comply with all their requirements. The Doukhobors generally accepted his wisdom that individual registration on behalf of their community supported their communal principles. The oath of allegiance had not yet become a problem and was not dealt with by the parties.

Verigin settled quickly into the leadership and management of the Saskatchewan communities. Discerning the need for some spiritual discipline among a group of people who had been rudderless for too long, he issued inspiring guidelines and directives to focus them on their faith and beliefs. A pragmatic man as well as a natural leader, he also employed such sound economic strategies that within less than twelve months he turned a situation of borderline poverty into a substantial asset base, increasing the communal land holdings in Saskatchewan by a further twenty square kilometres and adding substantial numbers of stock, farming equipment, and mills to the inventory. He even managed not only to pay off the loans that had been provided to the Doukhobors to emigrate but to send cash to Tolstoy to help other dissident groups in Russia. It was a remarkable achievement – a vision made reality by the sweat and faith of the Doukhobor community, who for the most part seemed willing to do whatever Verigin wished.

All the same, individuals who sought the independence they saw their non-Doukhobor neighbours enjoying began to leave the villages in increasing numbers. Some started to take up their own land and settle into mainstream Canadian society. And just as disturbingly, Verigin – by now commonly referred to as "Peter Lordly" by his followers – was unable to persuade the small but powerful group of purists in the community to align to his moderate views and his approach to amassing wealth in the name of the community. The word "zealot," which has frequently been applied to this group by historians, carries in contemporary meaning a pejorative element. But the *svobodniki*, or "Sons of Freedom," simply preached a potent doctrine of adherence to the stricter interpretation of their beliefs. The accumulation of assets, the wearing of fine clothes, the submission to even the most fundamental requirements of the government, were in the eyes of the *svobodniki* a betrayal of their faith and the road to perdition. So strongly held was this belief they felt compelled to demonstrate in the most elemental fashion they could think of. On May 11, 1903, casting off their clothes to stand naked before their God and nature, fifty-two men, women, and children marched through the Doukhobor villages in an unsuccessful effort to persuade their compatriots of the error of their ways.

This act of faith was the first chapter of a long and bitter rift between the *svobodniki* and their kin that would not heal for decades, if even then. The men among the protesters were beaten and jailed. But as the Doukhobors in Russia had done when oppressed, the *svobodniki* drew strength from their martyrdom and remained more convinced than ever of their righteousness. By the time they were released from prison, three months later, some of the men had determined that the only way to remove the twin demons of scientific progress and materialism from the communities was to destroy their concrete manifestations. They attempted to set fire to some equipment as a way to renounce the demons and purify the community. Their reward was three-year jail sentences for arson, advocated by Peter Lordly himself, perhaps in an attempt to nip the problem in the bud.

As Verigin consolidated his hold on the leadership in the prairies – decision-making was notionally by democratic votes at community meetings, but effectively everything Verigin recommended was approved – he still faced significant challenges. It was becoming increasingly untenable to avoid the issue of the Canadian government's wishes. Not only was the date approaching upon which the Doukhobors would have to swear allegiance to the Queen or forfeit their homesteads, but the government was becoming progressively more insistent that the Doukhobors also start to comply with registration requirements regarding births, deaths, and marriages, something they had successfully avoided to date. After the incorporation of Saskatchewan as a province in 1905, the enforcement of compulsory school attendance was also coming to a head.

In 1906, the Doukhobors lost one of their greatest defenders, Clifford Sifton. He was replaced as Canadian minister for the interior by Frank Oliver, a man with no great love for the Russian immigrants. Oliver immediately took a much harder line than Sifton had. In 1907, the government cancelled well over half of the homestead holdings of the Doukhobors in Saskatchewan on the pretext of the failure to swear allegiance to the Queen. As intended by the government, it precipitated a further break away by independent Doukhobors who decided to take the oath rather than lose the land they had been working on, and register it in their own names. There was also an immediate grab for the remaining land by non-Doukhobor settlers who had been waiting in the wings for the highly desirable developed ground to become available.

The government's actions revived the passions of the *svobodniki*, now freed after serving their jail sentences. A number of them set out to eastern Canada on a land march in protest, only to be shipped back without ceremony when they reached Ontario. The government there had no intention of tolerating such an intrusion in its orderly and already well-settled society. By 1908, it was clear to Verigin that staying in Saskatchewan was putting the survival of the Doukhobors as a community at great risk, and he turned his eyes westward to British Columbia. The advantage in moving to that province was the ability to purchase land, rather than settle it. The immediate problems of communal registration of land and the swearing of allegiance would become instantly redundant – and the other matters of school attendance and the registration of statistics could not be any greater a difficulty to manage in British Columbia, he imagined, than it had become in Saskatchewan. The other advantage was the relative isolation of the area that Verigin was considering – the west Kootenays, in the southeast interior of the province. There perhaps, he hoped, the Doukhobors might be left in peace to pursue their chosen way of life, and he could continue to lead them in a role he clearly relished.

In 1908, Verigin started buying land in British Columbia. Five thousand Doukhobors, including the *svobodniki*, packed their meagre possessions and the amassed assets of the communities and started their next journey, this time to the west Kootenays. Over the next five years they would migrate in groups small and large, dreaming of the peaceful life to come. Some could not travel immediately: "We had to wait for my grandmother to die," explained ninety-four-year-old Bill Lawrenow quietly. It was 1912 before the three-year-old and his family came first to Glade, a small group of Doukhobor villages on the CPR railway line

Thousands of Doukhobors migrated west to the Slocan from Saskatchewan, starting in 1908. Some, like the Lawrenow family, had to wait until elderly relatives who could not make the trek had passed on. Frank and Molly Lawrenow and their sons Ed, Bill, and Peter pose for a photograph before their departure in 1912, when Bill was three years old.

between Nelson and Robson; then to a growing settlement in the Slocan Valley itself, on community land west of Crescent Valley called Krestova.

Verigin embarked on an aggressive campaign of land acquisition as far west as Grand Forks, one hundred kilometres west of the Slocan. He bought in Nelson and Trail, at Champion Creek south of Castlegar, at Glade and at Thrums, and through Pass Creek. He purchased a series of properties up the Slocan Valley in addition to the land at Krestova, amassing lots in Crescent Valley, at Lebahdo Flats north of Slocan Park, in several places along the west bank of the Slocan River near Winlaw and as far up as Perry Siding. In 1912, consolidating the community holdings at the confluence of the Columbia and Kootenay Rivers, he

Walter Stoochnoff's great-grandfather and family, Ootischenia, date unknown.

bought the land at Brilliant that Baptiste Christian had so desperately wanted to keep as an Indian reserve. In the flat bench lands below the confluence, the biggest Doukhobor settlement of all was created: Dolina Ooteshenie, or Ootischenia, the valley of consolation. Within two or three years Verigin accumulated nearly six thousand hectares of land, using the proceeds of sale of some of the community's Saskatchewan land holdings and raising finance for the balance, and over the next ten years he would add another three thousand hectares of property to the community's asset base.

It seemed at last that life could be as it had always been intended. Continuing to apply his masterful mix of economic wisdom and divine guidance, Verigin took the community from strength to strength. In 1917, he even incorporated the Doukhobors as a company called the

Doukhobor women at Ootischenia, probably around the mid-1920s.

Christian Community of Universal Brotherhood – the CCUB – with himself as the first president. It solved an awkward problem for him. Prior to incorporation, the communal assets had been held in his name personally – on behalf of the community, assuredly, but nonetheless a position wide open to attack by any critic. On each CCUB property were settled a number of families, living in villages comprising two large houses built around a horseshoe-shaped courtyard and connected to a bathhouse and shared barns. Community members set to work, and in an astonishingly short time they had not only planted numerous fruit trees and begun producing crops for exporting east but had also built complex irrigation systems, flour mills, warehouses, office facilities, sawmills, and electrical plants. At Brilliant they built a jam factory, and throughout the long, clear summers, the smell of hot strawberry jam and boiling sugar would permeate the air. In 1914, a bridge was built to connect Brilliant to Ootischenia that would survive in general use for more than fifty years. Unlike their experience in Saskatchewan, their

Members of the Chernoff family, probably in Brilliant, during the 1920s.

neighbours were impressed with their diligence and persistence in, as Doukhobor chronicler Larry Ewashen put it, "bringing fruitfulness to the wilderness." Some outsiders marvelled at the lack of sophistication in their techniques, suggesting they could do much better using more advanced technology. But the expense of moving west had taken its toll, and the greatest asset the Doukhobors had at the time was their own free sweat.

Although it was a grand new beginning for them, life was also austere in many ways for the members of the CCUB. Those who could be spared were sent to work on the railways or as contract labour for other farmers. Everything that was earned went into the communal coffers, and even such personal items as clothing were supplied from CCUB warehouses. Frivolities were not permitted. There were no musical instruments, no ornamentation, no jewellery. There was on occasion little to eat, and that only vegetarian, providing limited sustenance to people who had been working in the fields for twelve or more hours. On the other hand, there was consolation in the security of living on land owned by the CCUB and in the steadily growing asset base of the community. In particular, there was great spiritual strength to be gained from the gatherings held on Sundays to sing and to pray together, and to discuss their children and their future. Peter Verigin's strategy of removing the group to the more isolated valleys of British Columbia seemed also to be working. While on the prairies the independent Doukhobors increased in strength and formed their own Society of Independent Doukhobors by 1916, in the west Kootenays the few dissenters remained quiet, fearing their inability to survive should they be forced to leave the community. Verigin forbade any communication with the Saskatchewan independents and kept a tight fist on the functioning of the CCUB, travelling frequently from Brilliant to Grand Forks and to the Slocan properties to visit the villages and renew the spiritual vigour of the people living there.

It seemed that at last the Doukhobors might be free to live under their adopted banner of "Toil and Peaceful Life." But the marriage of this little group with the province they adopted as their new home had been executed in some haste. The honeymoon would quickly be over.

10

WAR, LAND, AND CHILDREN:
the seeds of alienation

No matter how peaceful and well behaved they may have been, for the Doukhobors it was a false hope from the start to imagine they might continue to live in some sort of unregulated haven from the laws of British Columbia. Notwithstanding the isolation of the Slocan Valley and even Brilliant and its environs, it is difficult to imagine a group of more than five thousand people escaping the eye of the authorities. By the time they arrived in 1908, the province already had in place a well-established system of laws governing property-holding, taxation, registration of statistical information, and school attendance, as well as a robust law-enforcement system. It thus seems inevitable that the Doukhobors and the provincial government started clashing over the issues that were important to them almost immediately.

The concerns held by the Doukhobors regarding education were still not particularly clear-cut. On the one hand, most Doukhobor children had never been to a school and did not yet speak any English. What skills they were being taught – agriculture and construction, for example – were at the hands of their parents and elders rather than designated "teachers." On the other hand, a number of Doukhobors, especially among their leaders, were reasonably well educated themselves. Certainly Peter Verigin was highly literate, and he had been rigorously trained in preparation for taking on the mantle of authority. Many individuals, especially those wavering towards separation from the communal lifestyle in favour of the benefits of going it alone, saw the benefits in their children attending Canadian schools. Verigin could not afford to take a hard line against the government on the issue, knowing he would lose what limited leverage he had achieved as a perceived moderate. On the whole, therefore, by the time the community had reached British Columbia, its members were more or less prepared for their children to go to school and had even gone as far as building schools on communal lands. But when compulsory military training was introduced into provincial schools in 1912, the policy was too directly in conflict with their fundamental beliefs. The Doukhobors objected en masse and withdrew their children immediately on the grounds that it was immoral to subject the families of pacifists to such a regime – pacifists, moreover, who were protected by a government exemption from military service. They also refused to participate in the registration of births, deaths, and marriages, considering this none of the provincial government's business and completely unnecessary to boot.

At that point, the government employed the usual delay tactics brought to bear when it has no idea what else to do – it called a royal commission of inquiry into the issues. The benefit of such an inquiry at least was that the Doukhobors were provided an opportunity to explain their beliefs to some neutral authority. They expressed the view that when they had arrived in Canada, the government had promised to leave them alone. This promise, they submitted, had been broken. In their presentations they did not distinguish to any great degree between the federal and provincial governments, both of which they considered had treated them poorly in this regard; it was all the same to them that any authority should be taking it upon itself to pry so deeply into their personal affairs and peaceful existence.

Commissioner William Blakemore listened to the Doukhobors' submissions, eventually issuing a conciliatory report that called for patience on the part of government in dealing with these hard working people. They were, he said, adding considerable value to British Columbia's economy and infrastructure and were sincere in their beliefs. Blakemore then made a number of suggestions for compromises that he thought would be viable in reducing the tensions, including the employment of Russian-speaking teachers and a simplification of the curriculum to accommodate the steeper learning curve of the children in relation to subjects that were completely new to them, like mathematics and English. They were excellent ideas; but unfortunately, Blakemore also included in his report an astonishing recommendation to rescind the Doukhobors' exemption from military service. As a result, they rejected all the recommendations. Nothing further of any substance came of the report, and the authorities simply renewed their efforts to bring the Doukhobors to heel.

The gap grew steadily wider. In 1914 World War One broke out, and while the miners and loggers and farmers of the Slocan Valley and the west Kootenays set off for Europe to fight for Canada, Doukhobor men stayed at home – as of course they were not only entitled to do, but felt compelled to do by their beliefs. Nonetheless their refusal to enlist created animosity and soured relations with many of their neighbours, who were outraged that the Doukhobors would not fight for the country that had offered them protection. There was also a perception that the Doukhobors had gained an unfair advantage in being able to continue to grow and manage their agricultural enterprises while those belonging to soldiers deteriorated or foundered completely in their absence.

In the same year that the war began, the provincial government passed the Community Regulation Act to enforce the registration of vital statistics and the attendance at schools of Doukhobor children. Both matters were considered by the government to be critical components of the integration of Doukhobors into the mainstream life of the province. The tension increased exponentially, and the *svobodniki* again grew restless. The provincial government, however, did not particularly want to spark open conflict internally at a time when the country was at war. Attorney General William Bowser managed a carefully negotiated compromise on the educational front in 1915: acknowledging the right of the Doukhobors to conscientious objection, the government agreed there would be no military exercises in Doukhobor schools. However, the children must start attending school again immediately. The Doukhobor leadership agreed, and peace in the valley had been bought, at least for the interim. It would not last for long.

While the Doukhobors were able to stay on their land and cultivate it throughout World War One, any advantage they may have gained over their neighbours in doing so was of no great value. Like other hard-pressed farmers in the west Kootenays, they struggled from the sheer difficulties involved in carving out a living from agricultural undertakings. Land-clearing for crops continued to be expensive and back-breaking. The weather was rarely in their favour. Competing orchards in the more accessible Okanagan region were able to operate more cheaply, and the marginal returns that fruit-growing were generating in the early years of production, combined with the scattered locations of the relatively small orchards, made shipping costly and inefficient. Prices were also falling as their best markets disappeared. The decline of the mining towns in the north part of the Slocan and their falling populations contributed heavily to the financial stress on farmers in the region. On top of this, in the immediate aftermath of the war, anti-pacifist sentiment continued to run high against the Doukhobors. War veterans pushed hard on the federal government to expropriate the CCUB lands for the use of returned soldiers, but minister of the interior Arthur Meighen recognized the inherent unfairness of such a move and refused. However, in a concession to public opinion, further Doukhobor immigration to Canada was prohibited in 1919. At the same time the government of British Columbia disenfranchised the Doukhobors, preventing them and all other conscientious objectors from voting in provincial elections.

Things went from bad to worse. In 1922, a provincial school trustee by the name of E.G. Daniels decided to take a harder line against the CCUB on education. New public schools were built at Brilliant over objections from the community members, and another boycott of school attendance began as a result. Daniels did not hesitate to enforce the law to its limit, and by April 1923 the government began seizing CCUB property in lieu of the unpaid fines imposed for the boycott. In May, in retaliation, a school was burned to the ground. A dozen more burnings would follow in quick succession in the Brilliant school district.

The protests were not in each case necessarily against government action alone. As well as the schools, community property was attacked, and even Peter Verigin's home was threatened. Implicit in the attacks was a criticism of Verigin's moderate policies and his attempts to negotiate with the government; but the perpetrators, if known, were not caught. Verigin disassociated himself and the CCUB leadership from the arsons and pleaded with the government for help, but was ignored. The painful divisions within the community deepened, along with resentment at the way the government was behaving. And on October 29, 1924, the biggest disaster yet to befall the Doukhobors in Canada occurred. Riding the CPR train from Brilliant to Grand Forks, Peter Lordly Verigin was killed when the coach in which he was riding exploded with no warning. The shrewd and charismatic man who had guided and protected the Doukhobors for nearly forty years was now gone, and the members of the Universal Brotherhood were plunged into mourning. In the aftermath of the explosion, many suspects were considered and discussed around dinner tables. They ranged from the self-styled "Tsar of Heaven," a local lunatic who wore a crown of oranges wherever he went but who was later exonerated, to Verigin's own son Peter, who had come to Canada just once while his father was alive and was considered by some to be estranged from him. The *svobodniki* were of course held in deep suspicion. But none were convicted, and the identity of Verigin's assassin remains a well-kept secret. Thousands upon thousands of community members assembled for his funeral, and Peter the Lordly was laid to rest in a tomb of polished black marble on a small ridge overlooking the confluence of the Kootenay and Columbia Rivers and Dolena Ootishenie, the Valley of Consolation. His followers still gather to mark his passing. The potential for complete

The funeral of Peter "Lordly" Verigin on November 2, 1924. It was attended by thousands of his grieving followers.

Doukhobor community meal at Brilliant, possibly late 1920s. Bill Lawrenow's recollection is that the woman at front in the black skirt is Evdokia Grigorevna, Peter Lordly Verigin's widow.

disarray in the CCUB was huge. The abiding question was, who could possibly succeed the leadership. The dead leader's son, Peter Petrovitch Verigin, was spending a great deal of time behind Bolshevik bars in the U.S.S.R. As a rallying point for the anarchistic Doukhobors left in the republic, he was no more popular with that regime than his father had been with the Tsarist authorities before him. In any event, however, even if he had been free to come to Canada, the anti-immigration law of 1919 would have prevented him from entering the country. An ambitious woman in Brilliant named Anastasia Golubova threw her hat in the ring, but there was little appetite in the community for this woman – who is described in contemporary Doukhobor literature as having been the "devoted maid and companion" of Peter Verigin – to step into his revered shoes. The CCUB instead voted that Peter Petrovitch should succeed his father, notwithstanding his enforced absence. Golubova left for Alberta with her supporters, and a caretaker administration was established until the new leader could come to take up his role.

They did not have long to wait. The Canadian government had been at a loss when Peter Lordly Verigin died so suddenly. His moderating influence had at least held most of their problems with the Doukhobors at bay. Hoping that his son might be as moderate, the government decided it would be useful to let him come to Canada. The anti-immigration legislation was quietly repealed in 1926 and the way smoothed with Bolshevik officials, who were readily persuaded to rid themselves of the headache the younger Verigin had become. On October 11, 1927, almost three years to the day after his father died, Peter Petrovitch Verigin arrived in Brilliant to a welcome from several thousand people gathered there. Like his father before him, he came unaccompanied by his wife Anna Fedorovna or by either of his children, although they would later join him, as would his long-suffering mother. Instead, by his side on that

Peter "Lordly" Verigin was accompanied toward the end of his life by a "handmaid and companion" named Anastasia Golubova, who made an unsuccessful bid for the leadership after his death.

day was an intellectual Russian dissident named Pavel Ivanovich Biryukov, who recorded the proceedings. As Biryukov described it in the notes he scribbled by hand upon his knee, they were all "singing in full voice...the usual items of greeting were present: a small table with a white tablecloth, on which were placed bread, salt, water..."

Peter Petrovitch was a clever man and appears to have understood well the fractured community that was gathered before him, and what he needed to do. The record of his speech that day in Brilliant indicates a leader with not only a good strategic sense but also strong political survival instincts. He launched into a lengthy oration infused with passion and vigour, exhorting his followers to stay united in their faith and their way of life. Most importantly, he said, they must obviate the need for violence by adhering again to the fundamental tenets of their faith – discarding both compromise and fanaticism. Peter Petrovitch earned for himself that day in Brilliant a new name: Chistiakov – the Purger, or the Cleanser.

Any Canadian government officials listening may have felt their hearts sink into their leather lace-up boots at the tactical error they could be forgiven for thinking they had made. Despite his rejection of violent protest actions, Chistiakov appeared to be much harder-line than his father: a fundamentalist who would cause them far greater problems than they had experienced so far if his followers took his exhortations literally. But taking the approach that he did was the wisest strategy the new leader could have employed, under the circumstances. His speech was general rather than specific. He did not make the mistake of laying out a set of hard and fast directives at his very first meeting with his constituency. Instead, by using universal policy statements that could be broadly interpreted to fit any of their viewpoints, he appealed directly to both the mainstream and the fringes of the Universal Brotherhood, and assured them of his commitment to the principles governing their way of life. Had he wavered or attempted to go down the middle of the road in his very first address to his people, he would have simply cemented the existing divisions in the community, convincing none; and very quickly he would have lost control. As it was, he instead attracted the instant loyalty of all the factions and successfully established himself as an unequivocal leader with a very firm hand. He also bought himself the time to assess the situation and decide his long-term strategy.

Like his father before him, Peter Chistiakov was not only an intelligent and strategic politician, he was also resourceful and capable. He immediately plunged into an ambitious economic program to improve the efficiency of CCUB operations. Although all the assets were still owned communally, Verigin decentralized much of its work to the individual member communities, allowing them for the first time to manage their own business affairs. In Saskatchewan he created a new organization called the Society of Named Doukhobors, with the notional goal of finding common ground between the breakaway Independent Doukhobors, the *svobodniki*, and the orthodox members of the CCUB. Its real function, however, was to serve as a fundraiser for paying down the community's debts. He consolidated the organization's debt burden into one blanket mortgage of $350,000 to the National Trust Co. of Canada. The size of the debt was negligible, compared with the $6.5 million worth of communal assets that had been accumulated in just twenty years, but it would, all the same, remain the weak link in the CCUB's chain that would ultimately bring about its downfall.

For although Peter Chistiakov was a compelling and imaginative visionary capable of extracting large amounts of money from CCUB members towards communal causes, the CCUB's income never quite seemed sufficient to clear the debts. He built a dream amongst his people, for example, that a "white horse" would come to lead them out of Canada to a land of peace and prosperity, and in doing so he solicited hundreds of thousands of dollars towards a migration fund to some unknown destination; but it was for a migration that would never occur. Where the money went is also unclear. According to critics, Peter Chistiakov was also prone to violence, profanity, and drinking heavily – deliberately, his defenders rationalize, so as to deceive his enemies and test his followers. The official literature of contemporary Doukhobor organizations speaks more generously and reverentially of the "many difficult experiences that undermined his health."

Notwithstanding his skills as a leader, his behaviour was certainly mercurial, whether or not he was guilty of any of the sins described. But he was struggling against steadily mounting challenges that were not necessarily within his control. Internal dissension continued to grow within the CCUB. More and more Doukhobors left to strike out on their own. Young Bill Lawrenow married his wife Vera on February 6, 1931, on community land in Winlaw, then took a job logging and rented a home in Slocan Park so that they could be independent of the communal way of life. At the same time, the strength of the *svobodniki* grew proportionately. The incidents of protest burnings and nude marches to demonstrate the passion of their beliefs to both their leaders as well as the government became more commonplace. Riled by the media reports, indiscriminate public antipathy towards the Doukhobors was rising again. Brilliant schoolteacher Hazel O'Neail was more critical of what she termed the hypocritical voyeurs from Nelson, who would rush out to see the "show" with picnic baskets and cameras in hand.

To protect the rest of the community from internal hostilities and

Vera Gretchen, before her marriage to Bill Lawrenow in 1931.

government retaliation, Peter Chistiakov decided to banish the *svobodniki* from community lands. It proved to be a tactical error, creating enough sympathy among the more conservative Doukhobors that a number of them joined the outlawed group, now becoming known in the Slocan Valley and British Columbia as the "freedomites" or "Sons of Freedom." And when he also expelled a number of CCUB members for failure to pay their membership dues, they too joined their brethren, now gathering in increasing numbers on unoccupied land in Thrums and in Krestova. Their debts were growing; the community was starting to split apart in an intensely painful division of loyalties that went even into the hearts of families, setting brother against brother, as the orthodox and the *svobodniki* castigated each other for their actions. Meanwhile the leader of them all was struggling to hold the mainstream CCUB to his vision of the future.

Regardless of their self-sufficient way of life in the west Kootenays, as the Depression years loomed, the prospects looked as grim for the Doukhobors of the Universal Brotherhood as they did for anyone in the Slocan Valley.

*"When people in the Slocan heard my
father was moving us to Victoria back in
the thirties, they said, 'The man'll starve.
Tell him to come back.'"*

—Katherine Clay Hutton, Victoria
(formerly of Slocan City)

II

A GOOD PLACE IN HARD TIMES:
the depression years

In October 1929, when the bottom fell out of stock
exchanges in New York City, London, and other centres of
commerce around the globe, it would not have the same
impact on the Slocan Valley as it would in most other
regions of North America. Times would be hard, but they
had always been hard in the valley – and usually for reasons
that had less to do with economics and a great deal more
to do with weather or human nature. In the years immediately prior to the Wall Street crash, British Columbia

Not all work and no play: Bill Lawrenow, the Fominoff brothers (upside down), and one of the Chernoffs.

Courting in Appledale: Bill Lawrenow and Fred Chernoff (in the pinstripes) with Vera Gretchen, Anne Chernoff, and friends, circa 1930.

had been on the whole extremely prosperous: it enjoyed the highest per capita income in Canada, a doubling in the value of its minerals, and forestry values that rose by 50 percent in just seven years.

But those figures did not apply to the Slocan Valley during any part of the 1920s. The communities there had instead learned to diversify and make a living in any way possible from the resources at hand and by their own sweat. Ironically, then – while bank foreclosures were steadily emptying the dusty spaces of the prairies, homeless unemployed men slept on the concrete steps of government buildings in Vancouver, and families on the coast and in the north of the province tried to eke out an existence on relief cheques of twenty-eight dollars a month – in the Slocan, things were not much changed. If anything, people in the valley were suddenly better off in comparison with their city cousins.

It hadn't necessarily been easy for those in the Slocan during the stock market heydays of the 1920s. Forestry fortunes had risen and fallen again in an unsustainable fashion. The Patrick Lumber Co.'s sawmill in Crescent Valley had been forced into closure in 1919 because of the

Previous page: Stable and barn buildings on John Owen Clay's Valhalla Ranch near Slocan, 1920s.

depletion of readily accessible timber. The use of aircraft for forest reconnaissance, enthusiastically introduced into the Nelson District in 1927, was almost immediately curtailed at the onset of the

Great Depression. But during the 1930s, the demand for cheap timber rose: Peter Koch even built a new sawmill, between Slocan Park and Passmore, while the Cady Lumber and Pole Co. built one on the Passmore–Slocan West side road. Some of the bigger operations simply could not find enough men to fill their labour requirements. Castlegar sawmill operator Bill Waldie reminisced in an interview with Peter Chapman in 1990 that "in the woods, we did have trouble, just get enough bodies there, never mind how good they were...I re-member making trips around the area to see if I could find some men – get the name of a fellow who wasn't working, and go and see him if he wanted to go to work. Well,

Wilbert "Buck" Hicks, horse-logging near Slocan, 1929.

In the 1920s, old-growth timber was still relatively plentiful, although not for much longer: John Clay and Monty Morley, Slocan.

Below right: Joe Pawsky and giant cedar, Gwillim Creek, 1930s. One of the tortures for loggers throughout the valley's history has been the ubiquitous presence of mosquitoes. While latter-day residents hotly debate the spraying of BTi for mosquito control in the valley, loggers in the "old days" would spread motor oil on their skin to keep the bugs away. Women stuffed newspapers under their stockings and suffered the heat and discomfort instead.

what the hell, if he wanted to work, he was already working. It was tough." The year 1930 itself, recollected Waldie, was the best one for William Waldie & Sons Ltd., of whom he was one of the three sons involved in the business. Things got tougher as the thirties progressed, but there was generally enough work for those who wanted it.

New Denver's socialist captain, J.C. Harris, recalled the Depression years as among the happiest in his lifetime, according to his son Richard. Harris threw himself into his socialism with a vengeance, fuelled by the conditions of the thirties. He was a paid-up member of the relatively successful socialist Co-operative Commonwealth Federation, or CCF, and his son recalled prominent CCF leaders like Herb Herridge and Dorothy Steeves visiting the family home. Although he remained a staunch CCF member, in the 1930s Harris also started his own political group: the Useful People's Party. The manifesto of the UPP decried parasitical capitalism as absurd, while blaming no one for wanting to be a capitalist. But his tax policies had few supporters. "The Useful People's Party," Harris admitted wryly at one point, "is probably the smallest political party mankind has produced hitherto. In fact one pair of boots is suffi-cient for the present organization." In 1937 he published "The Cook's Strike," a humorous allegory to illustrate his political philosophy. On the back of the pamphlet he declaimed: "The USEFUL PEOPLE'S PARTY will consist of those who sincerely desire to lead USEFUL, HONEST lives in CANADA...We must sacrifice our absurd worship of LIBERTY and place JUSTICE and well-proportioned effort in place of our wild scramble for WEALTH, POWER, and PLEASURE."

Although Harris's exhortations would largely fall on deaf ears, he worked ceaselessly – and evidently with pleasure – to promote his social-ist agenda. The other main source of his happiness during the Depression was the fact that family members long separated by careers and marriage gathered together again on the Bosun Ranch to live and work on the farm. There was plenty to eat, and a safe and secure environ-ment far from the harshness and poverty of city life. The Harrises had been relatively well off to start with, and their investments were in land and food production, not in paper. But all along the wealth spectrum, the Slocan offered sanctuary during the hard times of the 1930s. At Crescent Valley, the Kosiancic brothers concentrated on their dairy business and by

It was hard for women, but not always: Marion Olstad (at left) and Ida Enquist, holding trophies they had won at the Slocan Fair in the early 1920s.

1937 had even purchased two new milk-delivery trucks. There was plenty of work for teachers, and many women became the breadwinners for their families. Young Yvette Bourgeois moved up to Winlaw from Crescent Valley in 1929 to teach at the Winlaw school, and Marion Olstad, the daughter of Norwegian immigrants from North Dakota, taught at Ootischenia and Perry Siding, as well as other schools scattered up and down the valley and in the Arrow Lakes district. When she married Hans Smedbol from Slocan City, she didn't think a married woman should be teaching. But they needed her wage to survive, so the young Mrs. Smedbol continued to trudge on foot for kilometres every day, through the snow and

Olstad family, 1935. From left to right: Marion, Clarence, Birgir, Ralph, and Frieda (Ralph's wife). The family is standing in front of the Slocan home still occupied by octogenarian Marion Smedbol.

Slocan City Presbyterian Sunday school class. Left to right – *back row*: teacher Mr. Elder, Muriel Hicks, unknown Japanese visitor, Slocan Mayor Peter McGill Swan, teacher Mrs. Parkinson; *second row down*: Shirley Buchan, Fern Cooper, Elsie Russell, Beth Hicks; *third row down*: Alan Ewing, Billy MacDonald, Bill Ewing, Innes Cooper, Roy Ewing; *front row*: Bud Rae, Marlene Hicks, Vivian Russell, Carmen Caniff, Barbara Hicks, Leslie Sherwood. Thought to be taken in the late 1930s, although the Japanese presence suggests early 1940s is more likely.

freezing rain of the Slocan winters to her students. Before she left the house each morning, she would stoke up the fires as high as she could; but the pipes would always be frozen again by the time she got home, often after dark. Smedbol remembers having to chip ice off the water buckets in the schoolhouse, too. But work was work, and the students needed a teacher. Like other young women in the valley who were struggling to hold their homes and families together, she did what she had to do.

Itinerant labourer Sydney Hutcheson describes in his book *Depression Stories* how he gave up as useless the struggle of trying to find work on the railways in 1931: "To get away from the running and the semi-starving on the main lines...I and my partner moved into the Slocan...at least there you ate, as there was not much competition in the scramble for food." Over the space of several weeks Hutcheson and his partner walked all the way from South Slocan to Nakusp Hot Springs, about thirty kilometres directly to the north of Hills. They caught trout from the Slocan River to eat on the way, and found work wherever they wanted it:

Slocan City musicians, date unknown, but likely circa late 1920s or early 1930s.

tearing down derelict houses in Slocan City, helping out on Harry Casemore's "Chicken Ranch" near Silverton, and finishing the road between Rosebery and Summit Lake, halfway to Nakusp. They ended up looking after the cabins at the hot springs, a popular health spa in the 1930s. One woman who came to the spa was so huge, Hutcheson claimed in one of his stories, that neither he nor his partner could muscle her through the door into the steam room until they had stripped her down, slathered her in bacon grease, and squeezed her inside.

But such entertaining memories were interspersed with sadness. Hutcheson also spent much of his spare time doing the rounds to check up on the "crippled old bachelors" – miners too old to work and too poor to move away, living in tiny huts scattered throughout the hills. Between the end of World War One and the beginning of the Depression, mining had become all but redundant in the Slocan Camp. Metal prices had fallen once more in the aftermath of the war. The worldwide Spanish influenza epidemic a year later had a dramatic effect on working populations and the economic well-being of small communities. In the Slocan, as various mines petered out and the market incentives to continue steady rail service declined, the CPR gradually reduced both its passenger and freight services into the valley. Forest fires and avalanche damage were combining to win the battle over the rail infrastructure in any event, and from time to time whole mine operations would be razed to the ground. The glow in the sky from the burning of the Standard Silver-Lead Mining Co. in Silverton in 1926 was so bright, writes John Norris in his history *Old Silverton*, that it was visible from Sandon. Further down the valley, in August 1937, the Winlaw sawmill was completely destroyed in a conflagration that wiped out all the loading platforms and the entire deck of cut lumber, and Nelson Winlaw abandoned the valley for good. Just the previous year, the nearby Winlaw school had also been burnt to the ground; whether by accident or design remained unclear.

Sandon was already essentially a ghost town by the mid-1930s, despite the best efforts of the eccentric Johnny Harris and one or two others to keep it alive. Labour problems had dealt further blows to its fortunes in 1919. With prices falling and their jobs once again threatened, both the Sandon and the Silverton Miners' Unions joined the "One Big Union" and struck for their demands: an increase of a dollar a day in wages, a closed union shop, and blankets in the camps for the men. Headquartered in Calgary, the goal of the OBU was to unite Canadian workers and, in doing so, to reduce the influence of the less radical American union federations in Canada. But in the Slocan region the OBU was up against a powerful cabal that had been successful further south, at Trail. Backed by mine owners and the Consolidated Mining and Smelting Co. in Trail, the Trail Smelter's union-breaking general manager, Selwyn Blaylock, had split the employees by promoting a competing union that was working in support of management interests – the Union of Mine, Mill, and Smelter Workers – thus successfully pushing the OBU out of the Trail Smelter in reasonably short order.

OBU leader T.B. "Tommy" Roberts was no more successful in Sandon or Silverton than he had been further south. The Union of Mine, Mill, and Smelter Workers inserted itself as smoothly into the negotiations as it had in Trail, bringing in alternative labour and accepting the terms of the mine owners with no resistance. At the same time, the mine owners successfully painted the striking miners as rebels and anarchists in the public mind. Faced with starvation – and no option to move to other mining camps, since the economic downturn was universal – the

Difficult as it was, everyone was always out to make a buck from mining if they could. Here near Silverton, Seamen Dewis, Bob Dewie, and Frank Mills are considering a salesman's miracle "ore finder" – date unknown, but likely early 1930s.

miners eventually not only caved in on their demands but accepted a wage reduction and went back to work, at least for as long as the work would last. Although other industries in the Slocan would fare consider- ably better during the Depression years, mining would not. Claims continued to peter out, mine owners continued to abandon their opera- tions for lack of the financial resources to continue, and the days of the Slocan Mining Camp appeared to be coming to their long-drawn-out end.

Along with the miners, the communities they had supported suffered as well. One by one, businesses started to withdraw from Sandon. The general stores, strung out on credit that had been given to prospectors and miners over the years, closed with their debts unpaid. The hotels emptied of their guests, and all but two also closed. Johnny Harris's Reco Hotel remained in operation, and his chief competitor, the equally eccentric Virginia Celente, kept his Sandon House open and the dining tables covered in clean white linen and fine china, even though it was quite empty. Celente and Harris had formed some sort of grudge against each other, Eugene Petersen noted in his memoir, *Window in the Rock*. Celente had the best gramophone record collection in Sandon, Petersen claimed, and it was not uncommon to hear the voice of Caruso booming up the mountain walls as Celente cranked up the volume to annoy his rival across the street. Harris and his indomitable attitude would prevail, however. He advertised for and found a wife, marrying Alma Harris in 1926, when he was already silver-haired and she was barely twenty years old; and although his Reco Hotel continued to offer rooms and food to the discerning public, Celente, on the other hand, "was forced to leave with a broken heart, the clothes he wore, and a little bag in hand" in 1935.

A small gold boom in the east Kootenays emptied Sandon further, as miners moved to the gold claims. By 1937, the last general store closed its doors. A brief surge in the price of silver stimulated some short-lived optimism, and there continued to be some attempts – as there had been sporadically over the years – to revitalize neglected claims. J.C. Harris in New Denver remarked in his correspondence with some pleasure that "a plucky little woman from Ontario came into the [Slocan] camp. Selected an old mine and actually started to work vigorously. Under her management the Viola Mac is turning out the finest sort of galena ore whilst the mining men look on with astonishment and admiration at that small determined personage." The temporary optimism was countered, however, by the pall cast when a devastating snow slide in 1937 took the life of six-year-old Evelyn Stewart, walking a few steps in front of her father George. By the end of that year, barely fifty residents remained in the town.

Minnie Stewart Thompson at the grave of little Evelyn Stewart, killed in a devastating snowslide in 1937. The Sandon cemetery is now barely discernible, and almost all of the headstones and markers have disappeared.

The same snowslide in Sandon that killed six-year-old Evelyn Stewart buried houses and demolished buildings in its wake: 1937.

Standard Mill mining crew, Silverton (undated).

As for Slocan City, the Depression did not have as big an impact as it might have had, commented historian N.L. Barlee in *West Kootenay: Ghost Town Country*. The city had, by then, been in a depressed state for nearly thirty years. By 1931, only two hundred people were left in the little town that only forty years earlier had witnessed Eli Carpenter's tightrope-walking antics and a cheering crowd of thousands. Those who remained

Slocan City hockey team, 1930s. Hockey was a perennially popular sport in the valley from as early as the 1890s, and several of the Slocan's native sons have gone on to win international fame in the sport.

looked for every way to keep making money. Phyllis Cooper's father, Walter Clough, bought a breeding pair of mink from Harry Avis at Perry Siding and tried his hand at fur farming, with some success.

But such diversity was not for everyone. By the 1930s John Owen Clay, the English minister's son who had come to the Slocan with high hopes and dreams of golden fruit orchards under his stewardship, was ready to turn his back on it all and move his family to Victoria. Clay had certainly tried hard enough, and at first it seemed that he and the other apple and cherry growers of the valley would prosper. Although, before the war, fruit growers had struggled with the challenges of start-up – the vacuum of years before the small trees would start producing, the expense of shipping fruit, and the impact of the variable weather on young growth – in the six years immediately following the war, production in the west Kootenays reached an all-time high. The largest apple crop in the history of the district was produced in 1922. So optimistic about his future was Clay at that time that in 1921 he sent his housekeeping sister Winnifred home and married a beautiful young Englishwoman whom he had met while vacationing on Pender Island. Selina Margaret Martin's father was also an English minister, and the family were friends of the Clays. The meeting had been carefully and successfully orchestrated by the two families.

Selina Martin Clay, 1918.

Dressed in her English silks and fine hat, the young bride arrived at Slocan City railway station, looking a little bemused by her new surroundings. She gamely traded her silks for rough cotton and was whisked up Lemon Creek to camp on the tarns high above on the mountainside – a not uncommon honeymoon for Slocan newlyweds. Before long, Selina's hands were as worn as her husband's, as she worked by his side in the orchard and clearing their land at Valhalla Ranch. They raised cattle and pigs, vegetables and children, as well as their beloved apples. They made friends with everyone, says their daughter Katherine Clay Hutton, because it was necessary

Selina Clay had arrived in the valley from a background as a well-brought-up minister's daughter in England. The adjustment to life in the Slocan wasn't easy: her first chore was to change from the silks she wore on arrival in July 1921 to the rough working clothes required for everyday life.

Lemon Creek was a popular spot for honeymooning – for hardy types. John Clay took his new bride Selina up Lemon Creek in July 1921.

For Englishmen like Clay, the remoteness of his environment and distance from Mother England did not mean that the niceties of Sunday tea could not be observed. Although the legend on the image states it is November 1921, the sunshine, shirtsleeves, and greenery suggest that it is earlier in the year.

to do so in order to survive. Selina, in particular, was nothing if not adaptable. Her little girl was always warned not to say anything if a well-known drinker they would at times be invited to visit acted "silly" – and her mother, the well brought up minister's daughter, would simply pour the fellow's awful homemade wine quietly through the floorboards of his cabin when he wasn't looking.

It was a hard way of life; harsh winters and the expense of shipping fruit out of the valley in those pre-refrigeration days affected the Clays as they did everyone attempting to operate orchards in the Slocan. The decline of the mining communities reduced the nearest available markets to an uneconomic level for the Clays, as it had for the Doukhobors. At the same time, an increasing number of provincial regulations governed the irrigation, spraying, packaging and marking of fruit, all increasing the costs of operation. A number of fruit growers had simply never tried again after their enforced absence during the war. As more and more gave up their business in the face of the hardships, fruit-packing plants started closing, creating more difficulties for those growers who were still operating.

John and Selina Clay in their fruit orchard, Valhalla Ranch, 1920s.

Horses were used in almost every aspect of working life in the early part of the 20th century: here, planting potatoes on the Valhalla Ranch.

Apples grown in the Slocan Valley had to be carefully packed for shipping in the pre-refrigeration days of the 1920s: John and Selina Clay in their packing shed, Valhalla Ranch.

Fruit also had to be graded in accordance with provincial regulations: the Clay Orchard, Valhalla Ranch.

The early years of apple growing were difficult ones in the Slocan. The young trees were up against inclement weather as well as a variety of pests and diseases: spraying, May 1921, Valhalla Ranch.

Extra hands were sometimes taken on at peak harvesting times in the apple orchards: W.S. Beames and family, fruit-picking camp, Valhalla Ranch.

There are no entries in the minutes of the Slocan Lake Agricultural Association between 1931 and 1940. The last entry is dated May 6, 1942: a simple terse statement to indicate that the association would not be continuing. By then, the population of New Denver, where the association had been based, had shrunk to a mere 350 souls. Fearful for his children's future, by the end of the 1930s John Owen Clay decided to move to Victoria in the hope that he would have greater success in growing fruit trees on a small plot on Beach Drive, east of the city. The Valhalla Ranch was sold to Eugene and Mary Hird, and the Clay's bee-keeping business was also sold, for twenty-five dollars, payable in instalments in tubs of honey. It was a mutually satisfactory arrangement for those difficult times.

Things were no better for Doukhobor farmers or the CCUB. By 1933, the same year Duff Patullo won a Liberal majority and took the Premier's seat, the CCUB's membership had dropped by a quarter in ten years. By 1938, it was less than half what it had been in 1923. The economic crisis had also had an impact. Many Doukhobor men, mistakenly believing they would find jobs with the railway companies, left the communities to search for work that they would not find; but they would not return for years, if ever. The strawberry-jam factory at Brilliant was one of the few enterprises that continued to thrive, and in doing so it supported a number of small strawberry farms in the Slocan Valley. But it was immensely hard work for the growers, and for miserably poor returns. Donald Sutherland of Winlaw recalled that his parents hired Doukhobor women to pick berries. Picking two hundred pounds a day would earn a good worker a cent a pound; the return to the grower was perhaps twice that, before shipping costs. Mabel Lawrenow Kabatoff's mother, Vera, told her daughter that she would pack five-pound pails of strawberries to carry up to the road for the fruit truck to collect. Both grower and picker, she was paid two cents a pound – provided the berries had not been damaged.

Notwithstanding Peter Chistiakov's efforts to curb the actions of the Sons of Freedom, burnings and nude protests had continued sporadically, to the dismay of most. In 1931, the federal government increased the penalty for public nudity by Doukhobors from six months to three years in prison, and in short order it incarcerated more than six hundred

The Kosiancics, like many farmers in the valley, would often hire seasonal help like these Doukhobor women to pick crops. This photo, and the ones below, are from the 1930s.

Ray Kosiancic's father Val, handloading corn.

Corn-cutting crew on the Kosiancic farm near Crescent Valley.

Sons of Freedom in an ersatz prison on Piers Island, a small rocky islet off the northern tip of the Saanich Peninsula on Vancouver Island. There they were left to their own resources, where they more or less spent the entire three years of their incarceration convincing each other they were right in what they had been doing. They eventually drifted back to Krestova, which was becoming somewhat of a heartland for the Sons of Freedom. Krestova was isolated from the main roads, poorly irrigated, and difficult to farm, and the more moderate Doukhobors did not appear to have raised any objection to the community land at Krestova being controlled by the Sons of Freedom. The children of those members sent to Piers Island had in the meantime been sent to institutional or foster care. Emotionally scarred by the separation from their parents, many of these children would also eventually rejoin the Sons of Freedom in Krestova.

Peter Chistiakov Verigin was not faring well. He was having great difficulty in reducing the debt that had been accumulating in the first few years of his leadership, the CCUB was starting to default on some of its loans, and he was also struggling personally on a number of fronts. In 1932, Verigin was convicted of perjury and sentenced to imprisonment. A year later, an attempt by the federal government to deport him failed when it was discovered by the media and civil-liberties groups, who took court action to prevent the deportation. But the stress was increasingly hard on Verigin, and he remained in constant trouble with the law for the next few years. In 1934 the federal government, as the province had done before it, withdrew the right to vote from Doukhobors. Perhaps it did this partly in retaliation for the frustrated deportation attempt, but it placed increasing pressure on community members to leave the CCUB.

And in 1938, the blow was struck that would spell the end of the Doukhobor community land-holdings and the gradual dispersal of the remaining CCUB members. The combined effect of the financial damage from repeated arsons, reducing membership, and non-payment of dues, together with the poor economic returns of the Depression years, saw the CCUB finally declare bankruptcy in 1937. Its two major creditors, National Trust and the Sun Life Co., together held mortgages for under half a million dollars – less than 10 percent of the assets of the CCUB – but the community had no cash flow to pay the debt, and the companies foreclosed. Assets were quickly and cheaply sold, and the land was about to go up on the block next. The government not only did nothing to help – it could have prevented foreclosure, but it refused to do so on a technicality – it wielded the hammer that drove the last nail in the CCUB's financial coffin. Rather than selling the land for its true worth, which would have been between six and ten million dollars, the government simply paid off the creditors and claimed the land for itself – leasing it back to any Doukhobor farmer willing to pay the nominal rent and withstand the indignity.

Peter Chistiakov's health was beyond recovery by that point, but he summoned enough strength to call a convention in November 1938, with the objective of holding the Doukhobor community together through the crisis, even if only as a religious organization. The Union of Spiritual Communities in Christ – the USCC – became the new representative voice of the Doukhobors, with Verigin at its head. It would be a short-lived reign, for on February 11, 1939, Peter Chistiakov's tumultuous life came to an end in Saskatoon after a long illness. He was laid to rest beside his father in Brilliant. As had occurred after his father's death, thousands came to say farewell to the mercurial and passionate character that had led them for twelve difficult years. The Verigin dynasty would continue, but its descendants would live in far different times and under a vastly different political sky. Their challenges as a cultural collective, however, were still not over.

Despite the Great Depression and the impacts it was having outside the Slocan, in the valley the residents enjoyed a number of modern developments that had started to take place as early as the beginning of the 1920s. Completion of a road between the City of Slocan and Silverton in June 1928 spelled the beginning of the end of the passenger steamboat service on Slocan Lake. Slocan residents were spared the trouble of learning to drive on the left-hand side of the road; the province had switched to right-hand driving six years earlier. But in many places on the highway, it would have made little difference. The road was little more than a narrow strip of rock and gravel. In some places – like the tunnel that had been blasted through sheer rock, immediately north of Slocan City – it was incapable of accommodating more than one vehicle upon it at a time. But at least the tunnel was short, and at lakeshore level.

The sheer bluffs above Cape Horn have always posed a thrilling challenge to motorists and their passengers. Shortly after the road opened in the late 1920s, members of the Clay family pose against the backdrop of the Valhallas.

A more daunting prospect was the one-lane, barrier-free curve around Cape Horn – its name derived, one resident theorizes, from the number of people honking their horns at the blind corner in the desperate hope that nothing was coming the other way. For, if so, the only option was for one party to back gingerly down the mountain. In winter, the ice and ploughed snow lent the exercise an even greater frisson. By the early 1930s, the road extended as far as north as Nakusp, and it had already been completed all the way south to Nelson via South Slocan since World War One.

Construction work on the Slocan to Silverton Road, circa 1928.

John Learmonth started a small bus company in the early 1920s that would go onto become Greyhound Coaches Ltd. The Learmonth bus depot was a major landmark at 221 Baker Street, Nelson, in 1934.

Not far from Nelson in 1921 an enterprising twenty-one-year-old named John Learmonth started his own bus service between Nelson and Willow Point on the west shore of Kootenay Lake, using a converted Oldsmobile one-ton truck called "Miss Balfour." By 1926, Learmonth's Motor Bus Line was servicing the Nelson–Slocan City route in "Patricia" (Chas. E. Clark, driver) daily. In 1929, under new ownership, the little bus company was re-incorporated – as Canadian Greyhound Coaches Ltd., B.C.

Construction of the Silverton road in the late 1920s eased travel in the north end of the valley considerably.

The original valley road in the early 20th century was a meandering set of wagon tracks that wound their way from door to door. John Clay stands on the section that passes by the Valhalla Ranch, 1900s.

By the beginning of the 1930s, the Slocan–Nelson route was also being serviced by a Slocan City businessman named Malcolm Cameron. Cameron drove his seven-seater stagecoach bus back and forth daily, carrying passengers and freight squeezed one on top of the other. His bus was rarely empty. Even without passengers, he could usually be guaranteed several daily shopping orders up and down his route, which initially did not follow the modern path of Highway 6 but meandered in the hoofprints of the former horse trail along the west bank of Slocan River. That trail roamed from settlement to settlement and frequently from front door to front door, a logical pattern for the days in which every passing pack train or supply wagon might stop at each cabin or farmhouse along the way. Despite the meandering route of the new road, it meant greater freedom for residents of the valley than they had previously experienced.

Towards the end of the 1930s, a faster and better route was built – this time on the east side of the river – from Winlaw as far as Vallican. Now it was feasible to make a day trip to Nelson to shop and to socialize, and people who had never left the valley for years now began to make regular expeditions to the bigger town. It was a change in pattern that spelt trouble for the smaller communities and the businesses in the valley that had sustained themselves from the passing traffic on the old

E.H. Chase General Store, Winlaw, 1920s.

Alf and Josephine (Winters) Newton were the proprietors of Winlaw's first gas pump in the early 1930s.

Above right: Alf Newton in front of the garage and warehouse at Winlaw, early 1940s.

Ab Willford, Alf Newton, Thelma (Winters) Willford, E. Chase, and J. Newton: May 1943, Winlaw.

road and from local custom. It was no longer necessary to make do with the limited and expensive selection of items in the local general store, and many of those stores started to disappear from the side of the road.

As they were driven back and forth from Nelson, bus passengers could also admire the West Kootenay Power and Light Co.'s latest electrical plant at Bonnington Falls, completed in 1925. Construction on the South Slocan plant began in the fall of 1926 and was completed by 1929. What the passengers could no longer admire were the waterfalls that had been lost forever after the construction of the original Lower and Upper Bonnington plants in 1898 and 1907, respectively. "One of the most magnificent bits of scenery in this country," wrote Robert Anderson to his uncle in Florida in 1903, comparing Bonnington favourably with

Niagara Falls, "is where the Slocan joins the Kootenay twenty-six miles from here. At the junction of the rivers is an immense fall known as Bonnington Falls...There is nothing to be seen but a whirling mass of foam dashing over a precipice and the white foam hurling itself high above the falls, the whole Slocan in fact tearing down into the Kootenay...The noise is simply terrific...It nearly took my breath away."

As the 1930s drew to a close, it seemed that many things were being lost to the valley. At the same time as long-held anti-Asian sentiments were consolidating in British Columbia, and politicians were becoming occupied with hostilities building once again in Europe as well as in Asia, the Slocan grew quieter every day. On December 7, 1941, by the time that American warships started to burn and sink in Pearl Harbor, the future of the Slocan Valley as anything but a forgotten backwater of eccentric prospectors and miners, misunderstood Doukhobors, and a handful of die-hard loggers, trappers, and farmers, seemed highly unlikely.

One of the original log cabins in Passmore, still standing in 1996.

Ralph, Marion, and Birgir Olstad fishing at Little Slocan Lake, early 1930s.

Silvertonians Sandy Harris, Turk Avison, and Art Jeffries, with baby Nancy Harris trying out their brew: late 1930s.

12

SHIKATA-GA-NAI:
the internment of Japanese Canadians

The outbreak of war has always been good economic news
for industry and the poor. This was no less true in the
Slocan than anywhere else in British Columbia after
England declared war on Germany in 1939 and the United
States of America entered World War Two in December 1941.
The army offered reasonable wages and benefits to people
who were previously unemployed. The demand for lead and
zinc rose once again and prompted the revival of the few
mines that still had workable ore veins. The smelter at Trail,

On the back of this photograph of a young woman in the New Denver internment camp is written: "Remember me always. Most sincerely, Mary Mishimura, 1943."

working on the production of deuterium oxide, or "heavy water," to assist with developing nuclear technology, lost many of its male employees to the Canadian army. Its doors, however, then opened to female workers in large numbers. For the first time, women were working not just as secretaries or food providers, but on the line with their male peers.

For the first time in many years, people in the valley actually had some disposable income instead of living at a subsistence level. Slocan resident Phyllis Cooper recalled that in 1942 her young children Glenn, Innes, and Fern were able to sell enough furs from their trapping efforts to buy her an end table as a Christmas gift. "Everyone had nice gifts that year," she writes in *My Dad*, her memoir about her father, Walter Clough. "Before that we were lucky if we were able to get them one nice toy or a pair of mitts for Christmas."

The Slocan Valley – along with Kaslo, Salmo, and two or three smaller communities further east along the old Dewdney Trail route – would also enjoy a unique economic boost as a result of the war, one that was not experienced anywhere else in Canada. In 1943, the population of the valley was increased by the sudden arrival of nearly eight thousand people, all of whom would stay for two years and some of whom would never leave. They were the *Issei, Nisei, and Sansei* – first-generation Japanese immigrants to the west coast of Canada and second- and third-generation Canadian citizens of Japanese descent. The latter were also known as *Nikkei Kanadajin*, or Canadian citizens of Japanese ethnicity. Unlike those who had come to the Slocan Valley before them, these people had not come seeking a place of refuge, or a place to find food, or a place to make their fortune. They had not come of their own free will, but because they had no other choice. *Shikata-ga-nai*, they said to each other as they rode on the train and in trucks up the valley. *Shikata-ga-nai*. It cannot be helped.

What follows is a litany of infamy that led to nearly twenty-two thousand people – more than three-quarters of them Canadian citizens – being forced by the government from their homes, farms, and livelihoods, on or near the west coast. They were herded into livestock pens at the agricultural exhibition grounds in Vancouver's Hastings Park, and then loaded onto trains and sent to the interior of the province, to be held in internment camps, or further east, some to work for white farmers for the duration of the war and others to be interned until after the war.

In January 1941, the federal Cabinet War Committee allowed public opinion to govern its decision to prohibit Japanese Canadians from enlisting in the armed services. In March of the same year, all Japanese Canadians over the age of sixteen were required to register with the Royal Canadian Mounted Police and carry photo and thumbprint identification at all times. After the bombing of Pearl Harbor, the federal government upped the ante. Using the 1914 War Measures Act – which among other things authorized the governor in council to "do and authorize such acts and things, and make from time to time such orders and regulations, as he may by reason of the existence of real or apprehended war, invasion or insurrection deem necessary or advisable for the security, defence, peace, order and welfare of Canada" – the government immediately confiscated more than 1,200 privately owned fishing boats, closed Japanese language schools and newspapers, and cancelled insurance policies held by Japanese Canadians. The government also required every person of Japanese origin – whether or not they were Canadian citizens, and regardless of whether they or their parents or grandparents had been born in Canada – to register as enemy aliens.

In January 1942, the government established a "protected area" – a one-hundred-mile zone covering the entire coast of British Columbia – and in February, the minister of justice was authorized to "evacuate" enemy aliens from the protected area. Within two days and with almost no notice, Japanese Canadians were ordered to leave their homes and make their own way to Hastings Park. They packed in boxes and placed in their basements their treasured possessions – china plates, heirloom silks, and family photographs. What little they could take with them was carefully crammed into suitcases and duffel bags. They locked their homes, and some gave the keys to their neighbours or to old friends who assured them that their possessions would be looked after until their return. Their cars and cameras and radios were taken by the police. A curfew was imposed on the few who were allowed to remain in Vancouver on "legitimate" business. Other Asian people in Vancouver took to putting up signs on their businesses to ensure that people knew they were not "Japanese."

In March, a gentleman holding the office of custodian of alien property took possession of all property owned by the people detained in

In 1942, the Custodian of Alien Property seized Japanese Canadians' commercial fishing boats by the thousands. These ones were being held at the Annieville Dyke on the Fraser River, prior to being sold for a fraction of their true worth.

Hastings Park. The government wanted to ensure that their property was kept safe, the detainees were assured. Some of them, the lucky ones, had hidden their life savings in rolls of old bills, tucked in their clothing.

These enemy aliens, including infants to eighty-year-olds, lived in ad hoc dormitory arrangements in Hastings Park and slept less than a metre away from their nearest neighbours behind curtains made of clothing and torn sheets. Coming from isolated farms and fishing villages all along the B.C. coast, they were mostly strangers to each other. The discomfort of such close proximity among a culture that was naturally reserved was intense. Contagion also spread rapidly whenever someone fell ill. That summer, hundreds of people became sick: it was revealed that directly under the floorboards of the buildings was the rotting manure of the cattle and horses that had been the previous tenants. Families could not always see their sick relatives, as the men and women had been separated from each other.

Protests started to occur, and a newly constituted body called the British Columbia Security Commission decided it would be best to relocate the Japanese Canadians to more suitable quarters. Since the prairie beet farmers said they needed help in the fields, several thousand doctors, fishermen, loggers, store clerks, musicians, teachers, farmers, and their families were sent east to Alberta and Manitoba to spend twelve hours a day weeding, hoeing, and picking beets in exchange for room and board. Younger men were sent under supervision to build roads and cut trees in the interior of the province. The first their wives and mothers often knew of the abduction of their husbands and sons was upon receipt of their first heavily censored letter from the labour camp. These men were at least paid for their efforts: just less than the lowest wage payable to Canadian soldiers. The "optics," the bureaucrats noted, wouldn't have been good otherwise. Some of the men refused to go to the B.C. labour camps. They went to prison in Vancouver instead, or were sent out east, to the prisoner-of-war camps in northern Ontario.

A few brave souls went independently to the handful of B.C. communities in the interior that had indicated they were prepared to receive them, like Lillooet or Kelowna. They kept a low profile there, all the same: local acceptance was slow to come. And the remaining twelve thousand-odd people were sent by the Security Commission to the internment camps of the west Kootenays. The Slocan Valley was an excellent choice, the commission felt: it was far from the coast, it was hard to get out of, and at its north end – a safe distance from the Trail smelter, which was also in a protected area – there were several small towns that had seen better days, with plenty of empty buildings that could be used as accommodation. The authorities could send lots of people there: nearly 3,000 to Slocan City; 2,000 to Lemon Creek; 1,700 to New Denver; and just over 900 to Sandon. The only problem was how to pay for it.

In January 1943, the government solved that problem. It sold all the Japanese Canadians' houses and farms and fishing boats, which it had confiscated a year earlier. As far as the houses went, that is, it sold what was left of them after they had been thoroughly ransacked and looted by thieves. The proceeds of sale were not enormous – about a third of the actual value of the property sold. The government didn't want to charge too much money for the property of enemy aliens, and the proper market price seemed a little steep in wartime. The sum was sufficient, however, to cover the costs of their room and board for as long as the war was likely to last, the commission reassured their charges in the internment camps; so they need not worry.

How did it get to that point? How could a country that now prides itself on the ethnic "mosaic" of its population justify the treatment of thousands of its own citizens and legal immigrants in this manner?

At the time, the government was responding to intense public pressure to restrain the activities of Japanese Canadians. Like the Chinese immigrants before them, Japanese immigrants to the west coast had quickly established themselves in some niche areas. They had owned the majority of the issued licences in the commercial fishing industry, until the government restricted the number they could hold; and immediately before the war, Japanese Canadians were producing 85 percent of the fruit from berry farms in the Fraser Valley. Threatened by that rapid economic success, many British Columbians of European and American descent held deep-seated fears about the Asian population and its ability to overtake the province economically, if not politically.

Meanwhile, the Japanese Canadian community – as is natural for most ethnic-minority populations, in the early days of settlement in a new country – tended to cluster together, both in "Japantown" in Vancouver and in small communities along the coast. "We are doing our best but we cannot change our colour in a day," explained Japanese Consul Ukita to the Vancouver *Daily World* in February 1920. As a result of public pressure, a number of anti-Japanese measures were already well in hand before the outbreak of war: limits on immigration and employment, segregation of youth in schools, the withholding of the right to vote in provincial or federal elections. Pearl Harbor simply gave the government the excuse it had been waiting for, to take direct action to disperse the Japanese Canadian population from the coast of British Columbia to the rest of Canada – and even, some hoped, all the way back to Japan.

There was a ready argument by the anti-Japanese faction that fishermen could easily "spy" for the Japanese government from their fishing boats and homes on the coast. Certainly British Columbia's coast was the most exposed of any part of Canada to threat from Japan. Some Japanese Canadians were reported to be boasting about what they would do when Japan won the war; whether or not those reports were true, there was also plenty of inflammatory material available to stir up fear among British Columbians about the way the Japanese had been behaving in China

Some of the "enemy aliens" who were so greatly feared – the Masuda family, at the Popoffs' Farm, in 1944. From left to right, *back row*: Toshi and Miyo; *front row*: Joe, Betty, Nancy, Mrs. Masuda, Mr. Masuda, Chris.

since 1937. The storm of anti-Japanese sentiment grew stronger, to the point that the federal government was forced to take action. Even the Department of National Defence added fuel to the flames, warning the government as early as 1938 of the Japanese threat across the Pacific Ocean.

Interestingly, the one strong "establishment" ally that Japanese Canadians had during this period was the RCMP. The police diligently investigated a number of reports of Japanese espionage and illegal immigration, even allegations of hidden weapons arsenals on Vancouver Island. With very few exceptions – and even those individuals were merely suspected of being a threat rather than being the subjects of actual evidence of wrongdoing – the RCMP found nothing to substantiate the allegations. They made a point of reporting the results of their findings publicly: that the Japanese of British Columbia constituted no threat at all to Canada.

Many arguments and reasons can be mustered to explain the government's actions during World War Two, and there remain a number of analysts, both professional and armchair, who still consider that those actions were justified according to the times. But for the men and women

The Obara family was forced to leave their home and logging business in the Comox Valley to go to the Slocan camps.

who were forced from their homes in 1942 – most of them forever – the reasons and arguments were merely empty words in the limbo in which they soon found themselves living. They arrived in the Slocan Valley in the thousands, in the winter of 1942–43. It was the worst winter in years, and snow was piled deep on the mountains and exposed areas of the valley. The nine hundred-odd who found themselves in Sandon thought themselves a little luckier at first than the others – there were buildings ready to move into, instead of the tents in which many people in New Denver and Slocan City were initially being housed. But Sandon's attractions soon palled, as the long winter wore on and showed no signs of abating. When the spring finally came, it revealed only poor, stony soil, difficult to cultivate and incapable of producing enough crops to live on.

On the other hand, the remaining fifty residents of Sandon were delighted with their new neighbours. Johnny Harris, still living in his dreams of Sandon regaining its former glory, suddenly had customers for his hotel again, and staff that he could hire to serve them. Thanks to the efforts of the new arrivals his aging power plant was repaired, and all the residents of Sandon were able to enjoy electric light and heat. Carpenters set to work to refurbish buildings, and scrap metal was collected for the war effort; a hospital and school was set up; even a Buddhist temple appeared in the abandoned Methodist Church. But the winters were really too difficult to endure. The B.C. Security Commission finally relented, to the dismay of the permanent residents of Sandon, and allowed the detainees to move into the New Denver camp instead.

The Japanese Canadians arriving in New Denver, Lemon Creek, and Slocan had a different experience. Although some empty buildings were available in all three communities, there were nowhere near enough to house seven thousand people. In order to build new housing in the area, the Security Commission had made arrangements to lease several farms, including the part of J.C. Harris's Bosun Ranch now known as the

It was traditional for Japanese Canadian internees to send signed photographs to friends, and Casey Obara had many such images given to him in the internment camps.

"Orchard" in New Denver. But construction had barely been begun when the first families started arriving in the valley. In any event, the housing that was being put up was of highly debatable merit. The standard-design structures were a mere four metres wide by eight metres long, containing two rooms at either end and a central space for cooking and washing. They were built of clapboard, with little or no insulation; and because of the haste with which they were constructed, they were also made with green wood that promptly shrank and left large gaps in the walls for the winter wind to whistle through. Into each of these dwellings were shown not just one, but two families – who in most cases had never before met and were now forced to share every intimate detail of each other's personal lives.

At least, most of the married men were now allowed to rejoin their families. But there were still some women who did not know where the men of the household had been taken, or if they were even alive. Elderly or ailing parents and grandparents were removed without their consent to care facilities in New Denver, and sometimes further away, making visiting difficult. Tuberculosis enjoyed a field day in the poorly insulated cabins, and a sanatorium facility in New Denver quickly became overcrowded. Some authorities chose to view these developments in a

The New Denver Japanese Canadian internment camp was built on part of the Bosun Ranch, owned by J.C. Harris. It became known as The Orchard, which it remains to this day.

positive light: "The evacuation of these people with…a minimum of hardship is a matter for congratulation," a royal commission report boasted in 1943.

Those who arrived too late the first year to receive a house spent the remainder of the winter in the tents, which was not as bad it might sound. Nobuyoshi Hayashi of New Denver remembers: "The tents were warmer than the houses. My family was in a tent that first winter. You could pile snow up around the edges to stop the wind coming in, and it was drier than in the houses." But Nobuyoshi – "Nobby" to his friends – was a child at the time, and for the children, things were different. "For my mother and father it wasn't so good, living in the tents and then in the cabins," reflects Sono Mukai Tully, now living in Manitoba. "But I enjoyed New Denver. I was young, it was so lively compared to the farm at Maple Ridge where I never saw anyone. In camp, there was ice skating, swimming, friends, girls from the city to talk to."

Proximity to a beautiful sandy beach at New Denver was not wasted: the Toyota sisters flank the Yano sisters in the middle.

Making music in the camps, date unknown.

It is a common sentiment among the people who were children in the camps. "We had great times," say Toshi Masuda Obara and Kazuyoshi "Casey" Obara, who were living on the Popoff Farm near Slocan. There were dances for them to go to, concerts to attend and perform in. It was good for the children, Tad Mori told Toronto's *Star Weekly* magazine in 1971. "We lost something, but our kids gained." All of the people interviewed by the magazine said the same thing: it was better in the long run for Japanese Canadians to leave their cultural ghetto in Vancouver and their isolated coastal communities, and take advantage of the opportunities presented to them after the war. It is a prosaic attitude; a strategy of acceptance of the situation and a decision to make the best of it rather than fight against it that is reflected in the majority of interviews that author Barry Broadfoot conducted for his 1977 book *Years of Sorrow, Years of Shame*.

Only a small number of Japanese Canadians continued to express bitterness about the experience: by far, most of those Broadfoot interviewed preferred to make the best of it, arguing that it was beneficial for Japanese Canadians to disperse themselves into the mainstream of Canadian society. *Shikata-ga-nai* – it can't be helped. Casey Obara, who ended up living in the Slocan Valley after the war, remarks: "The war was a funny thing, what it did to people. I know it was a bad thing but it worked out all right for us." His wife Toshi agrees. "It was a good thing it happened in the end. We got opportunities we wouldn't have had, staying on Vancouver Island." Neither of them can deny that it was very hard for their parents, however; and for some, like six-year-old David Suzuki, the

Schoolgirl Sono Mukai at the New Denver Japanese Canadian high school.

experience would leave lasting painful memories. Sono Tully believes she spent the rest of her parents' lives – as other *Nikkei Kanadajin* children she knew did theirs – trying to make them feel better about what had happened by working as hard as she could and constantly over-achieving.

The saving grace in this story is that for the people of the Slocan Valley in whose midst the Japanese Canadians arrived, they were on the whole a welcome arrival. Silverton was an exception initially, forbidding the internees entry into the town on the grounds that the Mammoth Mine concentrator might be at some risk. But even Silvertonians did not hold out consistently, after recognizing the prospective commerce that the new residents brought to the area, and the Silverton Miners' Union was only too pleased to invite the excellent Japanese Canadian baseball team that had been put together to come and play. J.C. Harris wrote on March 28, 1944, that "amongst the New Denverites there was considerable difference of opinion and much hot discussion; but even those who felt disposed to oppose their coming into the town on personal grounds, began to see that the poor Japs [sic] had to go somewhere, and that they had better surrender their own prejudices and make a virtue of necessity."

Various members of the communities in which the Japanese Canadians were to be housed rallied to help. J.C. Harris himself moved out of his home and into a smaller cabin so that the large house could accommodate the older men who needed better care. During that first hard winter, before the internees had had a chance to grow their own fresh vegetables, the Doukhobor farmers brought truckloads of produce and sold them cheaply. The Doukhobors, say the former residents of the camps fervently, are a very fine people. It was not necessarily easy to help the people in the camps, however. "Many community members broke the law to help the Japanese because the circumstances were so appalling," says Barbara Coghlan. "The government tried to stop it. They reprimanded my grandfather [Wilbert Hicks]. It was very mean-spirited."

The establishment of the internment camps spelled prosperity for the northern end of the Slocan Valley in a number of ways – the B.C. Security Commission employed Slocan men to supervise the work crews, and the money the Japanese Canadians brought with them and earned on relief was spent in local stores. The large and wrinkled old dollar bills that were

The Slocan High school class of 1944–1945. The school board paid for some local children to attend the Japanese Canadian classes instead of having to pay for a separate teacher: Muriel Hicks is in the front row, fourth from the left, and Bill Hicks is at centre.

being brought out to buy food and supplies – the life savings that the old people had hidden away in their clothes as they left their homes – were much bigger in size than the current currency and had not been seen in common circulation in years.

But the benefits went beyond money. The arrival of the Japanese Canadians also brought about relationships that would last a lifetime. Phyllis Cooper's family made firm friends with Dr. Hiroshi Kamitakahara, who relieved her mother-in-law's debilitating arthritis and sent his own assistant to live with them and look after the older woman. The friendship arose not so much from the care he gave the family, however, as from the mutual love of fishing and poker shared by Cooper's husband and Dr. Kamitakahara. Another doctor is fondly remembered for the work he did in the Slocan Community Hospital. His bitterness at the way he and his compatriots were treated meant that Dr. Uchida would refuse to ever work again with occidental people after he left New Denver in 1946. But in his time in the Slocan he not only worked with the Chief of Medical Services, Dr. Arnold Francis, and the half-dozen nurses who serviced the hospital; Dr. Uchida also toiled in the New Denver T.B. sanatorium treating both internees and locals, and never turned away a patient in need, regardless from whence they came.

The internees were allowed a relative freedom of movement, provided they did not go south of Appledale or north of New Denver, and provided they had the necessary permits. There were only a handful of RCMP officers watching them, for that was all that was necessary in the peaceful, law-abiding camps. There are many good stories about their way of life – the baseball teams that were so good that some of their members would go on to play professionally after the war;

Dr. Uchida and Nurse Gladys Reynolds outside the New Denver clinic, 1943.

Japanese Canadian high school class of 1943–44, New Denver. All left to right – *back row*: Tatsuo Sakamoto, Alfred Iwaski, Mitsuo Oikawa, Bobby Obara, Kazuo Osaka, Asamu Baba, Minoru Nagata, Akio Shudo, Jimmy Ito; *second row down*: Asae Mayeda, Kinuko Ikegami, Yumiko Morimoto, Lumie Ryoji, Sono Mukai, Riuko Kawamura, George Ito, Tom Onodera; *third row down*: Shizue Togawa, Hanako Ban, Mitsuko Kondo, Kazuko Kodama, Miyeko Wakayama, Taeko Ito, Minnie Kitagawa, Masaye Omatsu; *front row*: Kats Nakahara, Toru Sawada, Takeo Nakashima, Tom Emamoto.

Skating party. Sono Tully recalled that life was more fun for the young people in the camps than it had been back on their isolated farms on the coast of British Columbia.

the well-behaved students in the schools set up and taught by conscientious objectors like Stan Rowe, under the guidance of United Church women's missionary Gwen Suttie; the Japanese Canadian doctor who drove to the hospital in Nelson with an RCMP officer supervising him and, momentarily forgetting who his companion was when he came to a clear stretch of road, asked: "Any cops around?" – and started speeding, both of them ending up laughing "like hell."

In many ways, despite the hardships endured there, the time in the Slocan internment camps seems to have been the better part of the whole experience for many people. For as the war drew to a close, things did not immediately get any better for most Japanese Canadians. For many of them, things would get much worse before they got better. Prime Minister Mackenzie King gave Canadian citizens a taste of what was to come in his address to the House of Commons concerning the "Japanese problem," on August 4, 1944:

> "Now may I speak of persons of Japanese origin in Canada...the Japanese problem...is one to be faced by the whole of Canada as a Canadian problem...The government recognizes the concern felt by British Columbia at the possibility of once again having within its borders the entire Japanese population of Canada...In view of the concern, it is felt that it must be accepted as a basic factor that it would be unwise and undesirable, not only from the point of view of the people of British Columbia, but also from that of persons of Japanese origin themselves, to allow the Japanese population to be concentrated in that province after the war...The sound policy and the best policy for the Japanese Canadians themselves is to distribute their numbers as widely as possible throughout the country where they will not create feelings of racial hostility."

It is notable in the last sentence of King's address that he considered Japanese Canadians – rather than their neighbours – to be guilty of having the potential to create racial hostilities in the communities in which they resided. He also admitted in the speech that it had not been shown at any stage of the war that "the presence of a few thousand persons of Japanese race who have been guilty of no act of sabotage and who have manifested no disloyalty even during periods of utmost trial, constitutes a menace to a nation of almost twelve million people." Finally: "It is a fact that no person of Japanese race born in Canada has been charged with any act of sabotage or disloyalty during the war." Nevertheless, King set out three clear policy initiatives to be implemented after the war: first, the establishment of a commission to establish a list of those people who in fact had been disloyal, with the intention of deporting those people to Japan, regardless of their citizenship; second, the dispersal of Japanese Canadians throughout central and eastern Canada, rather than in British Columbia; and third, a temporary ban on further Japanese immigration into Canada.

The deportation and dispersal policies eventually manifested themselves as a notional choice for Japanese Canadians, set out in a notice dated March 12, 1945, and issued by the commissioner of Japanese placement in Vancouver: re-establish themselves and accept employment east of the Rockies as "the best evidence of their intentions to co-operate with the Government policy of dispersal" or choose repatriation to Japan. Many did go east of the Rockies: Sono Mukai and her family moved to the Tullys' beet farm near Winnipeg, where she would meet and marry her husband, Terry Tully. But confused and uncertain of any viable future in Canada, over ten thousand people signed repatriation applications, regardless of the fact that most of them had never been to Japan and many did not speak Japanese.

Two-thirds of those who signed would later realize that they were better off staying in Canada than going to what amounted to an alien country in the throes of recovery from its devastating losses in the war, and they would rescind their signatures in time. But more than 3,500 Japanese Canadians were deported to Japan before the combined weight of protests from civil-rights groups, churches, and the media would force the government to stop the deportations, and allow some who had been repatriated to return. Three-quarters of those who left never returned to Canada.

Some of the people in the internment camps would eventually return to the coast. They took with them the small amount of compensation they received from the government in 1947 – a sum amounting to a fraction of their actual losses – hoping to buy back their boats and their homes and find their precious belongings still hidden in boxes in their old basements. But the boxes were long gone, the boats and houses and farms in the hands of people who had no desire to return them to their former owners, or if they were prepared to sell, would only do so at prices that were not affordable.

In the Slocan Valley, the government's policy to disperse the residents of the internment camps east of the Rockies failed to some degree. The local residents had no wish to see the prosperity they had been enjoying during the war years vanish overnight, and they did nothing to discourage people they now regarded as friends and neighbours from staying. Gwen Suttie kept her school in New Denver open, at least until June 1946, when the government asked her outright to close it down because her efforts were impeding the progress of dispersal. Her institution, it seemed, was too good – the pass rate at the time it closed was 97 percent – and the parents of its students were reluctant to leave such an excellent educational opportunity behind for the unknown schools of the east.

And the reality for many of the former internees was that they simply could not afford to leave. Nobby Hayashi's father was dead. To support his mother and siblings he gave up a prospective but uncertain career in the American baseball major leagues to play semi-pro ball in British Columbia, achieving some notoriety and, more importantly, covering the bills back home in New Denver. "Where are you supposed to go after you've worked four years at twenty-five cents an hour?" Shoichi Matsushita asked the *Star Weekly* reporter. "To stay was the smart decision to make," Tad Mori told him. "The air's clean, the climate's good, the water's nice. There's nothing like a small town, you know."

A significant number of Japanese Canadian internees decided to stay in the Slocan. The Obaras moved to this farm near Vallican a couple of years after the war was over.

Very basic housing was hurriedly constructed on leased farm properties to house the majority of the Japanese Canadian internees. The Popoffs, whose leased farm was between Slocan and Lemon Creek, claimed against the government for the cost of the damage incurred to the property over the war years. They recovered only a portion of their claim.

Overall, more than one hundred Japanese Canadians would stay or return to the Slocan, either forced to by circumstance, like the Hayashis, or because, like Casey and Toshi Obara, they found it a good place to live and bring up their children. The tiny clapboard houses on the Popoff and Bay Farms and at Lemon Creek would eventually deteriorate or be torn down for other uses. Emilie and Konstantine Popoff brought their own compensation claim against the B.C. Security Commission for the damage they claimed had been done to the land from the occupation, with limited success. But in New Denver, many of the houses would remain standing, still occupied by some of the families that had been living in them, the gardens and fruit trees around them continuing to flourish as the sad decade of the 1940s drew to a close.

In 1948, the federal government finally removed the clause in the Dominion Elections Act that prevented Japanese Canadians from voting in federal elections, and in the following year British Columbia also relented and permitted not only Japanese Canadians but also Mennonites and aboriginal people to vote in provincial elections. In 1957, the government deeded ownership of the tiny cabins and the lots they were on to the remaining occupants, but it was another thirty years before any real recognition of the wrong done to Japanese Canadians was granted by the government of Canada.

Redress, in the form of an apology and financial compensation, was given by the government in 1988. For the people of the Slocan Valley, however, particularly New Denver, the lasting benefits of the terrible decisions that were made in 1942 would be stamped on the face of the community forever: in the tiny wooden houses in the Orchard, the blossoming gardens wrought by Japanese hands and hearts, and the absorption into Slocan society of a rich new cultural element. It is a source of pride now for valley residents – perhaps tempered with a sense of irony – that David Suzuki lived in their midst as a boy, regardless of the reason. Even more importantly, the friendships, working relationships, and marriages that ensued after the war would become a cherished part of life in the region.

As the 1950s dawned, however, the Japanese Canadian people of the Slocan Valley hoped just to be able to settle down into their new lives, and vanish – this time, they hoped, forever – from the forefront of controversy in Canada.

The Pavilion in New Denver was built for recovering Japanese Canadian TB patients in 1945. It later became a home for the aged.

13

THE TIMES THEY ARE
A'CHANGIN':
after the war

"I can't recall a better place to do nothing," said John
Owen Clay's new son-in-law Ted Harris of his visit to
Slocan City on his honeymoon in 1956. "The old-timers
were parked on the bench outside the store with their feet
up on the railing, watching the rest of their lives pass
them by, smoking pipes."

Slocan had continued to enjoy its up-and-down existence of progress and poverty as the war years came and
went. In some ways, once the internment camps for

New Denver, circa 1945.

Japanese Canadians were demolished, life had changed little from the 1930s. Some of the former internees stayed to work in the logging camps or open businesses, but most left, and at least initially life reverted to the pace of the slower pre-war days. Wayne Morrison won the prize for naming the New Denver "Lucerne" High School and received "five dollars and a handshake from the minister of education!" In his graduating class of 1954, there were twelve students, four of whom were *Nikkei Kanadajin*. Some mining continued in the New Denver and Silverton area – the Ottawa Mine in particular was relatively stable – but forestry had become much more of a mainstay for local employment. A great deal of logging was still done by hand, using horses to haul the fallen trees to the rail sidings.

Previous page: Perry Creek store, Appledale, J. Stooshnoff Prop. (date unknown).

202

Pleasures were still to be found in simple things, and children found their fun in the usual ways. Bill Hicks, born in 1933 in Slocan City, remembered as a boy of about twelve taking home his father Wilbert's 1,600-pound Percheron horse, also called Bill, from the logging camps. He would drive Bill along the main street of Slocan and past the same old-timers sitting on the same bench outside the store. The huge and flatulent animal would plod slowly all the way until he reached the store and then break into a gallop, "letting a giant one rip right in front of the old-timers," sniggered the seventy-year-old Hicks at the memory. "It was comical. Old Bill just kept on doing it, every time." Hicks' future brother-in-law, Laurence "Red" Sutherland – who claimed he met his wife Muriel when the pretty blonde threw a stone at him as he was passing by her on Main Street, ignoring her – was born further down the valley near Winlaw in 1930, the youngest of twelve children squeezed into a small log cabin. "They hadn't planned on having me," he confided with a mischievous twinkle in his eye, "so there wasn't any room left in the family Bible to write down my name. For a while I was known as 'Who's that?' because there was no space at the table for me at meals either, and I had to sit on the floor. My sisters and brothers would look down at me and ask my parents, 'Who's that?'"

The Sutherland family farm on the Slocan River Road, in Appledale, 1930s. The landmarks of the property are still visible from the road.

Laurence "Red" Sutherland taking a break from work on the *SS Rosebery* on Slocan Lake during the 1940s. "I must have done four hundred jobs in my lifetime, just to get by," said Sutherland.

Sutherland is as lively a story-teller about the old days as his brother-in-law is, and as liable to ham it up for the sake of a good joke. He claimed, for instance, to have hated school so much that he would hide from teacher Yvette Swanson every day in the cliffs across the river from the Winlaw school, running down at lunchtime to join in the games, then returning to his hiding-place afterward. He lasted at the Appledale school – where he was sent after his parents and Swanson agreed it was in everyone's best interests for young Sutherland to try other pastures – for one whole day. When he was late on the second day, he arrived to find his books and possessions on the steps outside. "And that," said the retired Greyhound Bus Co. manager triumphantly, "was my last day ever at school!" Recreational story-telling is a time-honoured tradition in the valley, and a trait that in Hicks's case at least was inherited from his father Wilbert. The older Hicks would casually stretch his bare feet up on the kitchen table in the hope that someone would eventually succumb to asking him what had happened to his missing big toe, and then "off he would go," sighed his granddaughter Barbara Sutherland Coghlan fondly. "He was such a wonderful man."

The comical stories of the Hicks and Sutherland boys could not, however, belie the hardships for their parents of trying to support such large families as the resource-based industries of the valley, mining and timber, struggled in the late 1940s and early 1950s. Nor can they hide the fact that the young men often joined in the dangerous work of their fathers at a very early age – even though, like Bill Hicks, they clearly enjoyed their temporary escapes from the schoolhouse. When he first started driving the huge horses at the age of about ten, Hicks was not

Wilbert "Buck" Hicks and daughter Beth, Slocan City, 1930s.

Right: A baseball game at Perry's school, 1942. Marion Smedbol was the schoolteacher, walking or riding all the way from Slocan and back every day to look after her own growing family.

even strong enough to unhook the chains that attached the animals to the logs and he would ask his brothers or his father to help him. And when he first started using one of the large two-man cross-cut saws with his father operating the other end, he remembered: "My Dad used to damn near pull me through the cut!" It was not at all easy for the women in the family, either. "It was terrible for the women!" exclaimed Dorothy Hird, from the village of Slocan. "I'd hate to go back and do it again."

For women in most parts of the valley, providing for a home full of growing children without the benefit of running water or electricity or nearby medical facilities had always been achingly difficult. Children would get sick, or hurt themselves, and there were no telephones and few vehicles to get them quickly to any help. A trip to Nelson was an infrequent pleasure. "The Sears catalogue was pretty popular up here in the valley," remarked Sutherland. The lucky few who were still finding work in the post-war period to supplement the household income still had to come home to clean house without the help of modern appliances and feed everyone on dried goods and whatever could be grown or hunted.

Above: Bill Hicks was born and brought up in Slocan City, worked there all his life, and retired there. This photo was taken in the 1950s.

Left: Burns Lumber Co.'s Camp #5, 1945.

Colleen McCrory's mother brought up her nine children in Silverton "on a diet of macaroni and deer meat." Venison was a staple for most: "I raised a whole family on deer meat," reminisced Hird. Bill Hicks, still an avid hunter at seventy, swore he had never eaten beef. And in the earlier days of settlement, it must sometimes have been heartbreakingly lonely for the few women in the valley – married, single, or as Robert Anderson had described them in 1903, "of degraded character who are always to be found in the mining camps." Anderson was explaining to his uncle in Florida why he was not yet married, not being "a great ladies' man, which is probably accounted for by the great scarcity of ladies out there. There are only three or four [single] young women in Slocan to my knowledge." Those few young women no doubt enjoyed their popularity for a short time at least, but their prospects for an easier life than their married counterparts were slim.

The days of any serious fruit-growing activity were largely over by the mid-1950s, and nothing had surfaced as an alternative. The commercial farms that remained – like the one further south at Crescent Valley that Jacob Kosiancic's grandson Ray and his wife Ida took over in 1955 – were largely focusing on beef and dairy products. There was a temporary burst

Chores were not necessarily as enjoyable as this image of Selina Clay on the Valhalla Ranch makes them look. For many women, life was brutally difficult in the early years of the 20th century.

of excitement in 1946, when Emilie Popoff was acclaimed as mayor of the City of Slocan, only the second woman in British Columbia to achieve that status; and again in 1948, when the Ottawa Mine began allowing residents of Slocan City to use its excess electrical power. The system was greeted with delight by the locals – especially the beleaguered women – but it was only ever intended to supply enough power for lighting. As people surreptitiously started plugging in toasters, irons, and electric kettles, wrote Louise Anderson in *Slocan City Legacy*, "the light bulbs became orange blobs producing less than three candle watts of light." The drain got worse as people added new refrigerators and vacuum cleaners into the mix, and "Monday mornings became especially grim when ladies started their washing machines, and the drain became so noticeable that the machines refused to operate." The power plant's maintenance man was a Slocan local, Tracy Cooper, and he would simply increase the output to accommodate the higher usage; but when the larger appliances started getting turned off as the day wore on, the unwary who still had theirs switched on would watch in horror as bulbs suddenly blew or wires fizzed and burnt out with the excess power surging down the line.

The Greyhound bus still passed through town every day on its way to Nakusp from Nelson, and again on the return trip. By the late 1950s young Red Sutherland was driving it, wisecracking happily with his passengers. Despite Slocan City's dwindling population, Gerry and Elsie

Hans Smedbol's boy scouts troop, Slocan, 1955.

Altman took a risk and bought the Greenlight Café and the gas pumps next to it, and eventually even started up a motel. In 1951, Wilbert Hicks and his brother Ted bought the Slocan sawmill and renamed it Hicks Bros. It was a reasonably successful operation employing dozens of men, including most of the Hicks boys, but by 1958 Wilbert and Ted decided to sell out. Wilbert, said his granddaughter Barbara

Bill Hicks driving one of the Hicks Bros. family logging trucks. His father, Wilbert Hicks, and Uncle Ted owned the sawmill at Slocan from 1950 to 1958.

Bill Hicks's nieces Barbara and Carolann Sutherland, 1955.

Coghlan, had decided "he would rather fish and hunt than work the mill...He was fifty-two at the time. A great age for retirement. All the Hicks boys had to scramble and find new jobs." They were not the only ones scrambling. Slocan City itself had barely stayed solvent over the previous forty years, hanging on by a thread, and in 1958, the smallest city in Canada finally applied for village status and became simply "Slocan" again.

By the 1950s, Slocan City was finally forced to relinquish its status and revert to becoming once more the Village of Slocan.

Diversity has been key to economic survival in the valley throughout its history. As mining became increasingly tenuous, in the second half of the 1940s, miner Frank Mills took to logging.

Sandon was doing no better. It had long before ceased to be incorporated, back in 1920. Truckers and loggers on the Kaslo–Slocan road would stop regularly at Three Forks to enjoy the hospitality of a resident diehard bootlegger still living there, but there was no reason for them to take the turnoff to Sandon. Intermittent mining activity continued throughout the 1950s, fuelled in part by the outbreak of the Korean War in 1950. Close to one thousand people surged again into Sandon, in a faint echo of its former glory – but they were of a different character altogether than their predecessors and had no intentions of staying. As quickly as the war ended in 1953, they vanished. And on December 6 of that year, Sandon's most romantic citizen of all finally passed away at the age of eighty-eight. Johnny Morgan Harris, with his grand dreams of building the Paris of the West, was laid to rest in his native Virginia by his widow Alma, who stayed for another ten years before she finally left Sandon for good. Harris's treasured Reco Hotel outlasted him by only a year. By then, only one train a week was operating into the little mining ghost town, and in 1955, with the town's population at an all-time low of about thirty people, rail service to Sandon ceased altogether.

The winter of 1954–55 had seen the usual deep snowfalls. The following June, heavy rain on the thawing snow pack finally brought down more water than the fifty-year-old wooden flume could handle. It had already been extensively repaired twice and was still serving as the "main street" of Sandon, but its essential design flaw could not be overcome.

Sandon, 1968.

Too narrow for the combined water and debris roaring down Carpenter and Sandon Creeks, and with too many right-angled turns to accommodate all the logs and rocks constantly washing down it, the flume was finally and irreparably torn to pieces and its planks scattered far and wide by the force of the water. The same heavy rains washed out the rail line in no less than twenty-eight places. The CPR needed no further excuse to shut down its service altogether, and shipped out its remaining boxcars on flatbed trucks. Sandon's post office stayed open as late as August 1962, by which time the federal authorities could no longer be convinced of its necessity to an almost non-existent citizenry. Artefact hunters began to strip the environs of Sandon bare of its old mining equipment – already being thought of as relics – and many of the town's buildings were sold for their timber and fittings and demolished. Only Eugene Petersen and one or two others – themselves now "old-timers" – clung stubbornly on, refusing to give up the precious way of life they had carved out for themselves in their isolated valley in the shadow of the Slocan Ranges.

As the 1950s progressed, however, things started to get much livelier further south along the Slocan River. Between 1942 and 1944, the West Kootenay Power and Light Co. had constructed another power plant on the Kootenay River, this time at Brilliant, and in 1957 the company – now also owned by the CPR's Consolidated Mining and Smelting Co. – had finally run operating lines up as far north as Slocan. Everyone along the road in the southern part of the valley was revelling in the luxury of having proper electricity for the first time. No longer would the ladies of

Jacob and Antonia Kosiancic, circa 1950.

The Brilliant hydro dam, near the confluence of the Kootenay and Columbia Rivers (date unknown).

Slocan have to rely on the Ottawa Mine to run their washing machines – and for the women south of Slocan, who had lived without power until then, it was a revelation. "I got rid of the gas irons straight away!" exclaimed Ida Kosiancic – who thirty years later would regret the impulse as she started collecting them again for her antiques store in Crescent Valley. At the time, however, it was simply an emphatic gesture to celebrate escaping the tyranny they represented. "It changed everything," reminisced Toshi Obara. "I got myself a washing machine and a fridge. I only wish I'd had them earlier." Those living further away from the road at places like Vallican would have to wait for their power and for running water in their homes. All the same, said Red Sutherland, who was living at Vallican with his wife, Muriel, the little community felt just the same as Winlaw to live in back in the early 1950s. Like Winlaw, where Arvid and Yvette Swanson had moved down from their log cabin at the top of Paradise Valley to start a garage and auto-repair shop in 1947, Vallican had its own garage, operated by Earl Fink, and a post office and general store to serve its needs. "It's different now, of course, because of the new people that moved in later," said Sutherland. "That's all gone. It's all hippies now."

In 1956 the word "hippie" was still a few years from being in common usage. The word "highway," however, was on everyone's tongue in the

Appledale school, class of (probably) 1953–54. Little Mabel Lawrenow, who became the Winlaw postmistress, is standing at left. Mrs. Murphy was the schoolteacher.

Mr. Chatfield and Mr. McGregor outside the Appledale general store, August 1955.

The Kosiancic turnip field once produced more than one hundred tonnes of vegetables a year. It now lies under Highway 6, near Crescent Valley.

Slocan Valley. In that year, work was begun by the province to pave the pot-holed, bumpy trail of rock and gravel that had served the valley as the main road to date; and by 1958, the paving would stretch the entire length of the valley, from South Slocan to the north end of the lake. No longer would constant clouds of dust hang endlessly over the trail, and the terror of Cape Horn was somewhat eased. But in gaining the relief of modern-day travel on a paved highway, something was also lost. The road engineers straightened out curves to more sensible gradients, blasted through rock to provide a more direct route, and flattened out the straightaways over turnip fields and gardens. The road did not even link directly to South Slocan, but joined the highway between Castlegar and Nelson a little further south, at Playmor Junction. And as the locals sped more frequently back and forth to Nelson to go shopping over the improved highway, the Sears catalogue – once the most popular reading in the valley, next to the Bible – became less useful; and even more of the small owner-operated stores along the old road fell into decline and eventually went right out of business.

Members of the Sutherland family enjoy the new lookout over Slocan Lake shortly after Highway 6 was paved in 1957.

As the fortunes of the small stores deteriorated, however, another form of business was on the rise in the Slocan. In 1956, according to Jan McMurray of the *Valley Voice* newspaper, Nick Osachoff and his wife, Mabel, started the valley's first credit union with ten members and $184.50, in the Osachoff's humble abode above Winlaw bridge. In 1957, the proudly named Slocan Valley Credit Union (which would eventually merge with the Castlegar Credit Union in the 1970s) was joined by the Slocan Valley Co-operative. The Co-op was started in Slocan Park by a group of Doukhobor farmers, originally with the intention of using their bulk purchasing power to obtain cheaper groceries and farm supplies without having to go all the way to Nelson. The initial membership was restricted to members of the Union of Spiritual Communities in Christ, or USCC – the successor group to the CCUB established by Peter Verigin in 1938 – and meat, alcohol, tobacco, ammunition, and fishing tackle were not for sale. Paul Markoff was operating a feed business at the other end of Slocan Park and did not feel par-

The *SS Rosebery*, tied up at Slocan wharf, 1940s. The tug was used for passenger service and towing logbooms as well as hauling freight. But as road improvements were made in the valley, the lake freight service became less useful and eventually vanished altogether by the 1980s.

The Nelson–Slocan Greyhound bus braves Cape Horn, circa 1948. The driver (and photographer) was Norman Warner.

ticularly threatened by the competition down the road; but within a few years he too was out of business, unable to compete with the large and thriving Co-op. The Slocan Valley Credit Union moved its "offices" into the Co-op, and in 1969 the membership was opened to anyone over the age of eighteen. The restriction on meat sales, however, would continue until the mid-1980s.

As the 1950s progressed into the 1960s in the valley, life changed for everyone on a number of fronts. There were major technological break-throughs in forestry practices: logging trucks were substituted for horses, and power saws replaced "misery sticks" – the old hand-operated cross-cut saws – but things were merely different, not necessarily easier, for individual logging contractors. Contractors were expected to supply their own gas barrel and oil, wedges, hammers, axes, and safety equipment. "If you didn't have it," retired faller Joe Wrangler told Peter Chapman in a 1993 interview, "then you just didn't work." They also had to have their own chainsaws. Wrangler, who worked for Passmore Lumber Co. from 1953 to 1958, told Chapman that the popular model of chainsaw in 1951 was a Vancouver Power Machine Co. saw. A "P.M." saw cost $407 at

Perry Siding, date unknown.

216

Sinnerud Truck and Tractor in Nelson. But when Hlookoff and Sons brought in the American McCulloughs only a few weeks later, everyone abandoned their P.M. saws immediately for the more expensive but also more powerful model. The McCulloughs must have been good; contractors who might only earn six hundred dollars in a month at the best of times suddenly laid out a great deal of money on them in a short space of time. And in 1960, the Passmore mill was sold to American Axel Erickson. Erickson showed up one morning, according to Ray Kosiancic, "as workers were punching the clock, not introducing himself and asking workers like Nick Osachoff, 'What the hell can you do?' Nick stated, 'What the hell do you want me to do?' They hit it off O.K."

The use of floatplanes and helicopters to observe the breakout of forest fires would also eventually replace the traditional use of Forest Service lookout towers. No longer would solitary observers spend months in their isolated wooden towers in the mountains, taming chipmunks and grouse for company and suffering from altitude sickness, bear depredations – and occasional lightning strikes. The problem, as forest

All of the Kosiancic boys have enjoyed collecting vehicles over the years. Improvements to the highway in the 1950s were a good excuse to add to an impressive collection, kept on the family farm near Crescent Valley.

ranger Bob Robinson discovered after the Lemon Lookout tower burned to a crisp – fortunately, during its occupant's absence – was that the "lightning arrestors" that the Forest Service had installed on the towers were in fact remarkably efficient lightning attractors. Once they were removed to one side of the tower rather than on the tower itself, no further problems were encountered. And as the lookout towers became redundant, the fires that would start after lightning strikes were no longer being fought on foot with axes and grub hoes, but with water-bombing aircraft and with bulldozers.

The days of reforestation as a priority after a fire or logging were still in the future. There were no attempts to replant then, retired Nelson District Forester Harry Forse told author Robert Turner in 1994, partly because the extent of logging in the west Kootenays was limited and partly because the logged areas seemed to reseed themselves fairly quickly on their own. The system of cutting was also different. "In 1954, you couldn't cut anything under a fourteen-inch base," said retired Winlaw forester Peter Kabatoff. "It wasn't economically feasible. So twenty-five years later forestry companies here could get beautiful second cut timber. It wouldn't be there if we had clearcut back then." That was about to change as well, however. Clearcutting – the practice of removing the entire forest canopy on a site – came into use in the valley in response to the introduction of new technology and the building of a pulp mill at Castlegar in the late 1950s. It was greeted with mixed feelings by loggers and Forest Service employees alike – welcoming the additional work opportunities, but dismayed at the sight of hillsides laid bare.

Like other industries, however, the forestry companies were responding to a massive increase in consumer demand following the war. Improvements in technology carried with them a corresponding need for bulk electricity supply. The small amounts that individual power companies like West Kootenay Power and Light could generate for both the industries they were created to support and the individuals purchasing their surplus power were proving – in the minds of politicians, at least – insufficient. In 1952, the same year that Doukhobor people in British Columbia were finally permitted to vote in provincial elections, a small man with giant plans became premier of British Columbia. Initiatives instigated under W.A.C. Bennett's leadership over the next twenty years would in their turn have direct as well as subtle effects in the Slocan Valley, and in both cases the changes would be permanent.

Towards the end of the 1950s, not for the first time, American officials approached Bennett's government to discuss the Columbia River. The United States wanted more hydroelectric power for its cities in the northwest states and improved flood control along the flat bench lands of the lower Columbia. Bennett wanted to go down in history. "I wanted to get the Columbia River developed as an international river," he told his biographer David Mitchell in *W.A.C. Bennett and the Rise of British Columbia.* "And to do that we needed an agreement." In 1961, with approval from Victoria but huge dismay from his constituents in the Kootenays, he got the agreement he had been seeking. The preamble to the Columbia River Treaty between Canada and the United States of America, ratified by Dwight Eisenhower and John Diefenbaker in 1961 and signed in its final form by Lester Pearson and Lyndon Johnson in 1964, was most positive in its explanation of the reasons for reaching agreement:

> "Recognizing that their peoples have, for many generations, lived together and co-operated with one another in many aspects of their national enterprises for the greater wealth and happiness of their respective nations, and
> "Recognizing that the Columbia River basin, as part of the territory of both countries, contains water resources that are capable of contributing greatly to the economic growth and strength and to the general welfare of the two nations, and...
> "Recognizing that the greatest benefit to each country can be secured by co-operative measures for hydroelectric power generation and flood control, which will make possible other benefits as well..."

As to whom the greater benefits of the treaty would accrue is debatable, but less so is the impact on people in the Slocan and Arrow Lakes region. In return for building three storage dams on the Columbia River that would be used for flood-control purposes as well as electricity generation, British Columbia would – eventually – receive a share of the downstream power generated by existing and new plants on the American side of the border. But that downstream power share was sold again almost immediately, in order to pay for the construction of the Canadian dams. Only in 2003 would the province start receiving its full share of the power to which it is entitled under the treaty – which may expire, at the election of either country, as early as 2021.

Meanwhile, people like Sheila Griffiths, who had moved into the Slocan Valley after 1968, were forced to find new homes when their houses on the Arrow Lakes filled with the rising waters created by the Hugh Keenleyside Dam. Bert Herridge, now the member of Parliament for the West Kootenay riding, had opposed the Columbia River Treaty vigorously in the House of Commons, but he too was forced to move his home away from the widening lake. The new dam flooded standing homes and living trees, and it flooded the long-forgotten graves of aboriginal people and buried their old village sites. The fish were already long gone. The building of the Grand Coulee Dam south of the border in the 1930s had also seen the last wild Pacific salmon make its journey from the saltchuck up the Columbia River to the Kootenays.

For the aboriginal people of the Slocan, things had not improved markedly in the 20th century. There began, after World War Two, what the Department of Indian Affairs called "The Age of Resurgence." Joint Committees of the Senate and the House of Commons held public hearings between 1946 and 1948 into the standard of living, health, and education of aboriginal people in Canada and made recommendations for change, although not nearly enough. Amendments to the Indian Act in 1951 removed some of its more overtly discriminatory provisions, including bans on activities ranging from traditional potlatch events to drinking in bars to the hiring of lawyers to help with land claims. In 1960, aboriginal people in Canada were permitted to vote in a federal election for the first time, and in 1968 Len Marchand became the first aboriginal Canadian cabinet minister and the second to be elected to Parliament; no doubt he hoped he would fare better than his predecessor, Louis Riel. In 1969, Indian agents were withdrawn from Indian reserves around the country. But many of these gestures were relatively meaning-less to people who not only had no reserves in the west Kootenays, but whose connections with the Slocan and Arrow Lakes area had, through no fault of their own, become increasingly tenuous in the past few decades. Since before the turn of the century, many aboriginal children had been taken from their homes and required to attend church-run residential schools around the province. Those few remaining in the west Kootenays were mostly directed east, to the St. Eugene Mission near Cranbrook. In their enforced absence, there would be no opportunity for reconnecting with the territory of their forefathers.

In the meantime, the membership of the Lakes Indian Band on the Canadian side of the border had continued to dwindle. The government was well aware of the fact, and by 1936 Indian agent James Coleman was already forecasting the demise of the band. Coleman and his colleague in the Okanagan, R.H.S. Sampson, appear to have made some genuine attempts to protect the interests of the last remaining member living on the Oatscott Reserve on the Arrow Lakes, a woman named Annie Joseph. Both of them were painfully aware of what was likely to happen if they did not take action to do so. Coleman first tried unsuccessfully to have her unmarried partner, Okanagan Indian Band member Joe Parker, admitted as a member of the Lakes Band. When that failed, Sampson suggested in 1952 that the Oatscott reserve be preserved by simply amalgamating the Lakes Indian Band with the Okanagan Band. It looked as though the latter initiative might succeed, as it had the support of both Joseph and the Okanagan Band; but Sampson's superiors were not so sure about the merits of the proposal and found reasons to delay making a decision. "It would...appear," the superintendent of reserves and trusts wrote querulously in June 1953, "that the Okanagan Band would be the only ones benefiting from the amalgamation." In October, Annie Joseph died.

On January 5, 1956, order-in-council 1956-3 was passed by the Privy Council in Ottawa. Citing a provincial order-in-council from 1938 that provided, among other things, "that in the event of any Indian tribe or Band in British Columbia at some future time becoming extinct, any lands hereby conveyed for such tribe or Band...shall be conveyed or repaid to the grantor," the federal government transferred the Oatscott Indian reserve back into the ownership of the provincial government.

The last officially recognized foothold of the Lakes people north of the border was gone. "We are satisfied," wrote the Indian commissioner to the British Columbia government a few days later, "that this band has become extinct."

14

SVOBODNIKI:
when freedom turned to tears

"I mean it's just taken away from your parents, Holy Christ, I mean we used to hide. We still remember the hay over where the cops have come with pitchforks, hey, and you'd see them, hey...and you'd run like crazy and six years old, you were running, you are still running, you are running..." That is how one individual remembers the times in the Slocan Valley after September 9, 1953. Over the next six years, more than 170 children, some as young as six years old and many of whom spoke no English at all, would be forcibly wrested from their parents' arms during midnight and dawn raids at Perry Siding and Krestova and confined at a residential school in New Denver. The pretext was to ensure that they received an education in the face of their parents' obstinate refusal to send them to school. The motive was more oblique: it was the provincial government's heavy-handed attempt to break the cultural spirit of the Sons of Freedom once and for all and to integrate the children into mainstream Canadian society. It was, in part, a desperate response to more than fifteen years of frustrated attempts to quell the Sons of Freedom: like every other initiative that had been tried, it would fail in every respect to achieve what the government hoped for. Instead, the events of those six years form a litany of sadness and despair. For some, those events left scars that will never heal.

After the collapse of the CCUB in 1938 and Peter Chistiakov's death in 1939, matters had remained difficult for the Doukhobors in the Slocan region. The newly founded Union of Spiritual Communities in Christ had a large membership of nearly eight thousand people, but without their communal land base to sustain them, the USCC's direction floundered temporarily. Peter Chistiakov's grandson, John J. Verigin, became secretary of the USCC in 1940 in the absence of his father Peter Verigin III, whose whereabouts in Russia were then unknown. The writing was on the wall, and John Verigin was able to read it as well as anyone. The effects of the loss of the communal land showed quickly in the scattering of Doukhobor families into the general work force and onto individual farms, and many Doukhobors started to leave the Slocan Valley. Hinging their survival to continued unity, Verigin vigorously promoted membership in the USCC and advocated active adherence to the principles of their faith. He was instrumental in easing his compatriots into the mainstream of Canadian landholding and becoming comfortable with Canadian society's expectations. Under his tenure, the USCC also started to reach out to other groups in Canada with similar pacifist philosophies, in the hopes of gathering strength through such connections. But during World War Two there had also continued to be a series of backlash protests by some Sons of Freedom in response to the loss of the community lands as well as the unfair confinement of some Doukhobors in work camps, notwithstanding their military exemption.

Although its members were only a small minority of the greater

Doukhobor community, the Sons of Freedom were resoundingly convinced of the injustice being perpetrated against the Doukhobors by government. They were dismayed that their compatriots did not support them in their protest actions. The protests were scattered and continued at times to be violent. On December 13, 1943, the Brilliant jam factory and a nearby store and garage were burned to the ground. The following year saw a steady series of burnings of schools, homes, and other buildings. The CPR railway station at Appledale went up in smoke; John J. Verigin's home was threatened. But even among themselves, the Sons of Freedom suffered from divided loyalties. Just as not all Doukhobors were or are Sons of Freedom, not all the Sons of Freedom necessarily approved of their compatriots' level of protest activity. By 1945, there were two main contenders for leadership of the group, now more or less based in and around the former community lands in Krestova: a man named John Lebedoff, from Saskatchewan, and a moderate named Michael Orekoff, who was Peter Lordly Verigin's third cousin. Renaming himself Michael Verigin, he preached in favour of a return to a communal life and against the protest actions that had been taking place. Verigin could not withstand the fervour of the more extreme faction of Sons of Freedom however, and by 1946 he had left Krestova for Vancouver Island with some of his supporters to establish what would be a short-lived community near Hilliers.

Not long after Michael Verigin left, yet another contender for the leadership appeared on the horizon: a Russian refugee called Stephan Sorokin. Although he was not a Doukhobor, some members of the Sons of Freedom convinced themselves that he was John J. Verigin's long-lost father, Peter. Doing nothing to correct that mistaken belief – Peter Verigin III had in fact died in 1942 in a prison camp in Russia – Sorokin enjoyed a form of ad hoc leadership of the Sons of Freedom and, along with it, a pleasant and well-funded lifestyle that was quite at odds with the beliefs of his followers. Sorokin decamped to Uruguay in 1952, where, according to George Woodcock and Ivan Avakumovik in their book *The Doukhobors*, he continued to lead that pleasant and well-funded lifestyle. Despite his departure, many of his followers continued to believe Sorokin was their true leader.

Buoyed by their passion and beliefs, the burnings and bombing of property by the Sons of Freedom escalated through the late 1940s. According to Gregory Cran in his Ph.D. thesis, "A Narrative Inquiry into the Discourse of Conflict Among the Doukhobors and Between the Doukhobors and Government," the destruction was targeted as often as not at their own homes as at schools and government property. The philosophy behind this strategy was hard to understand for their neighbours in the region, who also resented the disruption and emotional stress associated with living in the midst of unpredictable extremists. Occasionally, the protests would take the form of nude marches or sit-ins as Sons of Freedom shed their clothes to stand before their God, as they had been doing since their earliest days in Canada. John J. Verigin, as leader of the mainstream majority of Doukhobors, was enduring a painful dilemma. As reluctant as he was to cut loose any Doukhobor from the collective group, by 1947 he started to openly condemn the activities of the extremist Sons of Freedom. Like his grandfather and great-grandfather before him, he turned to the government for help. He was not the only one; many residents of the west Kootenays were placing increasing pressure on the authorities to intervene.

No doubt hoping for greater success than it had achieved the previous time, the government appointed Judge Harry Sullivan of Vancouver to head yet another commission of inquiry. But Judge Sullivan wound up the proceedings after only three months, as non-stop arson and explosions continued to reverberate up and down the Slocan Valley and in the Castlegar area. He could not continue, he stated adamantly as he beat a retreat back to Vancouver, "until the crazy people are put in the mental asylum and criminals locked up in the penitentiary." Following this less than helpful conclusion, according to Woodcock and Avakumovik, it was two police officers – Col. F.J. Mead of the RCMP and John Shivras of the provincial police – who suggested a different approach after talking to some of the Sons of Freedom in Krestova. Following their recommendations, a committee headed by Dr. Harry Hawthorn of the University of British Columbia was formed in 1950. The intention was to undertake serious and substantive research into the causes of the problem and to come up with some different and practical solutions for government to implement.

The committee suggested some excellent solutions. Supporting more than forty recommendations for change was the recognition of some fundamental values to all Doukhobors, not just the Sons of Freedom. The committee recommended the repeal of discriminatory anti-voting and criminal laws, such as the Criminal Code section providing for three years' jail for public nudity by Doukhobors – a far harsher penalty than for non-Doukhobors. Both matters were issues that local member of Parliament Bert Herridge had been unsuccessfully advocating were unfair and should be changed since after the end of the war. The committee also suggested acceptance of the Doukhobor form of marriage as legitimate (it required no licence or formal marriage celebration) and the return of the former communally held land to the USCC on behalf of its members. They were all good suggestions; the problem was getting the government to act quickly, if at all, upon any of them. Although the government had started a review of the land question by 1953, not until 1955 was the Criminal Code amended to remove the discriminatory penalties, and only in 1957 was the franchise restored to Doukhobors.

There was, however, no abatement in the level of violence throughout this period. Moreover, many of the Sons of Freedom were withholding their children from attending public schools, in a continuing protest against the heavy hand of government authority and a rejection of the state system of education. The Hawthorn report, while visionary, had also recommended that the government take a hard line on truancy and illegal protest action. That was one recommendation the government followed promptly and without equivocation. By 1953, hundreds of Sons of Freedom men and women had already been jailed and Premier Bennett was asking Ottawa to extend the application of the War Measures Act so that its provisions could be used with respect to Doukhobors. Members of the media sensationalized the protests with editorials as inflammatory as the protests themselves, demanding that Sons of Freedom communities be restrained behind barbed wire and that anyone leaving be shot. Although a considerable amount of property damage had occurred, the only human casualties to that date had been among Sons of Freedom themselves. But this fact was lost on the public – as was in most respects the distinction between the Sons of Freedom individuals undertaking the protest actions and all the other Doukhobors.

On September 9, 1953, the RCMP arrested nearly 150 Sons of Freedom

Doukhobor children at Ootischenia School, 1941–42. Pictin Village, with its traditional dual-family structure, is visible in the background.

men and women who were camped at Perry Siding on charges of public nudity. Their children – 104 in total – were taken on buses to New Denver to a residential school that had been set up in the old Japanese Canadian T.B. sanatorium. Some of the children ran and hid in the woods. "Somehow some of us kids got underneath the side of the tent and ran screaming in total shock across the fields," recalled a man who was eight years old on that terrible day. "I thought my parents were dead." But those children too were eventually found and taken away. Before a magistrate in New Denver a week later, a presentation was made by the provincial Department of Child Welfare to apprehend the children in custody under the Protection of Children Act on the basis that they had been found in the company of people "reputed to be criminal, immoral, or disorderly." At the hearing, the judge noted, "it was impossible to put the information to the children as they were praying, singing, and crying and would take no notice of the court order to keep quiet." It is not clear whether the magistrate was sympathetic or merely irritated. It does not seem to have occurred to him that the children, who spoke little or no English, could not understand anything that was happening around them, let alone instructions to be quiet.

To be fair to the child welfare officials involved in New Denver, apprehending the children was not their idea. In an exchange of correspondence between the officials and Victoria, they repeatedly demanded that the government come clean on their real motives for taking the children from their parents: not merely to ensure school attendance but "a broader belief that the religion and culture was what the child needed to be protected from." The value of education that the children might receive in New Denver was not in question, but "We do question their receptivity under conditions that to them and to their parents can only appear false and odious." The conditions in which the children were to be housed and "protected" were also highly questionable. The old sanatorium building could accommodate sixty people, at best; but more than 120 children and staff had arrived en masse and needed to be housed. Some hasty reorganizing saw nearly half of the children released back to their parents or to relatives, although on what basis is murky. Nonetheless, especially as more children were apprehended from Krestova in 1955 and brought to the facility, it remained vastly overcrowded.

The experiences of the Sons of Freedom children in the New Denver school have been well documented over the years since 1959, when the last child was finally returned to his family. But even as early as 1957, public recognition was being given to the oppressive conditions in which the children were living. "A disastrous failure," is how reporter Bert Whyte of the *Pacific Tribune* newspaper described it on July 19, 1957. "It is not only morally indefensible; it is also responsible in large degree for the complete alienation of Sons of Freedom parents from belief in Canadian justice and democracy. More than that it is embittering the children confined in New Denver and producing a crop of future juvenile delinquents." The term "school" said Whyte, was a farce. He interviewed a number of former staff who had quit, they told him, because they could no longer deal with the harsh way in which the children were being treated. Food was being withheld, children were being unfairly punished, and parents were being denied access. A chain link fence that some of the boys had been required to help build, notionally for a small amount of pay, surrounded the facility.

Visiting hours at the school were infrequent: one hour every second

Sunday, from ten until eleven in the morning. Not only was it severe in the extreme, it was impossible to get to in time for mothers and fathers travelling – in some cases – from as far away as Grand Forks. And on a number of occasions, parents who had travelled eighty kilometres or more for their precious one hour with their child would be told when they arrived: "Not today." The pretext would be that the child was being punished, or would be too unsettled by seeing their parents. The resulting toll on the adults was as high, if not higher, than on their children. Exactly one week after Bert Whyte's first article appeared, his newspaper reported: "A 32-year-old Freedomite widow whose nine-year-old daughter is held in the provincial government's special 'school' at New Denver hung herself from a beam in her home at Krestova on Wednesday of this week. A letter from her daughter Patsy was found near the body. It read: 'Mommy, I am lonesome for you – come and visit me. I love you. Goodbye.' "

Notwithstanding the dubious reasons for taking the children and the irreparable pain of separation from their parents, had the New Denver institution been run in accordance with contemporary standards of child care, some things at least might have turned out differently. The first director was remembered with forbearance by the former school residents as a kindly man who put considerable effort into caring for the children. But he was hampered in his abilities by a lack of funding and an inadequate facility, as well as by his belief that it was for the best that they were in the school. The second director, however, is remembered as a much harder individual who was responsible for things taking a distinct turn for the worse when he succeeded to the position. In her 1999 report on the New Denver school, provincial Ombudsman Dulcie McCallum quoted at length from reports of both of the directors, as well as staff, indicating that conditions were difficult but still acceptable and that the children's well-being of mind and body was sound. But McCallum dismissed all of the reports out of hand. She also set out in her findings in painful detail the shortcomings of the institution itself, often quoting from former school inmates that had been interviewed:

"The thing I hate about New Denver, is that, well, the physical abuse that was done to me by my own kind, which you have no place to go to for comfort...you have to tough it out." The chronic overcrowding meant

Although some still debate whether Doukhobor children were forced to stay behind a chain-link fence at the New Denver institution in which they were placed in 1953, the evidence of the forced separation of children from their parents is overwhelming: visiting day, 1954.

a complete lack of privacy and, children being children under any circumstances, many of the younger and weaker children were exposed to bullying at the hands of their schoolmates that they could not escape, or even complain about.

"There was only one person to so many kids and they could only supervise so much...The matrons never hugged us. They never gave us any comfort." The recognized staff-to-child ratio in similar institutions in 1955 was one to three. In New Denver, the ratio was less than one to eight, and those staff did not have the training they needed to work with the children.

"I was playing basketball...I dropped the ball and he started pounding

Sons of Freedom parents protesting at the provincial legislature against the incarceration of their children in a residential school system, January 1954.

[me] against the gym." One staff member was repeatedly accused by former inmates of having inflicted brutal physical punishments on the boys. One girl alleged sexual abuse.

"Of course, the parents would leave stuff like they'd bring avocadoes and cantaloupes and all kinds of fruits for you and mom would make tarts...it went into the kitchen and you never got to see the stuff." Both food and clothing and other types of gifts, the children said, would be taken from them and never seen again.

"The grounds and building are appearing dirty, unkempt, and run-down." The former sanatorium was in poor repair, and little effort seems to have been made to improve the situation.

"They were Russian books that my parents wanted me not to forget my language...that was destroyed." Not only were the recommendations of welfare officials to have Russian-speaking teachers at the school ignored, but under the leadership of the second director of the school, children were punished for speaking Russian and forbidden to wear decorative pins bearing the word "Moscow."

On July 31, 1959, after six years of raging against the injustice, the parents of the seventy-seven children remaining in the New Denver school swore an oath in court that they would send them to school, and on August 2 the children were freed. The weight of public opinion against the school had increased, and the legal basis on which the children had been held was debatable. It seemed wise to let them go. Once again they were herded onto buses, this time taking them home. The current director of the school was in Krestova to watch the children meet their parents, noted reporter Steve Scott of the Nelson daily newspaper. "He had been so upset by the loss of his 'family,'" observed Scott, "he could not eat. He passed some of the parcels out of the buses and then drove off." But Bert Whyte's predictions in the *Pacific Tribune* were unfortunately all too accurate. Far from serving as some kind of break in the link to their past, the treatment of the children had only served to harden Sons of Freedom attitudes, and many of the children themselves became entrenched in their beliefs, rejecting the New Denver experience utterly.

In the meantime the government was implementing a process to return the former community lands to community members for a token sum, even though the level of Sons of Freedom activity was also being ratcheted up again. The land review process that the government had initiated in 1953 had resulted in a decision to have the land surveyed into town-sized lots and offered back to the USCC. A Doukhobor surveyor named Nicholas Popoff was hired to do the surveying; it was hoped that he would be able to help smooth the way through the survey process with disgruntled community members. Somewhat surprisingly, and despite strong objections from Sons of Freedom representatives, Doukhobor families began buying the land individually in preference to it being held communally again. By 1963 much of the land, with the exception of Krestova, was once again in the hands of Doukhobor farmers. Other positive things were happening under the auspices of the USCC. In 1957, thirteen young Doukhobors attended the World Festival of Youth in Moscow, and in 1958 the USCC helped host a highly successful and widely publicized peace conference at the University of British Columbia.

These positive events were, however, overwhelmed in the public mind as the arsons and bombings by Sons of Freedom escalated, reaching a climax in 1962 with nearly three hundred reported incidents and a

Doukhobor village at Passmore, 1961.

corresponding number of prosecutions. Those convicted were sent to a prison in Agassiz, on the Fraser River, one hundred kilometres east of Vancouver. It was reasoned by the authorities, perhaps, that such a distance would serve to break the links that the prisoners had with their families and supporters hundreds of kilometres away in the Kootenays. But they had underestimated the Sons of Freedom yet again. On September 2, 1962, a feisty woman named Florence Storgeoff began a protest march to the prison from Krestova, followed by several hundred Sons of Freedom. It was an epic journey, part walked, part driven in buses and other vehicles, with many stops along the way. People joined the march for any number of reasons: to demonstrate their continuing anger, or in excitement. "A lot of people went because they were afraid of being left behind," says Larry Ewashen at the Doukhobor Museum in Castlegar. "Some thought they might get to go back to Russia if they were jailed and then deported."

It wasn't much easier for those left behind. "I didn't know what was happening to my friends," says one Doukhobor woman. Brought up as an independent Doukhobor, the gulf of understanding between this woman and her Sons of Freedom friends was vast. "I loved school from the first day I went there when I was five years old," she says, "even though I could speak no English at all. I never understood what the problem was." When her friends left on the land march to Agassiz that September, she had no way of knowing whether they would be all right, and no way to express her feelings about it to them later. "To this day, we don't speak of it." It is an apt reminder of the blurred lines of relationships between the Sons of Freedom and the rest of the Doukhobor family, and of the emotional difficulties experienced as a result. Neighbours and friends, even family members living in the same house, could have completely divided loyalties that made life very hard at times. Wayne Morrison of Silverton recalls a "Russian fellow" who had to leave the sawmill early one Friday afternoon to move his furniture out of his home. His father had spoken out against the Sons of Freedom; he was fearful that his own house would be burnt down that night.

But with the mass exodus of the land marchers in 1962, for a time relative peace descended on the valley. The protesters set up a vigil outside the prison when they arrived early in 1963, where some of them would remain for years and some, including Florence Storgeoff, would die. A few would drift away to Vancouver and become absorbed into the life of that city. Eventually most of them would return to Krestova, little better off than when they had left – still landless, and still facing a government that had no intention of giving in. The days of frequent violence in the valley were more or less over, however. And in the meantime, another group of people seeking refuge from an oppressive government had come to the valley, to escape an even greater violence occurring far away: the Vietnam War.

Three "generations" of Winlaw postmistresses, 1960. From left to right: Marilyn Jones, Nettie Zarchikoff, and Mabel Lawrenow Kabatoff.

15

HARMONY AND UNDERSTANDING:
the seventies

The Slocan Valley has always attracted both people looking
for something and people escaping from something. There
are those who came for the glint of silver and a fortune to
be made; hunters and gatherers of food; battered souls
seeking out a remote, sweet place to live in relative
freedom. In the late 1960s and early 70s, hundreds upon
hundreds of yet another generation of such immigrants
flooded into the valley. They were almost all uniformly
young – and they were all searching for something that

many of them would have had trouble defining.

They came from the United States of America – particularly California – in large numbers. They were conscientious objectors and draft resisters and their girlfriends, and hippies and flower children, and people who were simply afraid of the nuclear holocaust that threatened the planet. Some of them, coming "back to the land," were young people who believed they could build a better life for themselves and their children by living on their own resources. There were kids whose frightened parents had sent them north over the border with wads of cash to buy property and stay safe until the Vietnam War was over.

Bing Jensen, Helen Davis, and Gary Cramer of the band *Brain Damage*, started by the *Flying Hearts*.

Many of them were highly educated: "There were more Ph.D.'s per square mile here at one stage than at the University of British Columbia," jokes Fred Makortoff of South Slocan. They also came from Vancouver and Toronto and London, England, urbanites escaping the "doomed" cities of the world. Indeed, they came from all over Canada: "It's not correct to portray the counterculture in this valley as having been all about Vietnam draft resisters," insists Vallican resident and writer Rita Moir. "Many of the U.S. political refugees made a huge contribution here. But they also lived and worked side by side with a lot of Canadians, many of us from the prairies, from B.C., and from all over Canada. We brought our Canadian social values, our history, and our principles of co-operation."

Nonetheless, throughout the Slocan's history, people have also poured into it from the United States, and the 1970s were no exception. One of the predecessors of the movement north on this occasion was Californian David Orcutt, who had done his research and travelled to Ottawa in the 1940s to meet with local member of Parliament Bert Herridge. Herridge's glowing descriptions of the west Kootenays were convincing, and Orcutt moved first to the Arrow Lakes in 1949, then to 170 acres in Appledale that he bought for six thousand dollars in 1969. When he first arrived in the west Kootenays, Orcutt had just seen one terrible war come and go, and in the United States he had been facing the potential of a different war, this time in Korea. But Orcutt came to the Kootenays also because he was simply attracted by the wildness and natural beauty of the region, and he wanted to be a part of it: "Nature," says the slender, silver-haired man quietly from his small cabin tucked in the woods, "should not be a noun."

David Orcutt was followed to the Kootenays by a swathe of the back-to-the-land generation. By the mid-1960s, the Slocan Valley had taken on an almost mystical aura in southern California. "Everyone had heard of this great place to move to," says American expatriate Barry Lamare of New Denver. "It was over fifteen hundred feet in altitude, you see, so it was above radiation levels. You could grow root vegetables and survive." Lamare and his wife, Sally, came with their children to Winlaw in 1972 for a summer, to see what it was like. Three years later they returned to Perry Siding, and this time the Lamares stayed in the valley for good. "It was a philosophical choice as well," says Kathy Hart, whose parents came from Indiana in 1972, when she was fourteen years old, and bought a former Doukhobor farm in Appledale. "They were educated, artistic. They had heard about the Doukhobors here and the people dropping out. My father was older than most, but he still wanted to retire to a place like this."

For many residents, the reality remains that it was also an escape, a

In August 1972, Sally and Barry Lamare checked out the valley to see if it really was a safe place to bring up their children, renting a home near Drake's Beach, Vallican.

refuge from the jungles of Asia. Mary-Wade Anderson was a realtor in Castlegar who brokered numerous deals for American parents buying land for their sons to live on. "There was certainly a lot of cash around all of a sudden," remember the locals, who saw no reason to complain at the sudden surge in the economy of the valley. Author Richard Mackie was hitchhiking north in 1972 and was picked up by a couple of American hippies driving a big, luxurious van. "They weren't really hippies, though," he recalls, "more like acting the role." Their van was too expensive, too clean. "They passed a pot of honey back to me to eat and I spilled it on the plush carpet, and they were downright mad about it. I figured real hippies would have been a lot more laid back about that honey." Mackie asked them what they were doing in the valley, and the driver replied – drawing out the words in multiple layers of syllables in his southern American drawl – "We're looking for land." Says Mackie: "They may have had money, but they were desperate too."

A number of the new immigrants settled in communes on shared land. It was the Age of Aquarius, after all: the era of media-hyped free love and mind-illuminating drugs and rejection of the shackles of convention. It was a place to get away from typical parental expectations and to hang out with like-minded friends; a place in the sun where no one cared whether you had a job or not, and everyone loved one another: peace, love, and eternal grooviness, brothers and sisters. There are many, especially those who have remained in the Slocan Valley, who remember those days with nostalgia, for all the good things that happened and for their youthful freedom. "I'd give anything...I'd just love to get back to those times," former Flying Hearts Family member Peggy Hart told *Harrowsmith* reporter Frank Appleton in 1979. There are others who recall only the hard times and the sadness: how many people died, how many youthful names are inscribed on the worn headstones, decorated with beads and loving mementoes, in the leafy hidden glades of the Dumont Creek Cemetery. And despite the dreams of nirvana, how mundane and tedious life could be much of the time because people still needed to be fed, clothes washed, and houses cleaned. Human nature being what it is, there were as many squabbles over whose turn it was to cook and who wasn't pulling their weight as there would be in any home.

Some people prefer to believe that it was nothing but a brief and aberrant phase in the history of the valley. States one former commune resident: "More than passing mention that there were numerous attempts and mostly failures in the valley in the early 1970s to establish 'hippie communes' would not be appropriate or relevant. Most participants didn't stay in the valley more than a few months and had quite disparate ideas about what collective or co-operative living, sharing land and resources meant. These attempts have now passed into myths and legend."

But the experiences of people once they arrived varied as greatly as the reasons for their arrival in the first place. The Lamares had wanted their children to grow up in a better and safer place than California. They moved to Perry Siding and remained a nuclear family, living and working from their property for eighteen years before they moved to New Denver. Some, like David Orcutt, simply carried on what they had been doing in their previous life. Already a puppeteer of some renown, Orcutt established a credible career in the Canadian entertainment industry that allowed him the freedom to live on his property in Appledale and pursue his other interests.

After the birth of a son who suffered extensive brain damage, Orcutt began to investigate alternative pictoral and aural languages that his son might be able to learn and understand, a project that has since become his life's work. His property was not a commune in the sense of the media stereotype, he says – there was no sharing of partners, for example. "Most people," he confides, "don't have the background to be able to do that gracefully." But the good-natured American did seem to attract a disproportionate number of people who thought they could simply live on his land and commune with nature. "I had a hard time saying no," he muses. Orcutt saw many young people come and go over the 1970s. "A lot of the 'real' communes went under because they required too much energy to sustain them, too much hard work," he says. The flower children didn't seem to realize that meditating by the river was no substitute for making sure there was enough firewood for the winter or weeding the vegetable fields; and those who were working resented the freeloaders. "I've received numerous letters in later years by people apologizing for being such jerks back then," chuckles the laid-back Orcutt.

Orcutt's observation about the requirement for hard work is one with which Eric Clough and Nancy Harris, two of the founders of the New Family commune, agree wholeheartedly. "It was a lot of damned hard work," says Harris. "Some people weren't prepared for that." Harris and her former husband Joel had "dropped out" in 1968. "We were escaping life in California," she says, "All we knew was we had to get out. You have to remember, 54,000 Americans died in Vietnam, and who knows how many killed themselves after they got back to the United States. It was crazy ugly." Clough was a young architect also heading for the hills. Like the driver who picked up Richard Mackie, he was "looking for land" – and he found it at the top of Paradise Valley Road in Winlaw. In 1968, the New Family bought Arvid and Yvette Swanson's forty-acre farm for $1,400. "Yvette wasn't very popular locally for selling to the hippies," chuckles Clough now. But unlike many of the other shared-land arrangements in the valley, the New Family were a highly structured organization with strict anti-drug rules and an eight-hour working day. It was the key to sustaining the community on a long-term basis, but it wasn't the dream world of some. "One of our original members thought this life was going to be white picket fences, horses to ride and charming social evenings," Harris told *Harrowsmith's* Frank Appleton. The sheer hard work was an unexpected reality.

Nancy and Joel Harris with Rowdy, in front of the shared home at the New Family property on Paradise Valley Road, 1971.

The New Family also faced the same challenges as other communes – frequent visits from the police's "D Squad," who were fearful that the young Americans and the Sons of Freedom would form some sort of unholy alliance; the stares of passing voyeurs curious to see the naked hippies working in the fields; suspicion and hostility from some of the locals. But the core members of the New Family would endure on their land for nearly twenty years, succumbing only to economic reality rather than the social disintegration that quickly occurred in many other communes. Their relationship with other farmers in the valley was, on the whole, amiable. The Doukhobors taught many of the young back-to-the-land immigrants the skills and knowledge they needed to survive, and people like Ray Kosiancic were also happy to help. "[The hippies] would

Eric Clough and Carol Ladas-Gaskin, two of the founding members of the New Family, circa 1971.

come and bug us a lot with questions," he grins. "They didn't know a thing. We'd always try to be pleasant, to help."

As well as the New Family, there were other success stories. Yasodhara Ashram on Kootenay Lake, founded in 1962 by Sylvia Hellman, a woman by then calling herself Swami Sivananda Radha; Gestalt therapist Bethel Phaigh, who lived and worked in the Slocan for a number of years and attracted an international following for her work and writing, including

Nancy and Ananda Harris at the New Family shared property, 1972.

her famous book *Gestalt and the Wisdom of the Kahunas*. Joel Russ moved to the north end of the valley in 1972 to join a "vital little colony of back-to-the-landers" living in Hills, Rosebery, New Denver, and Silverton. These were mostly couples or individuals owning or renting their own properties, says Russ, but sharing socio-political values and a desire to live organically. "The jumble was exciting in some ways. But of course this miscellany could never be completely blended." Although a number of communal situations were tried, he recalls, there was "greater long-term success when the individuals were more mature."

Most of the communes, however, were short-lived, for one reason or another. In 1971, according to Frank Appleton, the then-radical Vancouver newspaper *The Georgia Strait* would proclaim the Harmony Gates north of Winlaw to be the "most successful open commune" in British Columbia. But within a few years it was gone again, along with the Sun Blossoms, the Flying Hearts Family at Perry Siding, the Funkwells, the Red and Blue Circus in Appledale, and the Many Skies. Despite receiving help from other farmers, surviving on the land was extremely difficult for the children of urban middle-class families, who had never experienced anything like this before. "There were...miscalculations," says Myrna Kostash in her 1980 book about Canadian communes, *A Long Way From Home*. They didn't know how to plant, how to fertilize properly; they could not bring themselves to slaughter livestock. They were isolated and often lonely, paranoid that the authorities were out to get them. "The whole communal thing was a disaster," Kostash quotes from an anonymous source. The young Americans, in particular, were "spoiled rotten" and didn't have any of the construction or other work skills they needed to grow a communal farm successfully.

Rosalinde Dettmar Compton, who ended up buying the Reds and Blues land in 1980, acknowledges the hardship and "weirdness" of the times – the drugs, the deaths from overdoses, the fear. "We were all completely convinced the Winlaw postmistress would open our mail and report us to the immigration people," says Compton. Heavily pregnant and knowing no one, the young Englishwoman had hitchhiked to the Slocan Valley from Toronto in 1971. Compton had read about it in a comic book and simply decided it was where she wanted to be. "The cities were doomed," she said. She camped temporarily in a Doukhobor cabin, heading to the hospital in New Denver a few weeks later in the company of a friend to give birth to her son Na-Kim. Young men and women like Compton roamed from friend's houses to communes to beach camps, making ends meet one way or another – seasonal work, unemployment insurance, growing some food. The tedium of that way of life in many respects surprised her, but she also recalls the excitement and the freedom and the good times. She was luckier than many – her husband in England, a musician playing for cult rock band Hawkwind, eventually sent her money to buy land in Retallack. Compton started to make a living as a graphic artist and never looked back. "I remember a sense of freedom to roam around and do whatever we wanted," she says of those early days. "Of course, there was a lot of negativity towards the 'longhairs.' I remember a friend getting thrown out of the Queens Hotel for reading in the bar – they told him it was a pub, not a library."

Rosalinde Dettmar Compton came to the valley to give birth to her first child, son Na-Kim. She had escaped the "urban doom" of London, England, for a better way of life in the Slocan. This photo was taken in 1972.

Brain Damage on tour, 1970s.

The counterculture in fact was anything but lacking in culture; it was simply of a different kind. "There is a cultural life in the valley now that stems from those days," says Compton. The Age of Aquarius may have quickly faded away, but its citizens brought with them the music, literature, and art they had experienced in their home communities and blended it into the valley's lifestyle in a way that has endured. In 1972 – the year that W.A.C. Bennett finally ended his twenty-year reign and New Democrat Dave Barrett succeeded him as premier – the Flying Hearts started their own rock band, calling it Brain Damage in a tribute, David Orcutt says, to his son. While it lasted – broken relationships would also break up the band eventually – Brain Damage enjoyed enough success touring and playing gigs both locally and as far south as Mexico (where they played under the tag "Los Damaginos") to cover the Flying Hearts' food bills. That year also saw the arrival in New Denver from Beverly Hills of watercolour artist Les Weisbrich to set up a studio. Textile artist J.C. Bradford moved to Winlaw in 1970, setting up the collective Threads Guild in 1981 at Perry Siding. And following on the success of an entertainment group in the New Denver area called the Valhallelujah Rangers, in 1976 a dramatic collective was formed that included Nancy Harris,

Hank Hastings, Buzz Bense, Meredith Bain Woodward, Judith Ceroli, and Catherine and Brian Marrion. Theatre Energy's first play, *Renderings*, was performed in December 1976, and the group – its members changing from time to time – went on to perform throughout the 1980s in various venues around the province, including national radio.

Alongside the more prominent artistic achievements in the Slocan in those years were the quiet, organic, cultural changes that started to occur, changes that would make an irrevocable difference – both positive and painful – to the way of life of the resource-extraction

Members of the Theatre Energy dramatic group, formed in the 1970s in the valley: Hank Hastings, Catherine Marrion, Buzz Bense, Ronnie Gilbert, Meredith Bain Woodward, and Nancy Harris, 1978.

mining and forestry communities in the valley. "The influx of Americans forced a different outlook that made people born and raised here look beyond the mountains that surrounded them," says American expatriate Leah Main of Silverton. An extraordinarily high proportion of literate and well-educated immigrants from all over the world had moved in, committed in turn to educating their children with freedom of thought and tolerance. Home schooling – not a novel concept, as some of the Doukhobors could well have pointed out – flourished. At the Vallican "Free School," groups of children went to various homes to be taught a range of subjects by experts in their fields, of whom there were many scattered through the valley. Libraries were put together with donated books. "On Fridays," recalls Kathy Hart, "we kids would walk to Vallican to borrow books. It would take us all day to get there and back from

Sally Lamare and her children waiting on the Winlaw back road for the school bus, 1972.

Appledale." The Vallican library, which was located in the former school-house near the river, also sponsored community workshops and a weekly Cinema Guild.

A little further west and still in Vallican, a group got together to build a community centre. It took several years to complete. The original project had been started in 1971, aided by government funding, but it was overly ambitious for a group of relatively unskilled workers and had not proceeded past the foundation. "People say that the building didn't go up because a bunch of lazy, American hippies were ripping off the government," reported *The Arrow* newspaper defensively in March 1974, referring to the unfinished project tongue-in-cheek as the "Vallican Hole." "The fact is that people, the major part of whom were Canadians, worked hard that hot, dry summer." But by 1975, the renamed Vallican Whole was complete and hosting concerts and dances and community meetings.

Artisans began taking the valley's resources and turning them into furniture and art to sell "outside." Organic gardeners, borrowing techniques from some of the older farmers and adding their own, revived the dying agricultural economy of the valley. So did marijuana growers. Supported by government programs, silviculture also became a regular seasonal source of income for newcomers and long-term residents alike. By the end of the 1970s the counterculture, it seemed, had simply become absorbed into the valley's way of life.

The Lamare family at a concert held at the future site of the Vallican Whole, August, 1972.

The flower children: the Lamares in a bed of sunflowers near Vallican, summer of 1972.

Things were changing for the valley's old-timers as well, but for other reasons; modern technology played its part, but so did the economic prosperity that the newcomers had brought with them. As the roads improved and the valley started to see its first real tourists travelling through, motels sprang up here and there along the highway. In 1970, Mavis and Bill Douglas opened the Maybill Café in Winlaw, and by 1972 they had added an extension with motel units as well as a gas station. Jones's store was doing a good trade. In 1981, Joan and Peter Duck took all of them over, renaming the café the Duckstop. By 1976, the old tunnel on the road north of Slocan fell into disuse, replaced by a brand-new four-lane bypass road that took drivers

The Krestova Confection served the local area for some time during the 1970s, although it is now long gone.

The icy challenge of Cape Horn in the 1960s was finally tamed, if only marginally, by a widening of the road and a barrier along its plunging length in the mid-1970s.

Before the bypass road connecting Highway 6 directly to Cape Horn was built in the mid-1970s, motorists would be required to squeeze through the old one-lane tunnel just north of Slocan. This image is taken sometime in the 1960s. The tunnel is now used strictly for recreational hiking or cycling.

straight past Slocan without ever having to stop. American forestry company Triangle Pacific was operating the rebuilt Slocan sawmill, having bought the Passmore mill complex from Axel Erickson at the beginning of the 1970s and consolidated the two operations. Only one or two independent logging operations were still in existence. Ironically – somewhat counter to the counterculture – a number of older Doukhobor couples like Bill and Vera Lawrenow were obtaining marriage licences and formalizing their original Doukhobor wedding vows. The older generation were starting to die, and since the government didn't recognize the status of their marriages, the normal laws governing wills and estates couldn't apply, explains Mabel Lawrenow Kabatoff. "It was a heck of a problem." In the meantime, Kokanee Glacier Provincial Park had been downgraded in its official status to a Class B park in 1964 – allowing mining – to the horror of hikers and conservationists, although not necessarily some of the locals. "The parks around here are for visitors," observed Bill Hicks from Slocan. "We don't need them."

One small group of locals disagreed vehemently with Hicks on that subject. A postcard from about 1979 shows the Valhalla Range and bears the following legend on its back: "The majestic Valhallas present myriad

In a letter John Clay wrote to England in 1927, quoted by Innes Cooper in *The Valhalla Mountains*, he spoke of climbing "to the topmost edge of Gimli Peak, and here I took photographs on the edge of an awful precipice."

wilderness vistas, ranging from icy glaciers and meadows ablaze with wildflowers, to foaming cataracts and moss-hung rainforests. Hopefully this pristine paradise will be preserved for future generations as a provincial or national park." In 1975, a small group of locals formed the precursor to the Valhalla Wilderness Society, a conservation organization created to get the Valhalla Mountains protected through parks legislation. It was a good time to be trying, with a socialist government in power (although not for very much longer), an influx of like-minded new immigrants in the valley, and the imminent growth of nature-based tourism. Nonetheless it was a struggle for its proponents. Colleen McCrory, the society's executive director as well as the deputy leader of the province's Green Party, recalls the days of taking press releases to Victoria – by bus. But after eight years of working eighteen-hour days and standing endlessly on the steps of the legislature, an ecstatic group of environmentalists and recreation-lovers celebrated the designation of Valhalla Provincial Park on March 3, 1983. Residents of the village of Slocan stood at the entrance to the new park that spring and looked up at the mountains, some with cynicism, and some with hope that it would mean new opportunities for the struggling little town.

For Sandon and the other ghost towns along the Slocan–Kaslo road, there seemed little reason to hope for anything. By the early 1980s, the

Relics of the old mining buildings along the New Denver–Kaslo road, 1972.

only relic of the old days in Retallack, says Sandon resident and jack-of-all-trades Hal Wright, was an old miner named Bert Eckhart. "Bert would pop out of his run-down old shack in his underwear and his long white beard and scare any passing tourist half to death," chuckles Wright at the memory. "Old Bert had no car, no running water, no hydro, just an old dog called Chubby, a leaky roof, and one new pair of underwear a year that he'd order from the Sears catalogue. You'd just about have had to operate to get the old pair off him." And in Sandon itself, the sole remaining resident was Gene Petersen, living with his memories of Sandon the way it used to be.

The Silverton ore tram and concentrator on the shore of Slocan Lake, just north of town: summer 1973. Today there is a subdivision on this property.

Griffiths family hiking Idaho Peak trail, 1995.

But the echo of hammer against rock had long been silenced in the steep valleys surrounding Carpenter Creek. It was replaced by the chatter of hikers heading up the trail to Idaho Peak in the summer to admire the views. What prosperity lay in the Slocan Valley's future would not depend on mining, and less and less on forestry, as the logging companies became increasingly entangled in regulations and protests against clearcutting. Its future rested on its people and their industriousness and creativity – as well as their willingness to stay and keep fighting for the ways of life they treasured.

New Denver, 1972.

*"I must've done about four hundred jobs
in my life, just to get by."*

— Laurence "Red" Sutherland, Kelowna
(formerly of Winlaw)

16

HEALING AND CONFLICT:
the end of the millenium

Things were tough in the 1980s. It didn't much matter
whether you were an independent logging contractor or a
small co-op or a multinational company: it was a struggle
to keep going. Inflation and interest rates soared, but
employment plummeted. Ray Kosiancic had long since
ceased the dairy business and was driving buses for the
Nelson School District to supplement his farm income
from beef cattle. In 1983, Robert's Restaurant, a popular
stop on the river south of Winlaw, closed its doors. By 1985,

Eric Clough couldn't find any work as an architect in the valley or its environs. "The economy was in the toilet," says Clough. The former patriarch of the New Family packed his bags and reluctantly left for Ontario, selling the forty acres at the top of Paradise Valley Road that he and his compatriots had bought from Arvid and Yvette Swanson back in 1968. Although Clough would later return to a property further down Paradise Valley, the days of the New Family were over. "I would never have left if I had any choice," he says wistfully. "But there was simply no work here."

Even the mighty CPR was having a hard time in the valley. In 1986 it sold its smelter operation at Trail to Vancouver-based Teck Corp. West Kootenay Power and Light was one of the few utility companies not captured under W.A.C. Bennett's program for government appropriation of private hydro operations by state-owned B.C. Hydro back in 1962; but by 1987 it too was sold, to an American company called UtiliCorp Networks Canada. In the same year, the CPR found itself facing what author Rita Moir in the *Kootenay Journal* called "ferocious" opposition, when it announced a weed control plan involving the spraying of herbicide Spike 80W – Tebuthiuron – on its rail lines through the Kootenays. The announcement sparked a massive community protest in the Slocan Valley. At a meeting held in the Appledale community centre, the Regional District of Central Kootenay condemned the spraying plan in its pesticide-free region. Organic farmers, schoolteachers, church members, river rafters, fishermen, teenage environmental activists and eighty-year-old veterans alike arose en masse to resist the CPR's spraying plan. In a triumph of community activism over corporate might, the CPR judged the negative-public relations impact against the value of the spraying plan and backed down. The provincial environmental ministry subsequently cancelled spraying permits generally throughout the region.

One of the considerations of the CPR may have been the fact that the end of its continuing operations in the Slocan Valley was in sight. On December 21, 1988, the last CPR train destined for Nakusp from Nelson was barged north over Slocan Lake to Rosebery on the tug *Iris G.* The final operating cog of the once-thriving lake and river transportation industry in the west Kootenays, the *Iris G.* had only been running weekly trips for a number of years. The service was a consistent money drain,

The tug *Iris G.*, pulling away from Rosebery with the CPR train on the barge after coming south from Nakusp, August 1974.

The CPR train crossing Lemon Creek, circa 1990. By then, the barge service over Slocan Lake had ended and trains just ran up to Slocan City. Their speed was limited to 16 kph and it took a long time for the train to waddle through the grasses over the deteriorated track.

Southbound CPR freight train between Slocan City and Slocan Junction, carrying poles and forest products from Nakusp and the Slocan sawmill: August 1974.

and it was inevitable that it would come to an end. And with the extensive improvements to Highway 6 and the resulting growth of the truck transportation industry, the final journey of a CPR train from the village of Slocan south through the valley to Slocan Junction occurred on September 14, 1993. Within a few years, even the tracks were gone. The only reminders of its existence for recreational walkers along the former rail bed would be occasional rusting iron spikes and bolts half-buried among the gravel and the weeds.

The strength of the anti-spraying action was not surprising. Since the 1890s, the Slocan Valley has been a crucible in which protest activity has flared again and again – the mining strikes of the late 19th and early 20th centuries, the Sons of Freedom actions from the 1930s to the 1970s. The 1980s and 1990s saw yet another surge of activism in the valley, deriving from several sources. As increasing numbers of people left the valley in search of work, those left behind drew together to protect the nature of the valley as they wished to see it remain. The flower children and back-to-the-land immigrants of the 1960s and 1970s were followed by the next generation of "hippie" – this time, wearing crocheted hats and wraparound tie-dyed skirts, but with the same desire to live in a cheap, organic environment that could support a freedom of lifestyle impossible to sustain in the highly regulated and overcrowded cities. They were accompanied by an older generation of people with independent means and the ability to pay cash for homes, but motivated by similar ambitions. The local cottage industry of pot-growing started to expand into more extensive commercial operations, as often as not instigated by new arrivals who had come expressly for that purpose. Forestry, the last real mainstay of any large-scale corporate business activity in the valley, was struggling with increased regulation, more expensive technology, fewer trees, and fewer jobs. Tensions escalated as loggers sought desperately to hold onto employment, environmentalists started to take radical action to protect their watersheds from degradation, and commercial marijuana growers took measures to protect their plantations, secreted in the hills.

Flip-flopping governments did little to help with the tensions. When staid Social Credit premier Bill Bennett stepped down in 1986, he was replaced by a colourful and controversial man named Bill Vander Zalm. The British Columbia public had had quite enough of Mr. Vander Zalm by 1991 and elected New Democrat Mike Harcourt in his place. Almost immediately, Harcourt's government initiated what is fondly – or perhaps not – remembered as CORE: the Commission on Resources and the Environment. The objective of CORE was to radically change land-use planning by giving regional residents a direct say in the plans affecting them. The outcome for the west Kootenays was a land-use plan released in 1995 that provided for nearly 80 percent of the region's lands to be available for commercial resource use and recreation activities, divided into different types of management zones, and about 11 percent devoted to parks. Naturally – as is common after processes of this kind – nobody was completely happy with the plan. Nearly a quarter of the lands zoned for resource uses – the "special management zones" – were subject to a requirement that these uses occur in "a way that respects sensitive natural and cultural values." That irritated many of the resource users, as did the doubling in size of the protected areas and parks. On the other hand, even within the special management zones mining exploration and development were deemed to be "acceptable activities." Conservationists and aboriginal groups, among others, were dismayed.

To be fair, the government was facing a serious challenge. While it professed itself dedicated to "ensuring jobs for workers, financial security for families, and stability for communities," it had to reassure communities that it was committed to safeguarding watersheds and, under the euphemistic title of "forest renewal," to cut back timber-harvest levels significantly. The existing unsustainable harvest levels were blamed on the "cumulative effect of...flooding entire valleys for hydroelectric projects, building wood-processing operations so numerous or efficient that they outpace nature's ability to regenerate our forests, increased harvest rates to salvage beetle-infested trees, and..." – always a clincher argument for a new administration – "...poor management or lax enforcement by past governments." Regardless of the reasons behind the changes, it was clear that already embattled forestry companies were facing a more highly regulated industry under the new Forest Practices Code announced in the land-use plan. From the perspective of the local residents not involved in the forestry industry, however, the plan itself gave little comfort that their individual interests would prevail over the corporate might of industry. The tensions did not decrease.

In its 2002 annual report, Slocan Forest Products stated matter-of-factly on page 2: "We have shifted production to lower cost facilities and our operations have become more efficient. Where necessary, we have curtailed higher cost operations. Our Slocan and Valemount mills," it continues, "did not operate in the third and fourth quarters." On page 27, it provided more detail: "The Slocan Division sawmill was curtailed in August 2002 because of its inability to operate at a profit. A new business plan has been developed for this operation to turn it into a specialty mill producing a higher percentage of high value products for both North American and export markets. The Division resumed operations early in 2003." But for the loggers and contractors on the ground in Slocan, that dry corporate reporting translated into job layoffs and no income for extended periods. "The question on everyone's mind," asked Slocan Forest Product's local company publication *The Sawmiller* a year later, on August 15, 2003, was: "Are we going to be working over the next few weeks?...We predict that we will curtail production in the sawmill as of shift end on August 21st." This time, the cause of the closure that did indeed occur was due to the high fire risk in the forest preventing any logging activity. The reason, however, was of little relevance to employees and contractors, who had suffered what seemed like a non-stop series of setbacks in the Slocan Valley over the previous decade.

In 1972, the owner of the Slocan mill was Triangle-Pacific Forest Products. In that heady year of economic well-being in the west Kootenays, the company had felt confident enough to claim in the May issue of its company paper, the *Triangle News*, that it was "one of the more rapidly expanding lumber producers in the Nelson area." The company was also boasting of its ability to take more wood out of the same-size cut blocks, thanks to the latest technological advances and a $1.1 million expansion. The company manager at the time, John Reibin, was quoted as saying that Triangle-Pacific was now able to log trees with a four-inch diameter: "We're using logs now that were left in the woods before," he states in the article. At the same time, reported the *Triangle News*, "Triangle-Pacific is deeply concerned about protecting the environment in the area covered by its operations...with regard to logging beside streams...the company's policy will be to cut alternate smaller strips right to the creek, taking care nothing is dumped into the creek...the environmental policy will be strictly followed as Triangle-Pacific is anxious to prove its concern for the environment." Unfairly or not, such promises of the forestry company (and its successor after 1978, Slocan Forest Products) were greeted with skepticism by many of the locals.

A group of independent watershed protection bodies merged to form the Slocan Valley Watershed Alliance in 1981, its main goal to protect water quality and quantity. Its main targets were forestry companies utilizing what it considered unsustainable and environmentally unsafe logging practices in the watersheds its members lived in, but it also buttonholed the government for allowing that to happen. Loggers, said the Alliance, aren't wrong to log; everyone is entitled to work, after all, and loggers live in the valley too. They just need to adjust their habits. "The loss of this valley by the calculated stripping of the last natural stands of trees in the next few years would be an enormous and unforgivable loss," wrote the Alliance in its literature. "We propose that loggers and environmentalists must work through the transition from an economy that includes clearcut logging to one that is diversified and able to withstand the trauma of a major reduction in logging in this valley." But the relationship between the logging community and the environmental group was strained. Rumours abounded that there was a conspiracy afoot to drive both logging and mining right out of the valley,

Triangle Pacific Forestry Ltd. preceded Slocan Forest Products as the owner of the mill in Slocan. These images of forestry operations in the valley in 1971 were donated by the company to the Selkirk College Archives.

according to the Valhalla Society Research Committee's 1984 report *The Conflict Between Mining and the Environment: Myths and Realities*. Although the Watershed Alliance also expressed a hope that there was willingness on both sides to co-operate, the gap between the primary forestry company in the valley and the provincial government and the water environmentalists was large. By the end of the 1980s, the lines had essentially already been drawn.

In the early summer of 1990, heavy rainfalls contributed to a number of slides in a logged-over watershed north of the village of Slocan that damaged homes and closed Highway 6, and tempers were running high. The flurry of correspondence exchanged between the Alliance and the provincial government on the issue only served to demonstrate what appeared to be an irreconcilable difference in opinion. "Conventional clearcutting," wrote Alliance co-chairman Herb Hammond to the Ministry of Forests in May 1990, "is not acceptable ecologically or socially." Hammond, an independent registered forester and alternative forestry methods proponent, was quoted in the media shortly after writing the letter as claiming that the spring slides "were a direct result of clearcut logging and logging road construction in the area." The local district forest manager replied promptly and caustically on June 6, 1990:

> "I find it interesting that your initial review indicates clearcut logging, compacted soils, concentrated clearcut logging, and inadequate culvert size to be the causal elements of the slides in question. Perhaps you could forward...your documentation which technically supports your allegations as I would assume that since one of you is a Registered Professional Forester in the Province of B.C., you would not make these statements without substantive, relevant on-site support documentation. I further find it most interesting that record precipitation has not been identified in your four causal elements. Is this merely an oversight?"

But he avoided the fundamental problem of the slides. The issue of clearcutting is a sensitive one for registered foresters in B.C. Retired forester Peter Kabatoff of Appledale frowns upon clearcutting, but adds: "There are two sides to every story. Without lumber, there would be no money in the valley." Retired Winlaw logger Casey Obara is less resistant, but rejects the way in which he has seen clearcut land left. "It takes a lifetime to grow a tree in the valley," Obara points out. "Not like the coast. Clearcutting is no good if the land isn't bulldozed and replanted. Nothing will grow." Many foresters simply see clearcutting as a legitimate and efficient way to log, and appropriate under the right circumstances. Slocan Forest Products' general manager of the Slocan Division, Cam Milne, explains it as simply being a better alternative in some conditions. On flat wet ground, he says, it would be "suicide" to selectively log because shallow-rooted species would be exposed to wind damage from the loss of protection. Loggers are better off, he says, to completely clear small openings and replant. It is also counterproductive, Milne adds, to

Clearcutting in the Slocan: like shaved patches on a dog's back. Clearcutting raises loud voices in the valley regarding its legitimacy (or lack thereof) as a logging technique.

selectively log where it is desirable to regenerate pioneer species, like lodgepole pine, that require full light. Nevertheless, in general, the benefits of clearcutting as explained in forestry publications and by foresters themselves are – naturally – expressed in terms of economic or forestry harvesting benefits rather than environmental ones: it's easier to grow the next stand to be cut down, it's easier to replant a more desirable species to be cut down, the next harvest will be of even-aged trees; it's a good way to get rid of beetle infestations that could damage future harvests, and so on.

Throughout the 1990s, it was impossible for Slocan Forest Products and the Watershed Alliance to see eye to eye on the issue. A series of angry protests took place between 1991 and 2000 at Hasty Creek, Bonanza Creek, Red Mountain, Perry Ridge, and Trozzo Creek. Dozens of Slocan residents were arrested on charges of preventing forestry company access to logging roads to cut. At New Denver in July 1997, a counter-protest was set up by the "Slocan Valley Equal Access to Public Resources Society" and members of the local IWA. "LOGGING FEEDS MY FAMILY AND PROBABLY YOURS," read one picket sign; "WE'RE

LOGGERS, NOT POLITICIANS," read another, "GO PROTEST IN VICTORIA." Speaking to the environmental protesters after arrests had been made, however, New Denver's John Anderson tried to be diplomatic: "Our quarrel is not with the loggers. The loggers want steady jobs and they want clean tap water for their children...Our quarrel is with the government." The Trozzo Creek protesters, however, felt betrayed by Slocan Forest Products; they believed the company had not let them know in advance of its plans to log in that watershed. The company metaphorically shrugs it shoulders in frustration: it considers that its community outreach record was excellent. Profit versus water purity; paycheques versus lifestyle. No compromise appeared, and in the interim, to their horror and outrage, several local residents involved in the protests – two of whom at least had suffered significant property devaluation in the wake of the slides – were sued by the government for trespass.

Not all logging in the valley is undertaken by large corporates like Slocan Forest Products; here we see Francine Griffiths, logger, Winlaw, in 1995.

Logs cut from the Griffiths property in Winlaw, July 1995.

While the rising activism of the 1990s was resulting in greater awareness of environmental issues and the creation and extension of provincial parks, aboriginal cultural and land-rights concerns were also re-emerging in the public consciousness. The 1970s court cases finding largely in favour of aboriginal rights, combined with the increasingly coherent articulation of their rights by First Nations groups, had forced both the federal and the provincial governments to consider the options for solving the "land issue." It was Premier Vander Zalm's Social Credit government that would finally take action to bring the province into

264

negotiations with the federal government and Indian bands to try and settle some of the issues being brought forward – issues such as the ability to carry out traditional activities within their territories, which had long been curtailed by the development of industry and by government regulation. Government officials and First Nations representatives worked together to recommend a formal process to undertake negotiations, and in 1992 the British Columbia treaty process was born. For the Ktunaxa Nation, it was an opportunity at last to enter into negotiations with both governments on a basis upon which it could expect to be treated with respect. They might, for the first time in years, come closer to the independence and well-being they had enjoyed in former times. In 1993, the Ktunaxa-Kinbasket Treaty Council started talks with government and submitted a map of its traditional territory to the British Columbia Treaty Commission. The western boundary of the map enclosed the Slocan Valley in its entirety within the Ktunaxa territory.

In February 1997, Ktunaxa chief of the St. Mary's Indian Band, Sophie Pierre – known also as *Kaquntkanusaqlam* – spoke about her people's aspirations for the treaty process in front of the provincial Select Standing Committee on Aboriginal Affairs, which was sitting in Cranbrook:

> "We want to share what we have with those people who have chosen to make this their home...but...the provincial government and the federal government have a responsibility to recognize the fact that we have a ten-thousand-year history here.

> "When the first settlers – your ancestors – were coming through, when the forty-ninth parallel was put in, our people were told it was to regulate the movement of the newcomers, it was not meant for our people...the forty-ninth parallel is an area we wish to bring to the negotiating table.

> "We feel we have a right to have a say in how the development is going to happen within our traditional territory."

Pierre also said something else important. "The Arrow Lakes area in the west Kootenays was an area that was shared by the Ktunaxa people with the Interior Salish people, people of the Shuswap language, people of the Okanagan language and the Colville language. That's an area that is very much an area of overlap...We must do our work in our own backyard and settle this overlap issue, because it is, after all, our issue and our issue only, and we must deal with it."

Sitting in the back of the room at the time was a resident of the Slocan Valley named Robert Watt. When Watt's turn came to make a presentation to the committee, he said: "My name is Robert Watt. I'm Sinixt, and I'm the caretaker of the Vallican burial ground." Watt told them shyly he should not be the one speaking to them: "We've usually got our own speakers and stuff, you know, I'm just like a caretaker...I usually don't do this type of thing. But we had such short notice of this going on." What Watt meant is that the Sinixt had received no official notice at all that the hearing would be taking place. In a 1979 paper to a conference of the Canadian Rock Art Research Associates, art historian Joy Bell had noted that the Lakes Indians were extinct: "Only rock art," she wrote then, "remains as testimony to a forgotten people." Forgotten by most, perhaps, but not by all – and the Sinixt living south of the border at Colville would have disagreed vehemently. However, despite making some progress in establishing a physical presence back in the Slocan Valley, they remained unrecognized by governments as having any official status.

The one small foothold that had been established by the Sinixt was on a piece of provincial crown land on the west bank of the Slocan River near Vallican. Archaeological explorations that had accompanied a planned road expansion in the late 1980s had revealed not only significant evidence of former occupation of the site, but the existence of ancient burials. When the Sinixt got wind of the discovery, they attempted to stop the road construction with litigation. When that failed, some of them simply moved onto the land in 1989. Among these people was Robert Watt, tasked by his colleagues and compatriots with the main responsibility for caretaking the site and protecting the burials from further depredation. By that stage, the road was complete, but the provincial government had provided the remainder of the Crown land with formal heritage protection.

The technically illegal occupation was causing government officials a giant headache, however. They had no authority to recognize the Sinixt, but removing them would be an exercise in bad public relations that could reverberate painfully well into the hallowed chambers of senior government in Victoria. On the other hand, the site was fairly well off the beaten track, and no one was beating down the door to see the occupants removed. The Ktunaxa were not making any move to force the issue. Heritage Branch officials hunkered down and deferred any decision-making until it would be unavoidable. In the meantime, the Sinixt managed to locate and have returned a number of human remains of Lakes Indians that had been held by institutions, and reburied them at the Vallican site. The Royal British Columbia Museum solved its conundrum in dealing with the unrecognized group in a creative fashion, by signing the remains over to the Okanagan Tribal Council on behalf of "the descendants of the Arrow Lakes people."

Although occasional references are included in documents such as the archaeological report attached to the Brilliant power plant expansion project – the Sinixt are referred to diplomatically as an "autonomous Sinixt organization aimed at furthering their people's aboriginal interests in B.C." – other government departments continued for the most part to ignore the Sinixt as an aboriginal entity in their official dealings with First Nations in the region. To do otherwise in conventional terms no doubt would have been to expose the government to the risk of legal liability for aboriginal rights, or to unwittingly lay the ground for the creation of another Indian band – a direction in which the Canadian government does not appear to be traveling in contemporary times.

By the time Robert Watt appeared in front of the standing committee, however, the Sinixt had been given much wider recognition by non-governmental groups and by people within the Slocan Valley itself. Watt was living more or less full time on the Vallican site in a small cabin, and he was often kept company by a series of travellers passing through from as far away as Tibet and Germany. James and other Sinixt people were also living close by in Vallican and spending time on the site as well as attempting to raise awareness of their ambitions as broadly as possible in Canadian circles. Watt stood up and told the select standing committee:

> "My people, the Sinixt people, were erroneously declared extinct in 1956. No one has the right to negotiate any of our land base with the Shuswaps, the Okanagans, or the Kootenays...We are

still repatriating and burying our ancestors in our homeland…It was our responsibility…to get those remains back and put them in the ground. It's part of our cultural law.

"When they talk about the Columbia Basin, down there by Brilliant and all up through the Arrow Lakes there, all those village sites and those burial grounds and everything that was flooded there. That was our people's, you know."

As the Ktunaxa began their treaty talks and the Sinixt struggled to have a hand extended to them by government, all kinds of outreach and conciliatory gestures were being made by various levels of government to other residents and former residents of the Slocan. In 1984, the National Association of Japanese Canadians (NAJC) had begun a comprehensive campaign seeking redress for the victims of the government's actions during World War Two. It had taken a full forty years for the tide of political will to turn enough that it was feasible to even consider the possibility of a settlement – even in 1964, when Prime Minister Lester Pearson had opened the Japanese Canadian Cultural Centre in Toronto, he had not been prepared to admit that the dispersal policies of the 1940s were founded on discriminatory decisions requiring compensation. "The distribution – even though forceful – over the whole country," said Pearson in his address, "undoubtedly hastened the full integration of Japanese Canadians into Canadian life."

By the 1980s, however, Brian Mulroney's Conservative government had campaigned and won an election on a platform that included a Japanese compensation settlement. On September 22, 1988, in the House of Commons, Prime Minister Mulroney offered to Japanese Canadians: "The formal and sincere apology of this Parliament for those past injustices against them, against their families, and against their heritage, and our solemn commitment and undertaking to Canadians of every origin that such violations will never again in this country be countenanced or repeated." On the same day Mulroney signed a formal settlement agreement with the NAJC providing for individual payments of $21,000 to each surviving victim of the internment camps, and an endowment fund of $12 million for human-rights programs and cultural and social activities. Additional funding was provided for administering the program and to create a new Canadian Race Relations Foundation. For those who had lost their Canadian citizenship during the war, a process was set in place to regain it.

Many Japanese Canadians greeted the settlement with relief and pleasure, accepting it as their just due. Others, still living with their memories, had mixed feelings. Slocan camp survivor Ken Adachi wrote in the *Toronto Star* two days after the settlement agreement was signed: "Of course, I feel better today as a Canadian than I did last week. But it doesn't assuage my anger. No, not quite. I cannot summon up tears. Our individual and collective experience lies too deep...It is too little and too late, for some of us."

In 1994, the same year that the Nikkei Internment Memorial Centre would open its doors to the public in New Denver, Slocaner Sharon Hicks Gibbons captured some of the war-year experiences in the film she wrote for the CBC about the Slocan camps that she called *Hakujin* – "white people." The fictional recreation of the internment camp story describes the relationship between a local woman and a Japanese woman, and a number

Young Barry Obara, posed ironically in front of a sign not far from the old Popoff farm, 1957.

of local Japanese residents who had been in the camps acted as extras in the film. Many of them broke down in tears repeatedly during the filming as they recalled their own real experiences. One man brought to the set the coat he had been wearing on the trucks when he was first interned. He had kept it for fifty years.

For the Doukhobors and the Sons of Freedom, government attempts to make peace were occurring on a number of fronts. In 1995, on the one-hundredth anniversary of the arms burning in Russia, an order-in-council was issued declaring October 24–31 "Voices for Peace Week." The provincial government recognized the persecution of Doukhobors in

Canada and stated in the order-in-council that "the government and people of British Columbia wish to recognize the important contribution of the Doukhobors to the Province's cultural, social, and economic development and to commend them for their perseverance in promoting global harmony through toil and peaceful life." Two more Doukhobor Heritage Weeks were declared in 1999, one hundred years after the first arrival of Doukhobors in Canada. In the meantime, attempts were being made by government negotiators to deal fairly with the Sons of Freedom regarding communal settlement lands in Krestova.

After their return from the Agassiz prison in the early 1970s, Stephan Sorokin – now back in the Slocan Valley – had successfully negotiated the resettlement of the Sons of Freedom in Krestova on a property that had become known as the New Settlement. Amid serious dissension within the ranks of the Sons of Freedom, however, a number of individuals had refused to pay the dues required to meet provincial taxes, and in 1984, the year that Sorokin died, the land once again reverted to government ownership. This time, though, the government did not abandon the settlement. In October 1995 a new agreement was signed, under which the land would be surveyed into individual lots but transferred to a holding society that would own the lots in common on behalf of the communal Sons of Freedom. By the year 2000, the properties were all in the hands of the society, payments for taxes were being made to government, and even some of the hardliners were succumbing to the attractions of putting in hydro and telephone connections. But in August 2001, eighty-one-year-old Mary Braun was convicted of arson in a Nelson court: earlier in the month, protesting the injustice of the treatment of the Sons of Freedom, she had set fire to Selkirk College's Adult Learning campus in Crescent Valley. It was clear that for some, the strength of their beliefs would remain undiminished regardless of the government's efforts.

While the land-issue negotiations were underway, a group of former residents of the New Denver school in the 1950s asked the provincial Ombudsman, Dulcie McCallum, to investigate the events of 1953–1959. In her 1999 report entitled *Righting the Wrong*, McCallum had unequivocally found that the acts of government had resulted in the mistreatment of the children and had made a number of recommendations. Writing to the government, she recommended that it acknowledge the wrongdoing of the past, provide an explanation, make an "unconditional, clear and public" apology, and offer reparation for the harm done. It was a huge step forward in the right direction for former school inmates like Fred Konkin, who wrote to the *Vancouver Sun* newspaper on April 12, 1999, urging its readers to look at the report and obtain "the true facts." Kathleen Makortoff told *Religious News Service* writer Douglas Todd on May 27, 1999: "The important thing is an acknowledgement it was wrong. If the government offers money, I wouldn't refuse it. But it's not something I'm holding my breath for."

In March 2002 a progress report was issued by Ombudsman Howard Kushner, commenting on the government's implementation of the recommendations in *Righting the Wrong*. Although only one recommendation had been fully implemented, Kushner praised the government for its efforts to explore "creative means of addressing the outstanding recommendations." Certainly government had immediately initiated a request to the RCMP to review its proceedings during that period, although no results were yet forthcoming. Officials had also travelled to New Denver on several occasions in an endeavour to start a dialogue with former school inmates on options to address the issues in an appropriate way. At one of the meetings, Deputy Attorney General Gillian Wallace had expressed "deep regret" regarding the experiences that the former residents had endured. It was not enough for some, however. By early 2001, flyers were circulating inviting former school residents to join in a lawsuit against the government to seek an apology and compensation, and in April the lawsuit was launched. Nevertheless, the government has persisted in its reconciliation efforts, continuing to meet with the claimants in New Denver while the litigation proceeds. "B.C. has been working with the Doukhobor community to address their concerns," Attorney General Geoff Plant told Eli Schuster of *Report* Magazine on October 8, 2001. "We really do want to achieve some reconciliation with this part of our history as a province."

In 1995, another form of reconciliation took place: the provincial government created the Columbia Basin Trust in response to recommendations made by the Association of Kootenay-Boundary Municipalities. Its purpose essentially was to make amends to the people of the Columbia

Basin for the impacts of the 1961 Columbia River Treaty, and to provide them with a fair share of the downstream benefits. The trust was set up with an endowment of $295 million plus an annual stipend of $2 million, to be paid until 2012; as well as a 50 percent share in power projects undertaken by the Columbia Power Corp., a provincial crown company, within the Columbia Basin. A set of local residents made up the board of governors overseeing the fund. The trust and the power corporation immediately bought the Brilliant Dam from Cominco as one of their first initiatives. The joint-venture partners also took on the Arrow Lakes generating station as well as a number of other facilities in the basin, and in 2003 they broke soil on the building of a second power plant at the Brilliant facility.

The trust provides funds for employment opportunities, economic development projects, research, environmental schemes, and the arts. From its inception it has been the pride of Kootenay residents. But in late 2003, the provincial government dealt the trust a body blow when it took away local control over the appointment of the trust's directors. Until then, two-thirds of the directors were appointed independently by the regional districts and the Ktunaxa-Kinbasket Tribal Council. The reason given for the change by Energy Minister Richard Neufeld was government accounting requirements. The government, said Neufeld, is an investor in the trust, not simply a benefactor handing over grant moneys. In that case, it needed to be accountable for its constituents' funds – therefore it needed to be able to control them. Whether or not the beneficiaries of the trust have anything to fear from the change remains to be seen.

What is certain is that the future of the Columbia Basin and the small valley that lies on its western border is one that the people of the Slocan, at any rate, view with mixed feelings of optimism, caution, and fatigue. But: "Warriors don't run away from the battlefield," says Marilyn James. Far from the bureaucratic corridors of Victoria and Ottawa, the people of the Slocan are working hard to preserve, and in some cases regain, the way of life they or their forebears sought in the first place. "If we can keep control in local hands and support local business, I think it's possible," says Winlaw's Kathy Hart. "I think it's possible."

The Griffiths children with chickens, Winlaw, 1996. The valley has always been a place where children could grow up with fresh air and adventure.

Fern Road in Appledale, 1995. It is this bucolic landscape that many people in the valley wish to preserve.

*"We must all give each other a hand up, to
exist for one more generation."*

— Marilyn James, Vallican

17

THE SLOCAN:
portrait of a valley

Tourism, pot, and forestry: these are probably three of the
most common dinner table topics in the Slocan Valley
these days. And all three represent both the challenges
and the opportunities that face the locals in the early 21st
century. Some things have changed profoundly, others not
at all. More than one hundred years ago Robert Anderson
wrote from his farm at Lemon Creek: "Americans are
flocking into the Dominion in thousands and what is
more are becoming British subjects." In response to what

may have been a query as to whether British Columbia might benefit from joining the United States, Anderson replied: "Canada is pretty well able to creep along by herself and when we need more Liberty then [sic] we have we will hardly ask Uncle Sam for it." If the American administration is taking notes – entirely possible, according to the conspiracy theorists who believe that the CIA has been stationed in the valley for decades – then it will have seen another large wave of Americans, as well as Canadians, embracing the Slocan's protection in the aftermath of September 11, 2001.

In 1975, a young American named Conrad Evans wrote in *The Arrow* newspaper: "In a month I will maybe be a Canadian. I will be a...never-let-on-where-you-came-from Canadian like so many. I will pretend. I have been pretending for these many long years already. [But] I would like...the right to admit to a history." Evans, like many of his compatriots, complained in *The Arrow* of the difficulty in finding jobs and acceptance in British Columbia. "I was grappling with my origins," says Evans now, "and the grief over what I had left behind. I felt like my country and family had been destroyed. But now I can look back and say Canada has been very good to me." In the twenty-eight years since becoming a Canadian citizen, Evans has found the acceptance he was looking for in 1975. Now living near Winlaw, he was a director of the Regional District of Central Kootenay for five years and was subsequently elected to the legislative assembly by the people of the Slocan in the Nelson-Creston riding. He represented them in Victoria for ten years – and even took a serious although unsuccessful run at becoming premier in 2000 – but lost his seat in the provincial election of 2001. Asked by *The Valley Voice* newspaper on June 12, 2003, whether he would consider running again, Evans replied cryptically: "You know, I'm a British Columbian. In British Columbia, life is politics." Questioned about the future of the valley, Evans responds: "The challenge in the Slocan is to come together on any particular vision of the future." There are too many divergent agendas in the valley, he believes. "Instead of sharing joy in each other's successes, we often react by thinking it's costing us. People need to learn to care about each other."

Respondents in a 2002 survey of the concerns of Slocan Valley residents conducted by the regional district illustrate the normal differences in opinion that occur in any community. "Wildlife protection" gets just one more vote as a priority than does the "elk problem." Government interference worries about half the number of voters that the concern with government cutbacks does. "Scrap the Agricultural Land Reserve" scrapes in right behind "preservation of rural community." Respondents identified the most important issue facing the community – by a considerable margin – as economic activity and employment. "Survey respondents," the report states diplomatically, however, "were divided on how they feel about the need for more industrial development or commercial services in their community." Indeed. In a valley where nearly two-thirds of the respondents also said that rural living was a key factor in choosing to live there – along with "natural beauty," "clean water and air," and "peace and quiet" – the ants' nest of commercial development and resource extraction industry is frequently stirred into exchanges of stinging rhetoric in the pages of *The Valley Voice* and at community meetings throughout the valley.

Surrounded by some of his trophies in his living room, hunter Bill Hicks, born and bred in Slocan, can't think of anywhere else he would rather live.

The marijuana industry gets only one mention in the report. Identified by a small number of residents as an issue requiring priority attention under the simple heading "Drugs," it is not something anyone in the Slocan wishes to dwell on, for a variety of reasons. The growers don't want the profile, and the valley's law-abiding citizens don't want it characterized disproportionately as a Mecca of the pot trade, which it isn't. Nevertheless, pot has grown – so to speak – into a much larger industry in recent years, and some fear and frustration has grown along with it. Hushed anecdotes circulate about new and unfriendly neighbours and about young people travelling through the airport with fistfuls of cash in their pockets. "They're not from here," the locals mutter. There is a distinct concern about "outsiders" coming in and bringing their harsher and harder habits. But Slocaners are right. It should not be given undue emphasis. It is simply yet another one of the challenges facing the Slocan Valley, where all the residents are struggling to find a proper economic balance in a rural way of life – a way of life that is increasingly under threat everywhere.

Many respondents in the survey wanted the regional district to encourage tourism, a distinct change from their opinions twelve years earlier. At that time, a Kootenay heritage tourism study commissioned by the provincial government found that among other reasons, the tourism industry was struggling because "Kootenay residents do not necessarily welcome an influx of visitors." But that observation may be less true now than the reality that locals simply have mixed feelings about it. Some are concerned about the impacts of tourism on watershed quality, and others worry that too many visitors will have a negative impact on the parks and the peace and quiet that they came for in the first place. Balancing economic benefits against the existing environmental status of the valley faces the same challenge for tourism in many respects as it does for the forestry industry. The Slocan is also still simply trying to work out how to put itself more solidly on the tourist map – even as I type, the Slocan Valley Economic Development Commission is helping fund the creation of a new marketing strategy for tourism and business in the valley via the Internet.

The valley has some distinct advantages over others in the Kootenays: it is closest to the coast, it is now accessible on major routes from four directions, and it is stunningly beautiful in a bucolic and tranquil fashion that other areas do not necessarily enjoy. While the Slocan has a long way to go before it is a Whistler or a Long Beach, with their built-in licences to print money and $500-a-night hotels, there is a concerted effort to attract more tourists into the area in a manner more consistent in fact with what residents want. The kind of development that has turned Whistler and Long Beach – and many Rocky Mountain towns like Fairmont Hot Springs – into condominium-and-golf-course tourist villages isn't necessarily what the Slocan is looking for. "Moderate prosperity and modest growth," says New Denver mayor Gary Wright, "is all we want. We don't want to see this beautiful place turned into some international resort."

Smaller operations are proving to have the successful formula for a place like the Slocan Valley as well as having the blessing of their neighbours, for the most part. A catskiing operation called Valhalla Powdercats started business in 2002 at the south end of the valley. People like Jane Leander of Arica Gardens in Appledale have come from places like Gabriola Island to set up new businesses and give the region a boost. Stuart MacCuaig and Tim Thickett of Lemon Creek have renovated the old Lemon Lookout fire tower and turned it into rental suites, renaming the tower the Skycastle Lookout. Saturday markets in most communities provide local artisans with the opportunity to sell their wares to the passers-by. Individual entrepreneurs shuttle hikers up to Idaho Peak, take them across Slocan Lake in boats to Valhalla Park, and tour sightseers around the Silvery Slocan loop.

Although a significant number of road trippers come through each summer, many of those who take advantage of Slocan venues are Slocaners themselves. Sophia Antoniuk doesn't worry too much about advertising her riverside bed-and-breakfast a few kilometres south of Winlaw. Many of her customers are locals. "Two years ago a couple from Winlaw came here for their annual vacation," she says. "They didn't need passports, they didn't have to fly or drive for ten hours, and they didn't have to worry about how their kids, ten kilometres away with their grandparents, were doing. They loved it." Slocaners are lucky, observes Kathy Hart. There is local support for businesses like the high-end, eclectic bookstore Jennie's Garden in Winlaw; art galleries do good business from one end of the valley to the other; and museums and community parks are tenderly maintained and used by volunteers. The events columns of the local newspapers are filled every month with festivals, shows, and exhibitions. The Vallican Whole enjoys a lively existence. Local artists and artisans are growing in number each year, producing fine furniture in their workshops, fine works of art in their studios, and organic beauty products from home-grown herbs, all for sale in the galleries and stores and co-ops from Playmor Junction to Hills. In Winlaw, world-class snow and ice sculptor Peter Vogelaar spends his summers designing his next models for international competitions. The village of Slocan entices drivers speeding past the turnoff on Highway 6 to take a detour and admire the Barry Coté murals of Slocan historic scenes painted on the village's public buildings and to have a bite to eat at the Herald Street Café. Volunteers on the "Rails to Trails" project are turning the old railbeds into walking and mountainbiking routes. Kayak and raft rentals are popular on the long hot summer days that the valley enjoys. Even Sandon sees more than five thousand people each year wander up into its ghostly canyons, says Sandon Historical Society president Lorna Obermayr.

Rumours of Sandon's death, says Obermayr, Twain-like, are exaggerated. The museum does good business, and the one small store, The Prospector's Pick, does a healthy trade selling pop and ice cream to hot, dusty walkers and books to armchair historians. The hamlet's population has increased, too. It now has five permanent residents. Store owner and author Veronika Pellowski has raised her two young children Catherine and Alexander in Sandon. Despite the hardships of weather and the danger of bears, she can't imagine a better place for them to be growing up. Six-year-old Alexander's idea of a good time is hiking the many kilometres up to see the old mine entrances, like the Altoona on the trail that follows the old Kaslo & Slocan Railway route. Catherine, only a few years older, already knows how to drive her parents' pickup truck, in case of an emergency.

But how long Sandon can last as a ghost town is a matter of strongly divided opinion. "There is a lot of conflict as to what to do," admits Obermayr. One developer wanted to build period-style summer homes, but there were strong objections from those who believe that Sandon should be preserved as a ghost town, with no modern embellishments. "The preservation of Sandon depends on the adoption and acceptance of an official community plan for a designated area to protect its historical integrity," states Ken Butler of New Denver firmly. But others, like Pellowski's husband Hal Wright – who has lived in Sandon off and on since he was fifteen years old – have dreams of it becoming once more a thriving community, this time based on mining the pockets of tourists. To that end, Wright has almost single-handedly kept Johnny Harris's old Silversmith Power plant in continuous operation – it now holds the record as being one of the oldest of its kind in North America – and has accumulated in Sandon historic memorabilia of all kinds, including old steam engines and rail carriages. More recently, Wright has acquired a collection of decommissioned trolley-buses. His intention is to have the old electric buses refurbished and sent to more suitable quarters; possibly even to be put back into use in cities like Vancouver. To his astonishment, however, Wright has been told by experts in London that this is the largest collection of its kind in the world. Visitors are flocking to see the buses; temporary interpretive signs have been put up on their windshields. New Denver mayor Gary Wright believes that the folks of Sandon must merge their common passion for the ghost town and the historic canyon in which it sits into a robust and sustainable vision for its future. For now, buses and mining memorabilia sit side by side in Sandon.

Mining's place in the valley, meanwhile, seems unlikely ever to reach even the post–World War Two levels it once enjoyed despite the optimism of some mining proponents. The Silvana Mine and Mill in Sandon, highly visible along the south bank of Carpenter Creek on the drive into the ghost town, have not operated since 1993 – although their ownership has changed hands frequently. According to the Ministry of Energy and Mines, however, there are plans for selective mining. "The Silvana could be invigorated at today's pricing," Pat Bell, the minister of state for mining, told *The Valley Voice* in the last week of March 2004. Bell also supports the reopening of the Willa Mine, near Silverton. In late 2003, when Orphan Boy Resources first announced its intention to reopen the Willa Mine, excited letters to the editor poured into *The Valley Voice*, both for and against: thirty new jobs in the valley versus environmental concerns, the usual suspects. On March 31, 2004, mine manager Steve

Silverton miner Frank Mills still defiantly at work, 1990s, on his claim near Silverton.

Phillips told *The Valley Voice* that exploratory drilling would be starting in the near future; its chances of success remained uncertain.

Meanwhile, further controversy was stirring around the proposed raising of the boxcars that had drowned in Slocan Lake at the beginning of the 20th century. Various attempts had been made to salvage the cars and their contents over the years. The former owner and operator of the tug *Iris G.*, Irvin Anderson, told *Canadian West* magazine in 1993 that he had been involved in locating barges for some of the unsuccessful attempts. According to Anderson, another attempt was made some time after 1975 – after he no longer worked on the lake – and several bars of metal were brought to the surface. The eighty-pound bars with the legend TADANAC stamped on them were taken to Trail to be assayed. "They were PURE LEAD!" Anderson told the magazine. "As one of the divers remarked in the bar of the Slocan Inn, 'it was a helluva leaddown!'" By spring 2004, another attempt was planned to raise the cars, with a view to having them displayed in public. Proponent Rick Tegeler thought the project would be of economic and historic value to the village of Silverton. But not everyone agreed that it should happen. "To raise one of the boxcars out of Slocan Lake is an irresponsible act of plundering one of the most unique historical underwater sites of the Kootenays," wrote Elisabeth von Ah and Michael Mardner of Lemon Creek to *The Valley Voice* on March 3, 2004. "The boxcar graveyard near Silverton takes us back to the great railroad days of this area in a very special way...On land, the boxcars would have rotted a long time ago."

Far to the south, in Trail, the Teck–Cominco smelter continued to do a thriving business. The company appears unfazed by looming legal action against it by the U.S. Environmental Protection Agency, which claimed the smelter is responsible for massive metal pollution of the Columbia River. In late 2003, the West Kootenay Power and Light Co. that Cominco had sold to UtiliCorp in 1987 changed hands again, this time being purchased by Newfoundland-based Fortis Inc. The Kootenay–Okanagan Electric Consumers Association (ECA) was watching the private utility company closely for rate rises, Donald Scarlett of Kaslo wrote to the newspaper, and the experience of West Kootenay consumers should serve as a warning of the disadvantages of privatization of power companies. "We're the canary in the coal mine," Scarlett quotes ECA president Bill Campbell as saying, "and we're not feeling all that good." Up in New Denver, on the other hand, even although preliminary approvals for a micro hydro plant on Enterprise Creek were obtained in 2003, the costs of proceeding mean plans were on hold.

Kootenay Canal Project at South Slocan, 1973. West Kootenay Power and Light in Rossland was one of the earliest producers of electric power in North America, and in its various incarnations it has remained one of the few privately owned utility companies in British Columbia.

The fortunes of Slocan Forest Products (SFP) remain a popular topic of conversation. Late in November 2003, logging giant Canfor Corporation bought the smaller company, making the mill owner at Slocan the second-largest forestry company in North America. The Slocan division has had to change the way it does things, says division manager Cam Milne; it specialized its products to carve a distinct niche in the market that make them worth buying, despite the expense of production. The Slocan Valley, says Milne, is an extremely difficult area to operate in from an economic standpoint. It isn't plantation logging, offering easy cutting; the terrain is steep and the cutblocks are smaller; and then there is what he refers to as the "social issues." Look up the hill above the golf course at Appledale, he says, and what you won't see is the company's cable-logging operation – a unique but very expensive selective-logging system aimed at minimizing visual impacts. Foresters in the 21st century, he believes, think more like artists than engineers in terms of "that portion of forest management that is most visible to all of us – harvesting." Compared with former days, when the forest was simply seen as a giant warehouse for trees and foresters concentrated their planning efforts on road building rather than visual impacts, says Milne, "the job of the forest manager today is to deal with many more of the issues of perception rather than just the technical issues of how to get the log from the forest to the mill in the most efficient manner...Foresters are much more sensitive to the visual aspects of how their activities affect the forest than they were in the old days. They have become engineers with an artistic bent."

On April 10, 2003, after a long shutdown, the first load in over eight months left the Slocan mill's yard. From left to right, Ralph Tomlin, Yev Maloff, Rob Gordon, Tim Yanni, Cam Milne, and unidentified driver.

Milne acknowledges that not everyone agrees with SFP's methods or his views. Although there is a diplomatically cordial dialogue between the Valhalla Society and SFP both sides, after all, have different agendas. Herb Hammond and his wife, Susan, continue to promote alternative forestry practices through their company, the Silva Foundation. The Kootenay

Centre for Forestry Alternatives in Nelson advocates "effective and enduring changes to forest management." In the village of Slocan, where the SFP mill is located, Canadian Women in Timber was founded in 1989. Its members support what they call "forest education." "Most of our members' families," states its literature, "are the first to experience the social and economic consequences of forest land use and harvest withdrawals. We have no use for actions and decisions motivated only by political correctness." Logging is not a topic most people in the Slocan are shy about saying how they feel. The mill at Slocan, says one resident, is a huge stumbling block to tourism at the south end of Slocan Lake. Others credit SFP for the jobs it has provided in the valley over some hard times, supporting close to five hundred employees and contractors. "The Valhalla Society is living twenty years in the past," sighs retired timberman Wayne Morrison of Silverton. "Things have moved on." SFP of course is by no means the only logging entity in the valley. In fact, many of the visible clearcuts in the valley have been undertaken by individuals on privately owned land, where the hand of government regulation lies a great deal more lightly. But it is forestry companies logging on crown lands that tend to attract the most criticism: "I have not admired the tree farming methods that have been performed in our public forests for the past fifty years and I strongly object to the sweeping changes that are being proposed by government as they only mean to damage our forests worse," wrote long-time Winlaw resident Frank Nixon to *The Valley Voice* on May 1, 2003. "I will fight clearcutting," says Silvertonian Colleen McCrory, "until I die."

In 1993, Eric Clough got into his car in Ontario with his cat and his plants and drove for three days to get back to Winlaw. "I got faster and faster as I got closer," he says. "I couldn't wait to get back home." Clough and Nancy Harris both live once again on Paradise Valley Road, now vastly changed from the days in which it was just "two sets of tracks with the bluff cambered the wrong way and no one living on the road except for us." From his acreage in Appledale, David Orcutt has observed many younger people moving into the valley again in recent years. "I am far more optimistic about the current generation," he says. "They are coming to change their lives for the better. They are here for the long haul." The octogenarian still has people coming to live on his land, and has many plans himself. He's in it for the long haul, too. But Casey and Toshi Obara have left the valley and retired to Victoria to be near their son Barry, who closed the circle by returning to his parents' birthplace of Vancouver Island to carry on a successful career as an accountant. The older Obaras still miss the Slocan terribly. "We never used to get sick there," says Casey. "We didn't have to worry about when we were going to see our friends. We knew we'd see them next trip to town."

J.B. Winlaw's grandson, Murray, also lives in Victoria, where he is a bank manager. Nobby Hayashi of New Denver is a minor movie star, appearing as an extra not only in *Hakujin* but also in the film *Snow Falling on Cedars*. In 1995, Ray Kosiancic finally decided retirement was his due. "The cultivation of the earth is the most important labour of man," wrote Kosiancic in a letter, but "I do not miss the old manure shovel, the pitchfork, milk cans, the dusty jute feed sacks, forty-five gallon gasoline and fuel barrels, or the heavy steel irrigation pipes and steel sprinklers." Kosiancic alternates his days between refurbishing his large collection of vintage vehicles ("He's not getting another one until he

"Nothing runs like a deer:" Ray Kosiancic at his home in Crescent Valley with one his favourite vehicles, 1982.

sells one of these," his wife Ida says adamantly), leading hikes up into the mountains, and paddling his kayak upriver on warm summer days. On breezy afternoons, Ray and Ida sit on the bluff above the oxbow bend in the river and gaze at the benevolent mountains, recalling the days when, below them on the riverbank, Ray's grandfather Jacob hand-shovelled enough dirt into place to make a railroad siding of his own.

In January 2003, the Doukhobor community led a large and vociferous rally in Castlegar to protest the Iraq war. They were joined by hundreds of their non-Doukhobor friends and neighbours. Prayers were said, songs were sung. It did not seem to occur to the authorities to be at all concerned. At the Doukhobor Museum at Ootischenia, across the road from the Castlegar airport, "professional Doukhobor" Larry Ewashen presides calmly over his small domain and ensures that the grass is kept bright and trim around the neat buildings, the flowers are thick and heavy with moisture, and the cats that sleep in the sunshine are well fed. Inside the museum, the tattered remnants of the clothes that Peter Lordly Verigin was wearing when he died in the train explosion of 1924 have been carefully laundered and displayed inside a glass case. The Sons of Freedom burnt the museum once, says Ewashen, because they believed it implied that Doukhoborism was dead. "Now people don't worry about all that anymore." In a speech given in Brilliant on January 12, 2003, current USCC director John "J.J." Verigin said: "We have the process of reconciliation happening within our Doukhobor family...because nobody, not the people in the Kootenays who are members of the USCC, not the people who were maybe former Sons of Freedom, or possibly call themselves that way still...we aren't trying to make people more like us and we aren't becoming more like them. No. We have begun to respect each other brother to brother and sister to sister, just as we are."

In May every year, a festival is held in the Brilliant Cultural Centre. Men in suits sit soberly at the sides of the large room speaking Russian to each other. Women in embroidered white headscarves, high heels, and a rainbow of silk and taffeta collect in the pews like a flock of tropical birds. The singing is fluid and strong and calming. "It is not just the future of the Doukhobors," said J.J. Verigin in May 2003, "but the future of the planet we need to pay attention to." But most of the people in the room are white-haired – the young folk can be counted on the fingers of one hand. "Coming from a Sons of Freedom background doesn't mean anything to me now," says a twenty-year-old from Krestova. "I'm not a hard-line Doukhobor," said Carey Voykin, who spoke at the 2003 festival about responsibility and the future. "I'm not even Christian. I *am* spiritual." But J.J. Verigin is optimistic about the future of the USCC all the same. "When I was young I was the same," says the kindly and gentle Robin Williams look-alike. "I was disconnected, disaffected. You can't force people to accept the wisdom of their heritage, it has to come naturally. The alarm clock will go off when they get older and realize they need to be involved." Fred Makortoff of South Slocan is blunter. "There has to be a recapturing of the imagination, of our spirituality. That's what gives life to everything we do, and the kids don't have a sense of that. There's no time for internal reflection. Actually," he adds, "that's what everyone in the valley needs to do." Verigin agrees. The future, he believes, is a matter less of following strong individuals than of taking personal responsibility. "It will not be a quick transition from following a charismatic leader to becoming a community that takes responsibility for itself, however," he says. "But that's something we are working towards."

In Vallican, Robert Watt continues to live on the provincial crown-designated heritage site that contains the bones of his ancestors. "Plans for the Vallican site," advises the Heritage branch of the government, "have not yet been made." Nothing further is forthcoming, understandably. Watt says government officials haven't been in touch in a long time. He just keeps looking after the place, "making sure no one's doing anything wrong." Twice a year the Sinixt invite the public to the site, hosting them to a Thanksgiving dinner to share their food and stories and give small gifts. "The giveaways at our events are so people will think about us and our struggles and wish us well," says Marilyn James. "By doing so they lighten our burden." Things remain difficult between the Sinixt and the Ktunaxa. "I used to be friends with Wilfred

Marilyn James visiting the southern part of Sinixt's traditional territory to dig for camas roots, a traditional food source, April 2002.

Paddling on Kootenay Lake during Ktunaxa annual traditional territory trek, summer 2002.

Contemporary Ktunaxa campsite, west arm of Kootenay Lake, 2002.

Ktunaxa treaty negotiator Cheryl Casimer and federal government negotiator Ken Warren at a treaty meeting at Harrop/Procter on the west arm of Kootenay Lake held during the Ktunaxa annual traditional territory trek, summer 2002.

Jacobs, [from Creston]," says Watt regretfully. "It's not so good now, because of the land claims." The Ktunaxa have a complicated time ahead of them, deciding upon an approach to take on the issue in treaty negotiations. They are painfully aware of the views of the Sinixt, but emphatic that the Ktunaxa, too, have a place in the Slocan. Regardless of the Vallican site itself, they remain determined that the valley is a place that is not only in their heritage, but in their hearts – and that it is also in their future.

In 2001, the Colville Confederated Tribes (CCT) in Washington state purchased the privately owned property directly north of the Vallican site on behalf of the Sinixt. The CCT, says James, is an artificially created body intended to support its member tribes. "There is no such thing as a Colville Indian," she states firmly. In the absence of a recognised Sinixt legal entity in Canada, however, it is easier for the CCT to undertake some activities on its behalf. The CCT, says Councillor Deb Louie, intends to support the work of the Sinixt in Vallican and bought the property to ensure that Robert Watt would have a place to live at the site. The confederation's Vancouver lawyer, Stuart Rush, says that the primary concern of the CCT right now is to make sure that its members are not impeded by government in conducting their cross-border activities. The courts, he says, have not yet put their minds to the issue. But they will be required to, before the issue is settled.

In the meantime, things with their non-aboriginal neighbours seem to be going well for the Sinixt. "I get along good with a lot of them," says Watt. "No problems there." The Sinixt and the Doukhobors are working on resolving any outstanding bitterness left by the 1912 purchase of Baptiste Christian's home. On National Aboriginal Day in 2003, the Sinixt, the Castlegar Doukhobor community, and Selkirk College collaborated to dedicate the Mir Peace Centre on the college's campus in Castlegar. "Nobody can give the perspective about the Sinixt that a Sinixt can give," says Marilyn James. "But the only way to begin the process of understanding my people and our place in this landscape," she wrote in *A Confluence of Cultures* with author Eileen Pearkes, "is to engage in the dialogue."

Just outside Winlaw, on the left-hand side of the highway heading south to Playmor Junction, is a small law office and a log barn with the roof missing. It is the old Avis place, and the roof has been missing for decades. One night around 1962, Red Sutherland and his buddy Axel Erickson were driving trucks and decided to stop at Slocan to warm up. "There was a fair bit of liquor in that coffee, I have to admit," recalls Sutherland. "But that's what you did in those days." Erickson, driving a half-ton, was heading to the Avis place and didn't think he could find it in the dark. Sutherland, driving a truck with a D-8 cat blade on the back, said he would go ahead and flash his lights when they came to it. But the old Avis place is also on a tight bend. When Sutherland flashed his lights, Erickson didn't see the turn and kept going into the ditch. Sutherland didn't notice immediately – he had spotted the lights on and decided to pull in and socialize for a while. "Around midnight, old Erickson came in all covered in dirt and grass and mad as hell because no one had come to find him," Sutherland cackles. "But we were all having way too good a time to bother."

Sutherland then decided he should really head home. Turning his truck around in the dark, the D-8 blade took the roof off the barn in one clean sweep. Sutherland didn't notice a thing. Bob Avis, he says, could never bear to fix the roof – it made him laugh too hard every time he looked at it.

"Hope," said Robert Anderson at Lemon Creek back in 1902, "is not a good thing to live on, although it is good to live on in hope." Long may the people of the Slocan Valley live on with their memories, and in hope.

Bonnington Falls, before the Kootenay River was dammed for hydro-electricity generation at the turn of the twentieth century.

"One remarkable thing about this country is the volume of its rivers. Here for instance is the Slocan River flowing from the Slocan Lake which is an extention of the Arrow Lakes which are the extention of some others and really all of them only one long wide river. The Slocan flows on into the Kootenay River and when you look at the Kootenay there is no perceptible difference in size from the Slocan. It has swallowed the Slocan up without any apparent increase in its size. Then the Kootenay in turn empties into the Columbia and hastens away through Washington to the Sea and still you would not know to look at it that it was bigger than the streams that have lost themselves in its own waters."

— Robert Thompson Anderson, Lemon Creek, February 9, 1903

Photography Credits

ABBREVIATIONS

AN: Anonymous
BCA: British Columbia Archives
BSC: Barbara Sutherland Coghlan
CTO: Casey & Toshi Masuda Obara
ESB: Edna Swanson Brown
FEM: Frank and Effie Mills
HF: Hicks Family
KCH: Katherine Clay Hutton
MBL: Mabel Lawrenow Kabatoff & Bill
  Lawrenow
MLK: Mabel Lawrenow Kabatoff
MPK: Mabel Lawrenow Kabatoff and Peter
  Kabatoff
MS: Marion Smedbol

NMU: Nelson Museum and Archives
QG: Quinton Gordon
RDT: Robert D. Turner
RIK: Ray and Ida Kosiancic
SCA: Selkirk College Archives
SF: Sutherland family
SFU: Simon Fraser University Library
SG: Sheila Griffiths
SHS: Silverton Historical Society
SL: Sally Lamare
SMT: Sono Mukai Tully
SSHS: Silvery Slocan Historical Society

COVER
Front: QG
Back (top to bottom): NMU; KCH; MBL; KCH;
SSHS; Bert Learmonth; Nappy Lamare; RDT.

FRONT MATTER
Title Page: AN / 4: QG / 9: QG.

CHAPTER ONE
Page 13: AN / 16: Katherine Gordon.

CHAPTER THREE
Page 33: NMU-61533 / 44: SHS, BCA C-02831.

CHAPTER FOUR
Page 47: SHS-BCA C-07157 / 52-53: BCA I-
60928 / 56: SCA / 57: FEM / 58: SCA / 59:
SHS-BCA B-06828 / 61: SHS, BCA B-07210.

CHAPTER FIVE
Page 63: BCA B-09507 / 70-71: BCA G-09489.

CHAPTER SIX
Page 73: SHS / 77: FEM / 83: SCA /
84: SHS / 85: SHS / 86: BCA A-00674 / 88:
NMU 793

CHAPTER SEVEN
Page 92: both, RIK / 93: both, RIK / 95: top
left, SCA; top right, NMU 68333; bottom left,
BCA C-09797; bottom right, BCA C-09798 /
96: NMU 37 / 99: all, KCH / 102: SHS / 103:
SSHS / 104: KCH / 105: both, Collis family /
106-107: SF / 108-109 all, KCH.

CHAPTER EIGHT
Page 111: NMU 68312 / 113: NMU 68311 / 115:
NMU 683110.

CHAPTER NINE
Page 131: SFU / 135: MBL / 136: SCA / 137: MBL /
138: MBL.

CHAPTER TEN
Page 145: SFU / 146: MBL / 147: SFU / 150:
MBL.

CHAPTER ELEVEN
Page 153: KCH / 154: both, KBL / 155: top, KCH;
bottom left, SF; bottom right, MS / 157: both,
MS / 158: HF, SF / 159: HF / 161: FEM / 162:
both, SCA / 163: top, SSHS; bottom, HF / 164-
167: all, KCH / 169: all, RIK / 172: top, KCH;
bottom, BCA C-03976 / 173: top, SF, Bert
Learmonth; bottom left, FEM; bottom right,

KCH / 174-175: all, ESB / 176: SG / 177: top, MS;
bottom, FEM.

CHAPTER TWELVE
Page 179: SSHS / 182: BCA C-07293 / 185-187
all, CTO / 188: SSHS / 189: CTO / 190: SSHS / 191:
SMT / 192 : SF / 193: SCA / 194: top, SMT;
bottom, CTO / 197-198: both, CTO / 199: SCA.

CHAPTER THIRTEEN
Page 201: Jack Edson / 202: Village of New
Denver / 203: SF / 204: SF / 205: left, HF; right,
MS / 206: left, SCA; right, Bill and Rita Hicks /
207: KCH / 208: MS / 209: top left, HF; top
right, SF; bottom, SF / 210: FEM / 211: BCA I-
27314 / 212: both, RIK / 213: top, MLK; bottom,
MPK / 214: top, RIK; bottom, SF / 215: top, SF;
bottom, Bert Learmonth / 216: Jack Edson /
217: RIK.

CHAPTER FOURTEEN
Page 227: MS / 230: BCA C-01724 / 231: BCA C-
01740 / 233: BCA C-06152 / 235: MLK.

CHAPTER FIFTEEN
Page 237: all, AN / 239: Nappy Lamare / 242-
243: Eric Clough / 244: Nancy Harris/Misha
Perkes photographer / 245: Rosalinde
Compton / 246: AN / 247: Nancy Harris / 248:
both, SL / 249: top left, Nappy Lamare; top
right, SL; bottom, Rosalinde Compton / 250:
left, SF; right, BSC / 251: KCH / 252: top, SL;
bottom, RDT / 253: top, SG; bottom, SL.

CHAPTER SIXTEEN
Page 256-257: all, RDT / 261: all, SCA / 263: QG /
264: SG / 269: CTO / 273: both, SG.

CHAPTER SEVENTEEN
Page 276: BSC / 281: FEM / 282: SCA / 283: Tom
Gilgan / 285: RIK / 287: Marilyn James / 288:
all, Ktunaxa Nation (Bev Hills) / 291: West
Kootenay Power and Light, photo archives.

END MATTER
Page 294: clockwise from top left, Nancy
Harris; SCA; MBL; MBL; SSHS / 295: SF / 296:
SSHS / 297: FEM.

PORTRAIT OF A VALLEY
Pages 305-319: all, QG.

AUTHOR PHOTO
Page 320: QG.

FAMILY HISTORIES

A striking experience in undertaking the research for this book has been my discovery of the many significant family records, photographs, and documents that were lying neglected or forgotten in the Slocan – in shoeboxes, old suitcases, envelopes, and plastic bags, gathering dust in basements and attics. This is completely at odds with the level of importance that people living and working in the Slocan Valley today attach to their forebears. The few existing local histories carefully record the names, places, and people directly linked to the narrator; memories and quotations fill the pages; and older Slocan residents can recall individuals and recite their exploits in cherished detail. This is true of all sectors and groups, from miners to Doukhobors, aboriginal people to Japanese Canadians, loggers to hippies. Many of them are one and the same people. With few exceptions, I found, it is less the "big picture" historical context of the area – interesting and relevant though it may be – than the individual and family stories that grasp and hold the attention of the locals. Without them, after all, there would be no history of the Slocan Valley to tell.

And yet there is also a corresponding sadness linked to the memories

and an acknowledgement that with the passing of the old folk, many of the family stories will be lost forever. This book will not change that, but I hope it has helped a little. In the course of many interviews, it was very rewarding to watch the faces of sons and daughters as their parent or grandparent identified long-gone relatives and friends in timeworn black and white images that had not been looked at, in some cases, for fifty years. Formerly unimportant photographs took on newfound significance, and names and dates were carefully recorded for posterity.

As a researcher, I was pleased that the records would survive. As a human being, I was heartwarmed by the pleasure generated at the sharing of memories within families. It motivated me to start recording my own family names and dates before it is too late, working mostly with my father's photographs, and to experience that pleasure for myself. When I see a photograph of my grandparents with a king and queen, of my great-aunt in front of a heritage building, or the construction of a massive and famous bridge being observed by my grandfather, it helps me understand not only my own story better, but also history in general.

Upon which note, I urge readers to check their own closets and basements for dusty shoeboxes and record the names, dates, and events you discover. If you are uncertain where to store historical records, local archives and museums will rarely turn away such treasure. Future historians will thank you for such a legacy. But I suspect the satisfaction you will gain from the exercise will be its own – and best – reward.

This image shows Frank Mills and Bill McEwan at the Galena Farm Mine, but is undated. Maintaining family records is essential to the work of historians.

SOURCES

The hardest part about writing a book of this nature is what has to be left out. For every story told, there are one hundred more. Every person interviewed can suggest ten more people to speak to. Entire books could be written – and some have been – covering every subject, every community, and sometimes even individual people. The question I had to consider was not "Is there enough material?" so much as "Where on earth do I start – and even more importantly, stop?" There is a wealth of detailed information, reports, family histories, anecdotes, community histories, Ph.D. theses; personal, corporate, government, and non-governmental organization Web sites; academic histories, textbooks, manuscripts, government records, and other material available. It would be possible, I believe, to spend a lifetime researching the Slocan Valley region and never get around to writing the book itself. There are, of course, as many books to write about the Slocan as there are subject matters to research.

A bibliography listing all the available resources would be almost as long as the book itself. Here instead is a selection of the books and other materials that I enjoyed and found useful during my research, including a number of general resources that helped set the context for this book. Although it is not a complete list, it provides an excellent start for those interested in finding out more about the subjects discussed in this book. I have also included a number of Web sites. Although it has its limitations, this marvellous tool of the 21st century allows armchair historians and travellers to gain access to information and images of which they would never have dreamed even twenty years ago.

Apart from noting the quoted sources, I also acknowledge those local and regional professional and non-professional historians, past and present, paid and volunteer, whose work is invaluable in piecing together stories like this one. The risk of naming anyone in particular is the unintentional omission of others; but with respect to this book, I include among their number First Nations elders and representatives, museum curators and archivists, journalists, students, academic historians, family historians, and everyone who has kept and cared for their family records. A number of people have recorded their memories over the years in a variety of publications, and I have included a selection of them here. Finally, among the unsung heroes of history and research are the civil servants – especially provincial ones – as well as local government officials who have, over the years, compiled and made accessible innumerable pages of government records. Far from being dry and boring, these documents are often as vivid and fascinating as the people who created them.

General

Akrigg, G.P.V., and Helen B. Akrigg. *British Columbia Chronicle 1778–1846, Adventurers by Sea and Land*. Vancouver: Discovery Press, 1975.

Akrigg, G.P.V., and Helen B. Akrigg. *British Columbia Chronicle 1847–1871, Gold and Colonists*. Vancouver: Discovery Press, 1977.

Bowering, George. *Bowering's BC: A Swashbuckling History*. Toronto: Viking Books, 1996.

Cail, Robert E. Land, Man, and the Law: the Disposal of Crown Lands in British Columbia, 1871–1913. Vancouver, UBC Press, 1974.

Cannings, Richard, and Sydney Cannings. *British Columbia: A Natural History*. Vancouver: Greystone Books, 1996.

Coull, Cheryl. *A Traveller's Guide to Aboriginal BC*. Vancouver: Whitecap Books, 1996.

Gough, Barry. "The Character of the British Columbia Frontier." *BC Studies* 32, 1976–1977.

Johnston, Hugh J.M. ed. *The Pacific Province: A History of British Columbia*. Vancouver: Douglas & McIntyre, 1996.

Ormsby, Margaret A. *British Columbia: A History*. [Toronto]: Macmillan, 1959.

Robin, Martin. *The Rush for Spoils: The Company Province 1871–1933*. Toronto: McClelland & Stewart, 1972.

Taylor, G.W. *Builders of British Columbia: An Industrial History*. Victoria: Morriss Publishing, 1982.

Woodcock, George. *British Columbia: A History of the Province*. Vancouver: Douglas & McIntyre, 1990.

First Nations

Bell, Joy F. 1977. *The Pictographs of Slocan Lake*. Fourth Biennial International Conference. CRARA. Heritage Record No. 8, Royal British Columbia Museum, Victoria.

Boas, Franz, and James Teit. *Couer d'Alene, Flathead and Okanogan Indians*. Fairfield, WA: Ye Galleon Press, 1985.

Bouchard, Randy, and Dorothy Kennedy. *Lakes Indian Ethnography and History*. Report prepared for BC Heritage Conservation Branch, Victoria, 1985.

James, Marilyn, and E.D. Pearkes. *A Confluence of Cultures: Integrating Indigenous and Settler Perspectives in the Columbia Basin*. Nelson, BC: Heyu Publications, 2000.

Keefer, Michael, and Peter McCoy. *All Living Things: A Ktunaxa Ethnobotany Handbook, Part One*. Cranbrook, BC: Ktunaxa/Kinbasket Tribal Council, 1999.

Ktunaxa Legends. Compiled and translated by Kootenai Culture Committee, Confederated Salish and Kootenai Tribes. Pablo, MT: Salish Kootenai College Press, 1997.

Mohs, Gordon. *Archaeological Investigations at the Vallican Site (DjQj1) Slocan Valley, Southeastern British Columbia*. Victoria: Government of British Columbia, 1982.

Pearkes, Eileen Delehanty. *The Geography of Memory*. Nelson, BC: Kutenai House Press, 2002.

Pryce, Paula. *Keeping the Lakes Way*. Toronto: University of Toronto Press, 1999.
Select Standing Committee on Aboriginal Affairs: Various transcripts of proceedings (Hansard).

DOUKHOBORS

Facts About "Operation Snatch": Personal Recordings of Doukhobor Mothers Whose Children Were Taken Away. Selkirk College Archives, Castlegar.
Righting the Wrong: The Confinement of the Sons of Freedom Doukhobor Children. Public Report No. 38 of the BC Ombudsman, April 1999 (and Progress Report No. 43, March 2002).
Maloff, Marjorie, and Ogloff, P. *Toil and Peaceful Life: A Portrait of the Doukhobors*. Sound Heritage, Vol. VI, No. 4. Victoria: Provincial Archives, 1977.
Mealing, Mark. *Our People's Way*. Ann Arbor, MI: University Microfilms International, 1985.
O'Neail, Hazel. *Doukhobor Daze*. Surrey, BC: Heritage House Publishing, 1994.
Tarasoff, Koozma J. *Plakun Trava: The Doukhobors*. Self-published, 1982.
Tarasoff, Koozma J., and Larry A. Ewashen. *In Search of Utopia: The Doukhobors*. Spirit Wrestlers Associates, 1994.
Woodcock, George, and Ivan Avakumovic. *The Doukhobors*. Toronto: McClelland & Stewart, 1977.
Yerbury, J.C. "The Sons of Freedom Doukhobors and the Canadian State." *Canadian Ethnic Studies* 16(2) (1984) 47–70.

JAPANESE CANADIANS

Adachi, Ken. *The Enemy That Never Was: A History of the Japanese Canadians*. Toronto: McClelland & Stewart, 1987; rev. ed. 1991.
Broadfoot, Barry. *Years of Sorrow, Years of Shame: The Story of the Japanese Canadians in World War Two*. Toronto: Doubleday Canada, 1977.
Granatstein, J.L. "The Enemy Within?" *Saturday Night* Magazine, November 1986.
Medical Aspects of Evacuation Days 1942–1946 (New Denver–Slocan). New Denver, BC: J & G Brighton.
Kogawa, Joy. *Obasan*. Toronto, ON: Lester & Orpen Dennys, 1981. (Novel).
Miki, Roy, and Kobayashi, Cassandra. *Justice In Our Time: The Japanese Canadian Redress Settlement*. Vancouver and Winnipeg: Talonbooks and NAJC, 1991.
Suttie, Gwen. *With the Nisei in New Denver*. Self-published, 1983.
Takashima, Shizuye. A Child in Prison Camp. Montreal: Tundra Books, 1971. (Fiction).
Ward, W. Peter. "British Columbia and the Japanese Evacuation." *Canadian Historical Review* 57 (3) (September 1976).

AGRICULTURE, INDUSTRY AND TRANSPORT

A Statutory History of the Steam and Electric Railways of Canada 1836-1937. Ottawa: Department of Transport, 1938.
Bealby, J.T. *Fruit Ranching In British Columbia*. London: Adam & Charles Black, 1909.
Doeksen, Corwin, and Gerry Doeksen. *Railways of the West Kootenay, Part 1*. Montrose, BC, self-published, 1991.
Grams, Brian W., and Donald M. Bain. *Greyhound Canada: Its History and Coaches*. Calgary: Kishorn Publications, 2001.
Harris, R. Cole. "Industry and the Good Life Around Idaho Peak." *Canadian Historical Review*, LXVI, 3 (1985).

Hedley, M.S. *Geology and Ore Deposits of the Sandon Area, Slocan Mining Camp, British Columbia*. Victoria: Queen's Printer, 1952.

Lang, Joan. *Lost Orchards: Vanishing Fruit Farms of the West Kootenays*. Self-published, 2003.

Learmonth, Bert. *From the Beginning: Kootenay Bus Transportation*. Nelson, BC: unpublished.

Melnychuk, D. *Agriculture Strategy for Ootischenia Area, 1984*. Victoria: Government of BC.

Mouat, Jeremy. *The Business of Power: Hydro-electricity in Southeastern British Columbia 1897–1997*. Victoria: Sono Nis Press, 1997.

Ormsby, Margaret. "Agricultural Development in British Columbia." *Agricultural History* 19 (1945).

Russ, Joel, ed. *A Life in the Woods: Oral Histories from the West Kootenay Forest*. Vols. 1 and 2. Nelson, BC: Kootenay Museum Association & Historical Society, 1994.

Sherrod, Anne, Wayne McCrory, and Craig Pettit (Valhalla Society Research Committee). *The Conflict between Mining and the Environment: Myths and Realities*. New Denver, BC: self-published, 1984.

Slocan Valley Planning Program Agricultural Resource Study: Technical Report. Government of British Columbia, 1981.

Taylor, Geoffrey W. *Mining: The History of Mining in BC*. Saanichton: Hancock House, 1978.

Taylor, Geoffrey W. *The Railway Contractors*. Victoria: Morriss Publishing, 1988.

The West Kootenay–Boundary Land-Use Plan. Victoria: Government of British Columbia, 1995.

Turner, Robert D. *Sternwheelers and Steam Tugs*. Victoria: Sono Nis Press, 1998.

Turner, Robert D. *West of the Great Divide: The Canadian Pacific Railway in British Columbia, 1880–1986*. Victoria: Sono Nis Press, 1987.

Turner, Robert D., and David S. Wilkie. *The Skyline Limited*. Victoria: Sono Nis Press, 1994.

PIONEER/COMMUNITY

Affleck, E.L. *Kootenay Lake Chronicles*. Vancouver: Alexander Nicolls Press, 1978.

Anderson, Louise A. *Slocan City Legacy*. Self-published, 1992.

Appleton, Frank. "Where Have All the Communes Gone?" *Harrowsmith* magazine, 1979.

Barlee, N.L. *West Kootenay: Ghost Town Country*. Canada West Publications, 1984.

Basque, Garnet. *West Kootenay: The Pioneer Years*. Surrey, BC: Heritage House, 1996.

Brighton, J., and G. Brighton. *New Denver's Frontier Doctor*. New Denver, BC: Self-published.

Church, John Spencer, and E.L. Affleck, eds. *A Young Scotsman's Adventures in Canada: The Letters of John Adam Watson*. Vancouver: Alexander Nicholls Press, 2002.

Coghlan, Barbara. *Slocan City Then and Now*. Unpublished. Whiterock, BC: 1995.

Cooper, Phyllis. *My Dad (The Family of Walter and Ada Clough)*. Slocan, BC: Self-Published, 1976.

Graham, Clara. *Kootenay Mosaic*. Vancouver: Evergreen Press, 1971.

Graham, Clara, Ed Picard, and Angus Davis. *Kootenay Yesterdays*. Vancouver: Alexander Nicolls Press, 1976.

Hodgson, Maurice. *The Squire of Kootenay West*. Saanichton, BC: Hancock House Publishers Ltd., 1976.

Kostash, Myrna. *Long Way From Home: The Story of the Sixties Generation in Canada*. Toronto: James Lorimer, 1980.

Nesteroff, Greg. Various unpublished articles re Slocan characters.

Norris, John. *Old Silverton*. Silverton, BC: Silverton Historical Society, 1985.

Pellowski, Veronica. *Silver, Lead & Hell*. Sandon, BC: Prospectors' Pick Publishing, 1992.

Petersen, Eugene. *Window in the Rock*. Fairfield, WA: Ye Galleon Press, 1993.

St. Denis, Denis. *My Recollections of Slocan City, BC, 1903 to 1911*. Unpublished, 1958.

Stevinson, Jean. *Old Pards*. Victoria: I. Cooper, 1988.

Swanson, Yvette. *A Look in the Past*. Winlaw, BC: Pigweed Press Ltd., 1983.

Turnbull, Elsie G. *Ghost Towns and Drowned Towns of West Kootenay*. Surrey, BC: Heritage House, 1988.

MISCELLANEOUS

Arrow Lakes Historical Society. Various publications regarding Nakusp and Arrow Lakes, 1989–2003.
Blake, Don. *The Valley of the Ghosts.* Kelowna: Sandhill Publishing, 1988.
Cooper, Innes. *The Valhalla Mountains.* Unpublished, 1996.
Farrar, K. Ed. *Castlegar: A Confluence.* Castlegar: Castlegar & District Heritage Society, 2000.
Kootenay Conference on Forestry Alternatives. *Forest Tenure Reform: A Path to Community Prosperity?* Assorted papers, 1999.
Kootenay Journal. *Kootenay Journal.* Winlaw, BC: Polestar Press, 1988.
McLeod, Murdoch. *Verse and Stories Through the Slocan, Arrowhead & Nelson, British Columbia.* Self-published, 1994.
Morley, Eldridge. *The Heritage Resources of the Slocan Valley: An Inventory and Evaluation.* Victoria: Government of British Columbia, 1981.
Nesteroff, Greg. *The Mayors of Slocan.* Slocan City, BC: Self-published, 2001.
Paterson, Thomas William. "Slocan Lake's Lost Silver Bullion." *History of the Canadian West,* August 1983.
Phillips, Paul. "The Underground Economy: The Mining Frontier to 1920." In *Workers, Capital and the State in British Columbia: Selected Papers,* Patricia E., Rennie Roy, eds.
Slocan City Centennial Cookbook, 1901–2001. Unpublished. Compiled by The Royal Canadian Legion, Slocan Valley Branch, Slocan. Historical introduction compiled by Karna Franche.
Norris, John. *Strangers Entertained: A History of the Ethnic Groups of British Columbia.* Vancouver: Evergreen Press, 1971.
Smyth, Fred J. *Tales of the Kootenays.* Vancouver: J.J. Douglas, 1977.
Woods, G. *Slocan Valley Wildlife: Technical Report.* Government of British Columbia, 1981.
Wright, Gary, R. Ochsendorf, and P. Menton. *Recipes & Rapscallions: Culinary and Other Secrets from the Apple Tree Sandwich Shop.* New Denver, BC: Twa Corbies Publishing, 1998.

GENERAL SOURCES

- *BC Historical News*
- *BC Mining Record*
- Newspapers (archival records)
- *Valley Voice* newspaper, New Denver – an invaluable and excellent publication!
- www.bccommunitynews.com

USEFUL AND INTERESTING WEB SITES

Archives and Historical Societies

Arrow Lakes Historical Society: www.geocities.com/alhistoricalsociety
BC Archives: www.bcarchives.gov.bc.ca
Fort Steele: www.fortsteele.bc.ca
Kootenay Gallery of Art, History and Science: www.castlegar.com/gallery
Kootenay Heritage: www.valleyoftheghosts.ca/heritage
Kootenay Lake Historical Society: www.kin.bc.ca and www.klhs.bc.ca
Museum of Civilization: www.civilization.ca
Nelson Museum: http://museum.kics.bc.ca/Museum
Sandon Historical Society: http://stats.slocanlake.com/sandon
Selkirk College Archives: www.selkirk.bc.ca
Silvery Slocan: www.kootenay.org/silverslocan
Silvery Slocan Museum: www.newdenver.ca/museum

Silverton Historical Society: www.slocanlake.com/silverton
Slocan History: http://selkirk.bc.ca
Slocan Lake history: www.slocanlake.com/heritage
West Kootenay mining history: www.mining.kootenays.bc.ca

Communities

Kootenay Resources: http://kootan.org and www.slocanlake.com/
Maps: www.kootnet.com/maps
www.slocanvalley.com
West Kootenay Regional Arts Council: http://wkarts.kics.bc.ca (arts)

Doukhobors

http://users.accesscomm.ca/doukhobor.genealogy
http://www.igs.net/~koozmataras
www.civilization.ca/cultur/doukhobors
www.doukhobor-homepage.com
www.kootenay.org/doukhobor

First Nations

Aboriginal historical and contemporary resources:
http://victoria.tc.ca/Resources/bchistory-disciplines-1stnations.html
Colville Confederated Tribes: www.colvilletribes.com
Ktunaxa: www.ktunaxa.org, www.kktc.bc.ca and http://photohunter.tripod.com
Selkirk College Archives: www.selkirk.bc.ca; www.bchistory.ca
Sinixt: http://sinixt.kics.bc.ca

Forestry

Kootenay Centre for Forestry Alternatives: www.kcfa.bc.ca
Slocan Forestry: www.slocan.com/forestry
Slocan Valley Watershed Archive: www.watertalk.org/svwa/

Japanese Canadians

Japanese Canadian National Museum: www.jcnm.ca
National Association of Japanese Canadians: www.najc.ca
www.japanesecanadianhistory.net

Miscellaneous

Cominco: www.teckcominco.com
Living Landscapes Project: www.livingbasin.com (Columbia Basin history resources)

Parks and Recreation

Kokanee Glacier Park: www.kokanee-glacier.com
Slocan Valley Heritage Trail Society: www.slocan-valley.org

Provincial Government

Kootenay Region Fisheries: http://wlapwww.gov.bc.ca
Ministry of Energy and Mines: www.em.gov.bc.ca
Ministry of Forests: www.for.gov.bc.ca
Provincial Parks: http://wlapwww.gov.bc.ca/bcparks
Sustainable Resource Management, Archaeological Branch: srmwww.gov.bc.ca

portrait of a valley

Marilyn James is the public face of the Sinixt people in the 21st century and an emphatic advocate of their rights to be recognized in the Slocan and elsewhere. Here at the Mir Centre at Selkirk College's Castlegar campus in 2003, James describes the building of the firepit through the placement of stones by friends and visitors.

Facing page, above: Larry Ewashen, author, filmmaker, and curator of the Doukhobor Museum, in the area once known as Ootischenia and now dominated by the highway and the Castlegar airport.

Facing page, below: Krestova, 2003.

Darcy Barisoff (left) and Ryan Verigin, both of Winlaw, working summer shift at the tombs of the Verigins, 2003. The original tomb was made of black marble; after it was destroyed in protest actions, the tomb was rebuilt in white cement.

Facing page, above: Alexander and Catherine Wright in 2003. They have a unique claim to fame: they were both born and bred in Sandon and have lived there their entire lives.

Facing page, below: Sandon, 2003.

Little remains to be seen of any of the original graves in the Sandon cemetery.

The trails surrounding Sandon are pockmarked with the entrances of disused old mines, like this one at Altoona on the old Kaslo & Slocan Railway track.

New Denver's colourful markets, quaint atmosphere, and beautiful setting now draw crowds of tourists each summer, in place of the hopeful prospectors and entrepreneurs that flooded into the area in their thousands in 1891, hoping to make a fortune from silver.

The former Bank of Montreal building in New Denver now houses the museum.

Nobuyoshi "Nobby" Hayashi was interned in the New Denver camp. His family stayed in New Denver after the war. To earn money, Hayashi became a semi-pro baseball player. He is now a guide at the Nikkei Memorial Internment Centre.

L.B. "Red" Sutherland on his old family farm at Winlaw, 2003.

Murals depicting historic scenes enliven the walls of many of the buildings in Slocan.

Before the bypass was built in the mid-1970s, traffic used the one-lane tunnel just north of Slocan that has since become a popular hiking and cycling trail.

Dumont Creek is a registered cemetery, but its quiet shade is well hidden from unwanted disturbance. It is here that many of the Slocan children of the 1970s and later lie in peace.

Mabel Lawrenow Kabatoff, Winlaw postmistress, 2003.

Kathy Hart, long-time Winlaw resident, at the former Hungry Wolf Café.

Appledale.

Eric Clough and Nancy Harris, founding members of the New Family, still living on Paradise Valley Road in 2003.

About the Author

KATHERINE GORDON, born in England in 1963, began travelling the world at the age of three months with her English civil-engineer father, her French mother, and the rest of her family, eventually settling in New Zealand.

There she worked in commercial law for several years before globe-trotting again, in South America, Costa Rica, and Canada. Settling in Canada in 1989, the lure of the ocean eventually drew her west to Victoria, B.C. where she worked in aboriginal treaty negotiations for a few years before moving to Gabriola Island with her husband, photographer Quinton Gordon.

Gordon is a full time freelance writer contributing to such international publications as *British Columbia* magazine, *North & South*, and *Action Asia* among others. *The Slocan: A Portrait of a Valley* is her second book. *A Curious Life: The Biography of Princess Peggy Abkhazi* was published by Sono Nis Press in 2002.